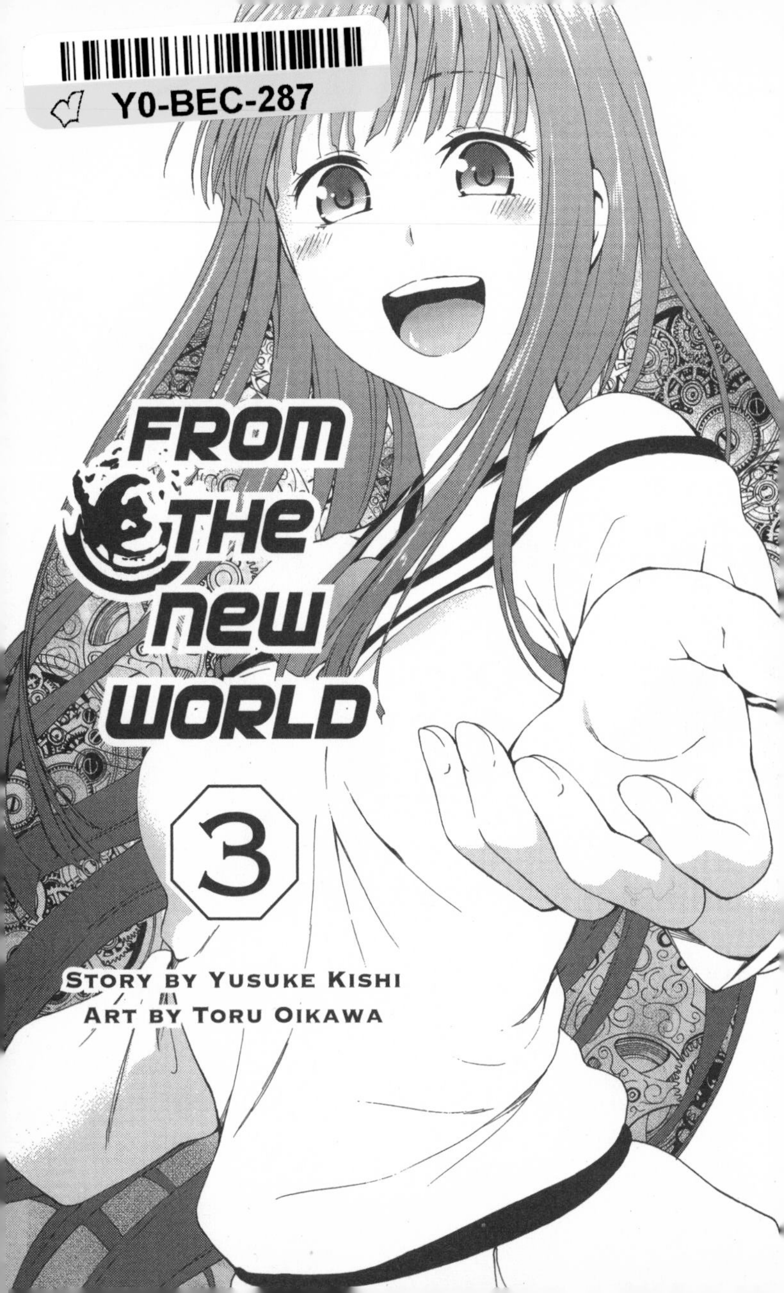
FROM THE NEW WORLD
3
STORY BY YUSUKE KISHI
ART BY TORU OIKAWA

CHARACTERS

FROM THE NEW WORLD

PROFILES

SAKI WATANABE

A curious and active girl. She lights up everything as the core of Group 1 in the Holistic Class. She can be very decisive and is mentally very strong.

SHUN AONUMA

Wise and trusted, his magick skills were superb, but he developed Karma Demon symptoms and offed himself once he realized his fate.

SATORU ASAHINA

Childhood friend of Saki. Exchanges taunts with her and likes to spook people with tall tales that may or may not be true.

MAMORU ITO

A meek, gentle boy. A graduate of Friendship Academy who became friends with Saki and the others at the Holistic Class. Good at drawing.

MARIA AKIZUKI

Best friends with Saki. A beautiful girl with flame-red hair. Strong-willed and blunt-spoken yet unaffected at heart.

SQUEALER

Prolocutor of the Robber Fly morph rat colony. Speaks excellent Japanese and shows obeisance to humans.

KIROMARU

Supreme commander of the Giant Hornet Colony, the largest and most powerful colony in Kanto. Marshals more than 20,000 troops.

THE STORY THUS FAR...

Caught up in a Morph Rat war, the five members of Group 1 escape the poison gas attack, but Shun suddenly collapses. After Kiromaru and his Giant Hornet Colony annihilate the overseas Rats, Saki and her friends can finally head home. Leaving Shun in the care of adults who have come for them, the other four are ready to leave. Saki learns, however, that Shun is turning into a Karma Demon and is about to be disposed of, so she sneaks out alone to try and bring him back. But his time is running out. As she is parted from her beloved Shun, Saki promises to inherit his dreams. Yet, when she returns to town, Shun has been deleted from her memories, while false ones of Ryo have been implanted in their place...

REIKO AMANO

Childhood friend of Saki.
Made it into the Holistic Class but struggled to control her magick. She vanished one day, from Saki and the others' memories, too.

SHISEI KABURAGI

The most powerful magick user in Kamisu 66 Acreage where Saki and the others live.

MUSHIN

Abbot of the Temple of Purity outside the Border Rope. A high priest and respected man of character.

CONTENTS

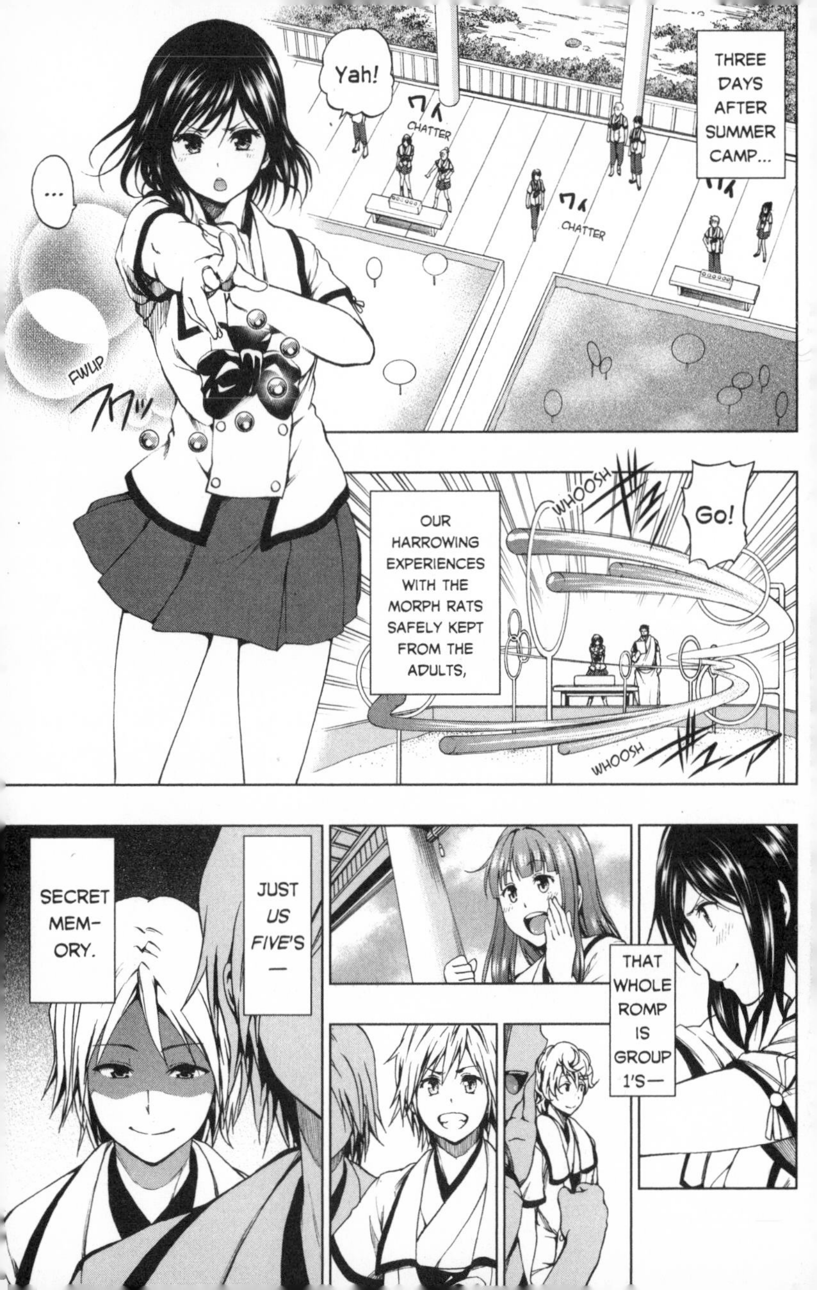

THREE DAYS AFTER SUMMER CAMP...
ワイ
CHATTER
Yah!
ワイ
CHATTER
Go!
WHOOSH
OUR HARROWING EXPERIENCES WITH THE MORPH RATS SAFELY KEPT FROM THE ADULTS,
WHOOSH
...
FWUP
THAT WHOLE ROMP IS GROUP 1'S—
JUST *US FIVE*'S —
SECRET MEM-ORY.

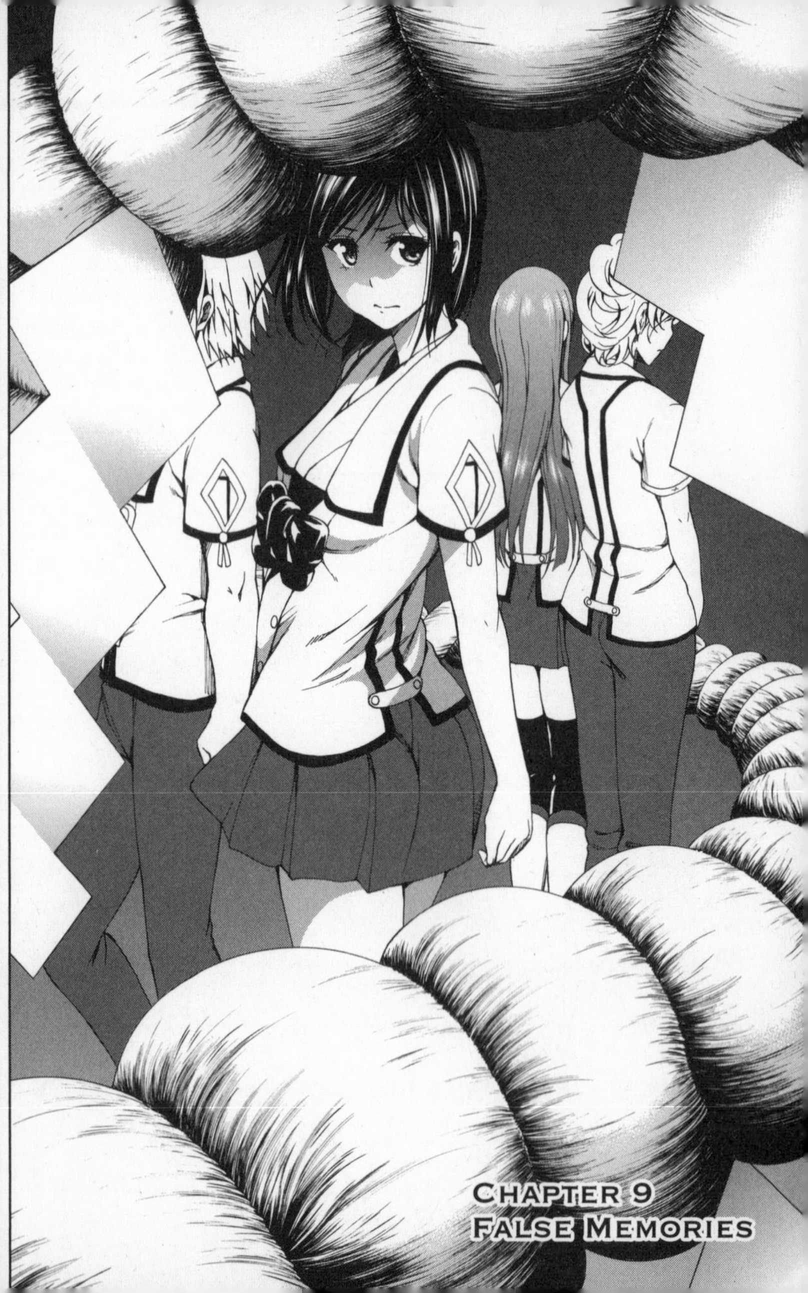
Chapter 9
False Memories

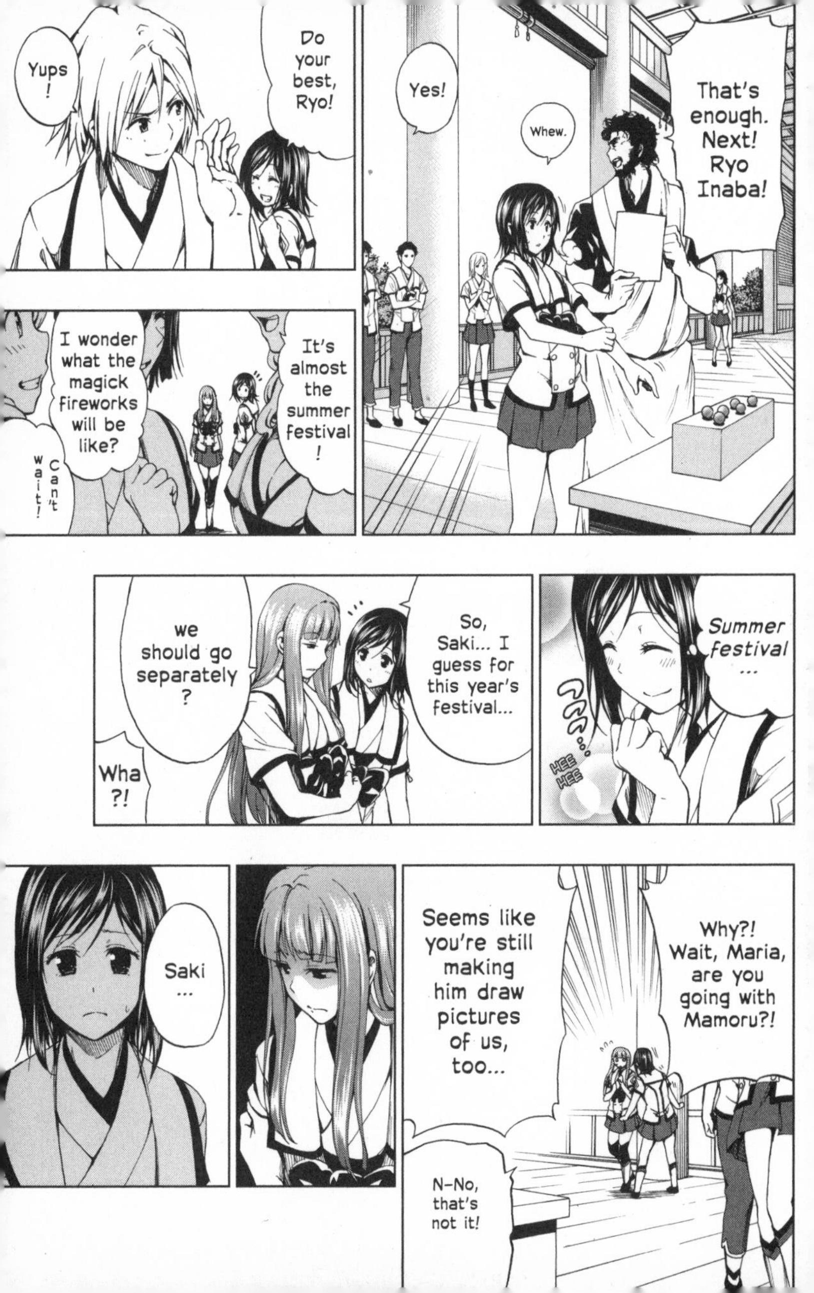
That's enough. Next! Ryo Inaba!
Whew.
Yes!
Do your best, Ryo!
Yups!
It's almost the summer festival!
I wonder what the magick fireworks will be like?
Can't wait!
Summer festival...
HEE HEE
So, Saki... I guess for this year's festival...
we should go separately?
Wha?!
Why?! Wait, Maria, are you going with Mamoru?!
Seems like you're still making him draw pictures of us, too...
N-No, that's not it!
Saki...

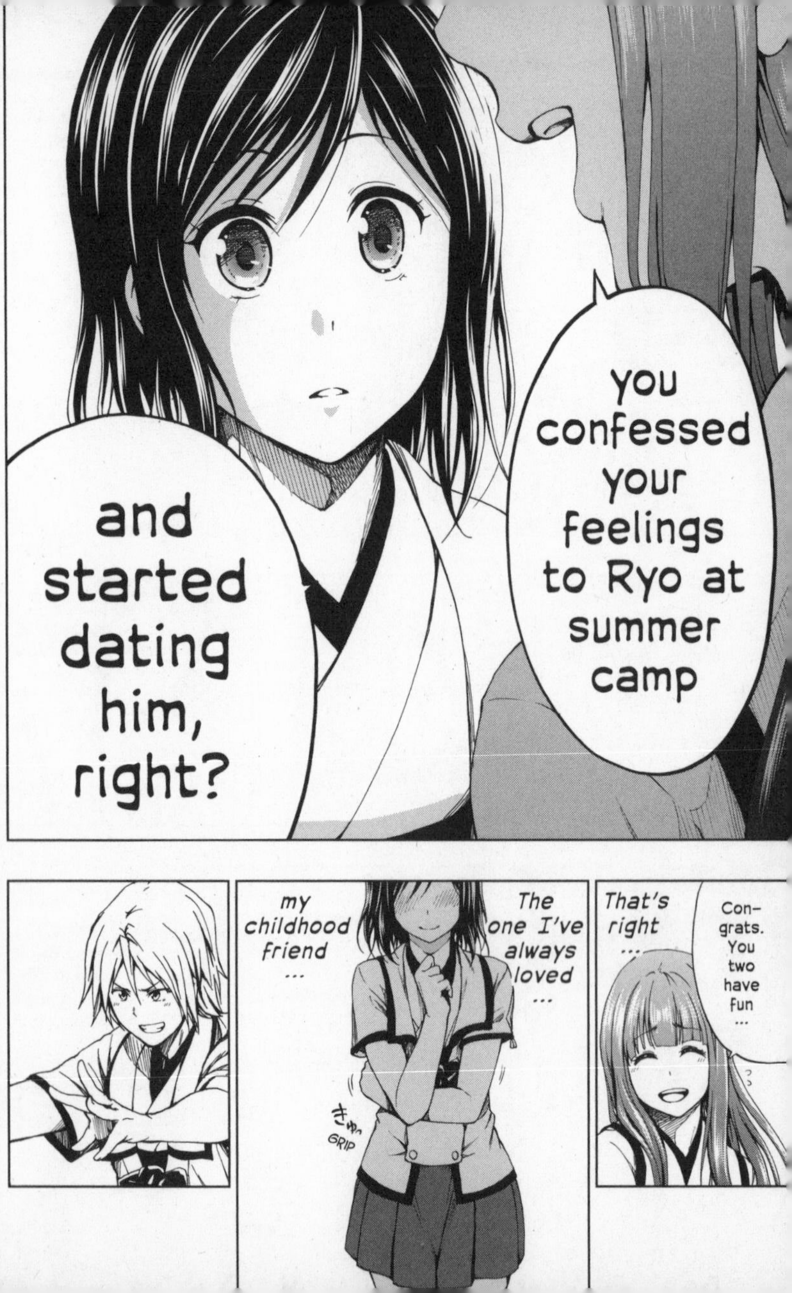
you confessed your feelings to Ryo at summer camp
and started dating him, right?
Con-grats. You two have fun ...
That's right ...
The one I've always loved ...
my childhood friend ...
きゅっ
GRIP

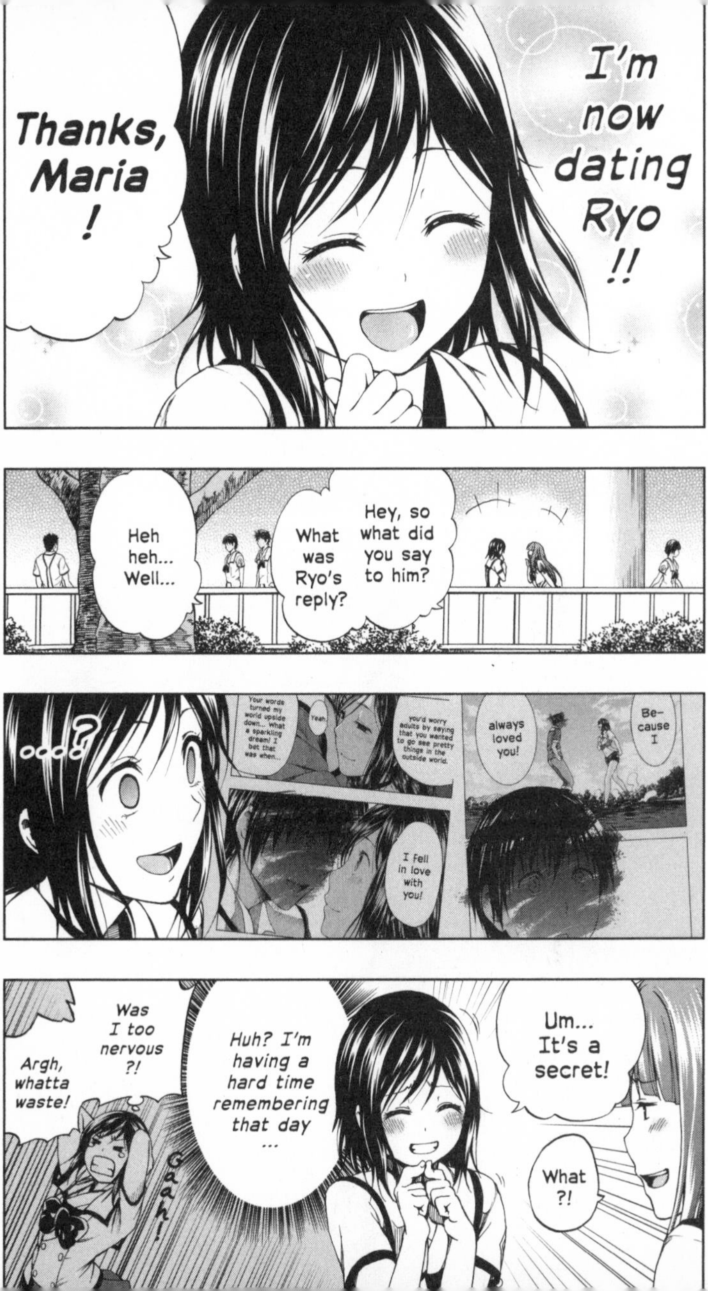
I'm now dating Ryo!!
Thanks, Maria!
Hey, so what did you say to him?
What was Ryo's reply?
Heh heh... Well...
Because I
always loved you!
you'd worry adults by saying that you wanted to go see pretty things in the outside world.
Yeah.
Your words turned my world upside down... What a sparkling dream! I bet that was when...
I fell in love with you!
oooo?
Um... It's a secret!
What?!
Huh? I'm having a hard time remembering that day ...
Was I too nervous ?!
Argh, whatta waste!
Gaah!

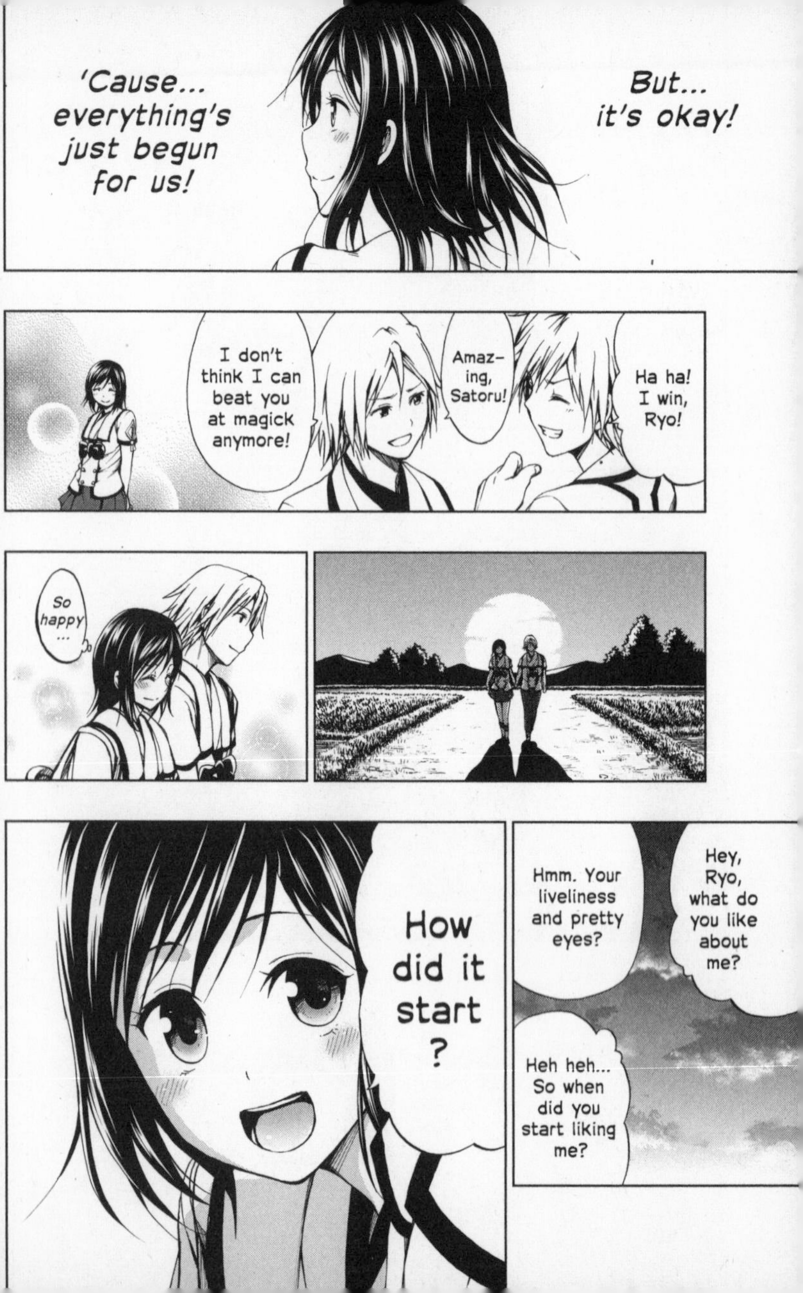
But... it's okay!
'Cause... everything's just begun for us!
Ha ha! I win, Ryo!
Amaz-ing, Satoru!
I don't think I can beat you at magick anymore!
So happy...
Hey, Ryo, what do you like about me?
Hmm. Your liveliness and pretty eyes?
Heh heh... So when did you start liking me?
How did it start?

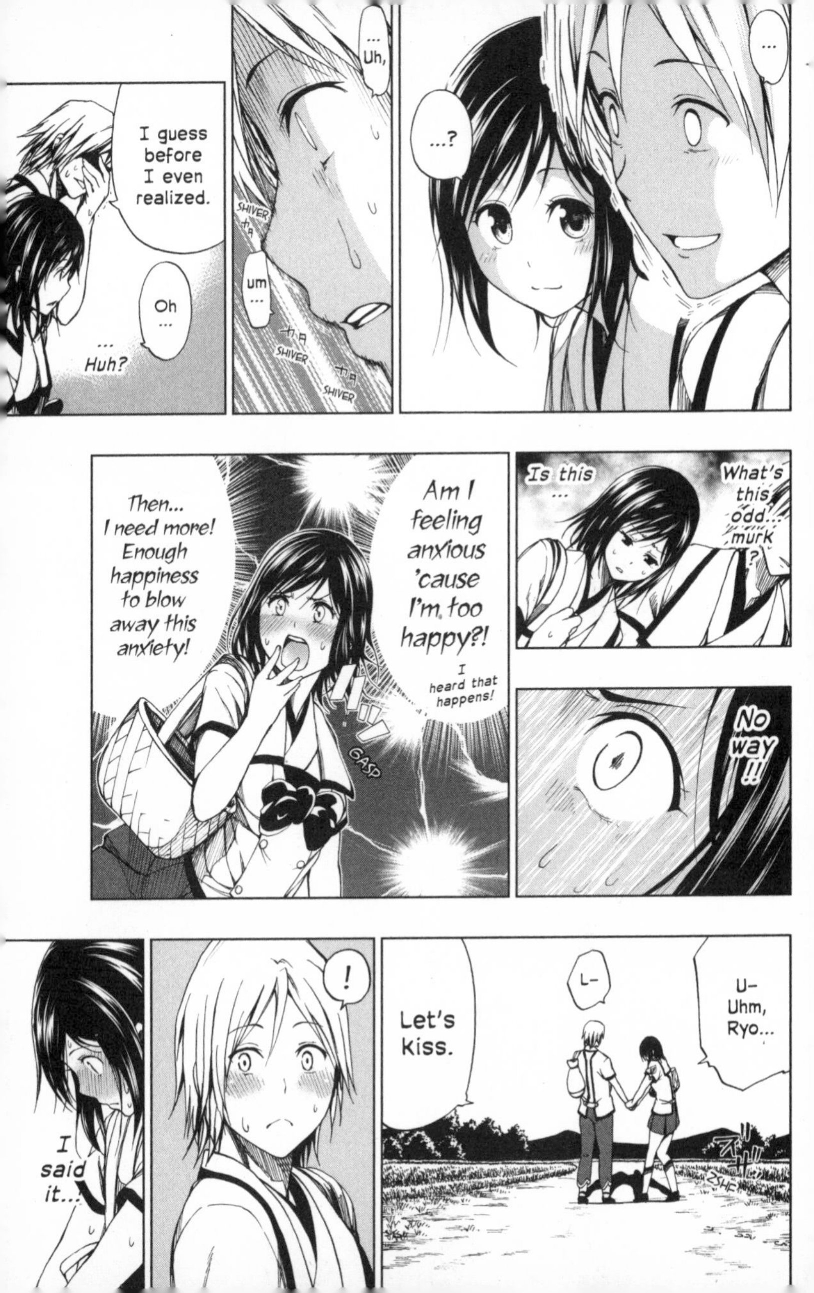
...
...?
... Uh,
SHIVER
um ...
SHIVER
SHIVER
I guess before I even realized.
Oh ...
... Huh?
What's this odd... murk?
Is this ...
No way!!
Am I feeling anxious 'cause I'm too happy?!
I heard that happens!
Then... I need more! Enough happiness to blow away this anxiety!
GASP
U-Uhm, Ryo...
L-
Let's kiss.
ZSHF
!
I said it...

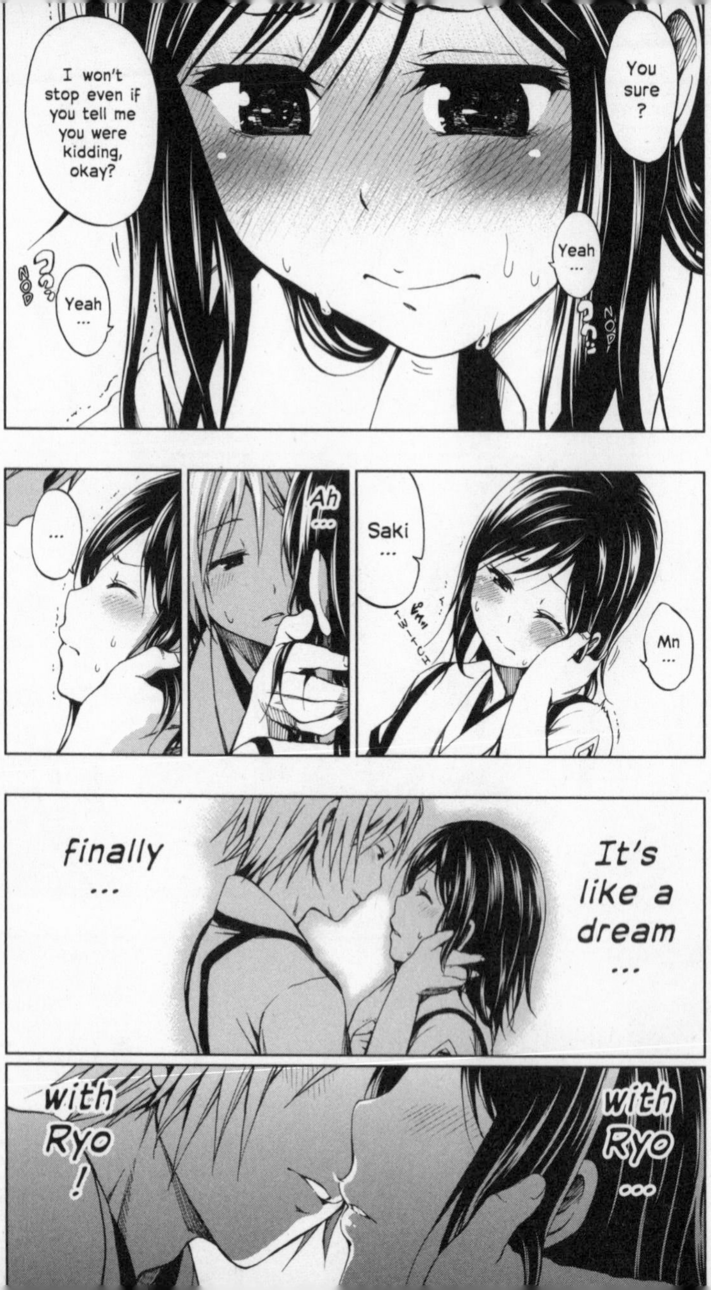
You sure ?
Yeah ...
NOD
I won't stop even if you tell me you were kidding, okay?
NOD
Yeah ...
Saki ...
TWITCH
Mn ...
Ah ...
...
It's like a dream ...
finally ...
with Ryo ...
with Ryo !

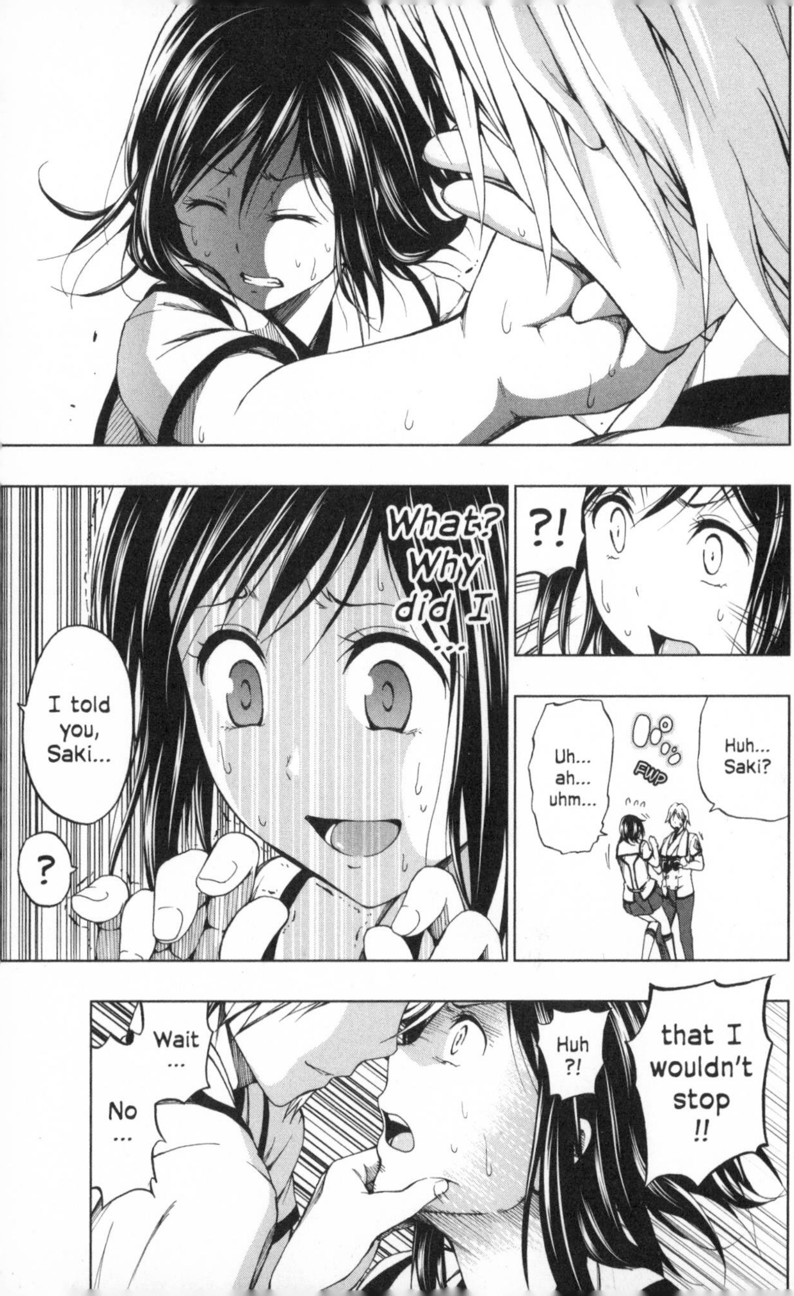
?!
Huh... Saki?
Uh... ah... uhm...
FWIP
What? Why did I ...
I told you, Saki...
?
that I wouldn't stop !!
Huh ?!
Wait ...
No ...

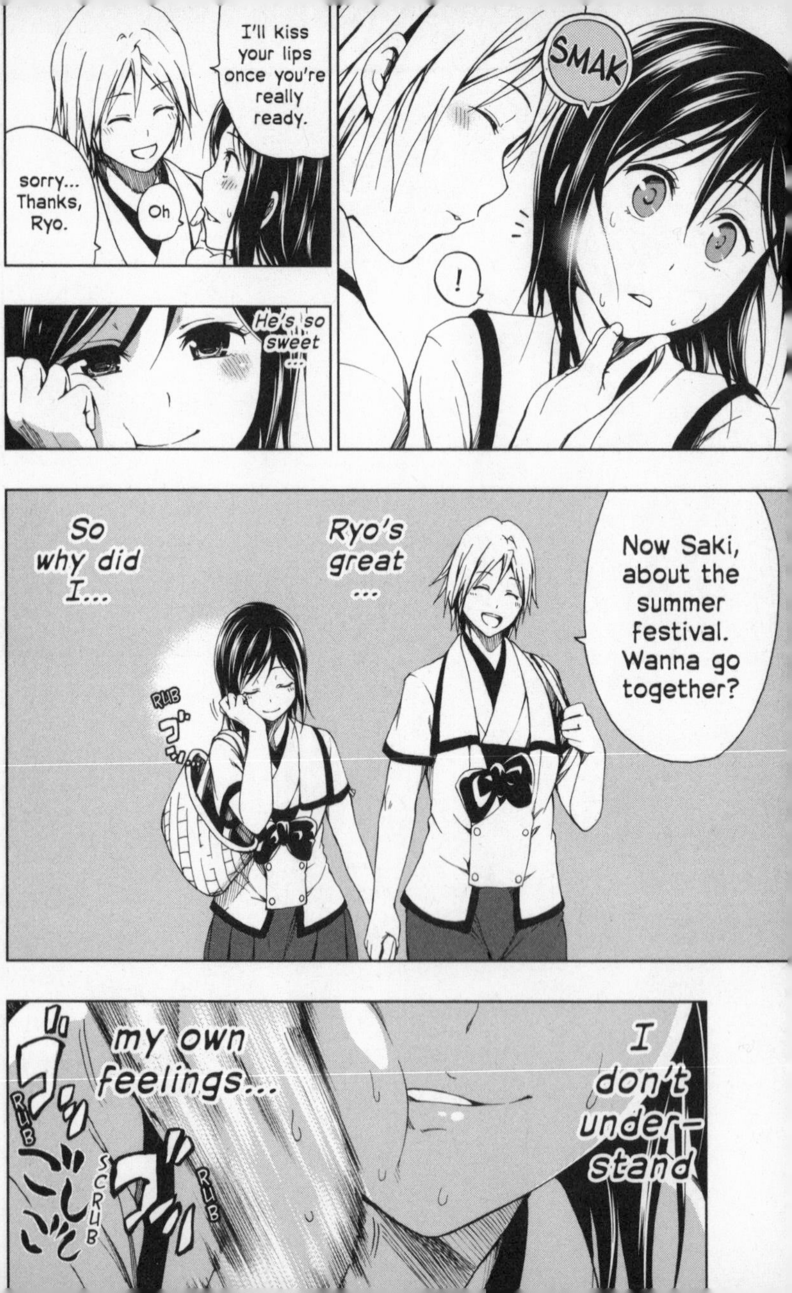
SMAK
!
I'll kiss your lips once you're really ready.
Oh
sorry... Thanks, Ryo.
He's so sweet ...
Now Saki, about the summer festival. Wanna go together?
Ryo's great ...
So why did I...
RUB
I don't under-stand
my own feelings...
RUB
SCRUB
RUB

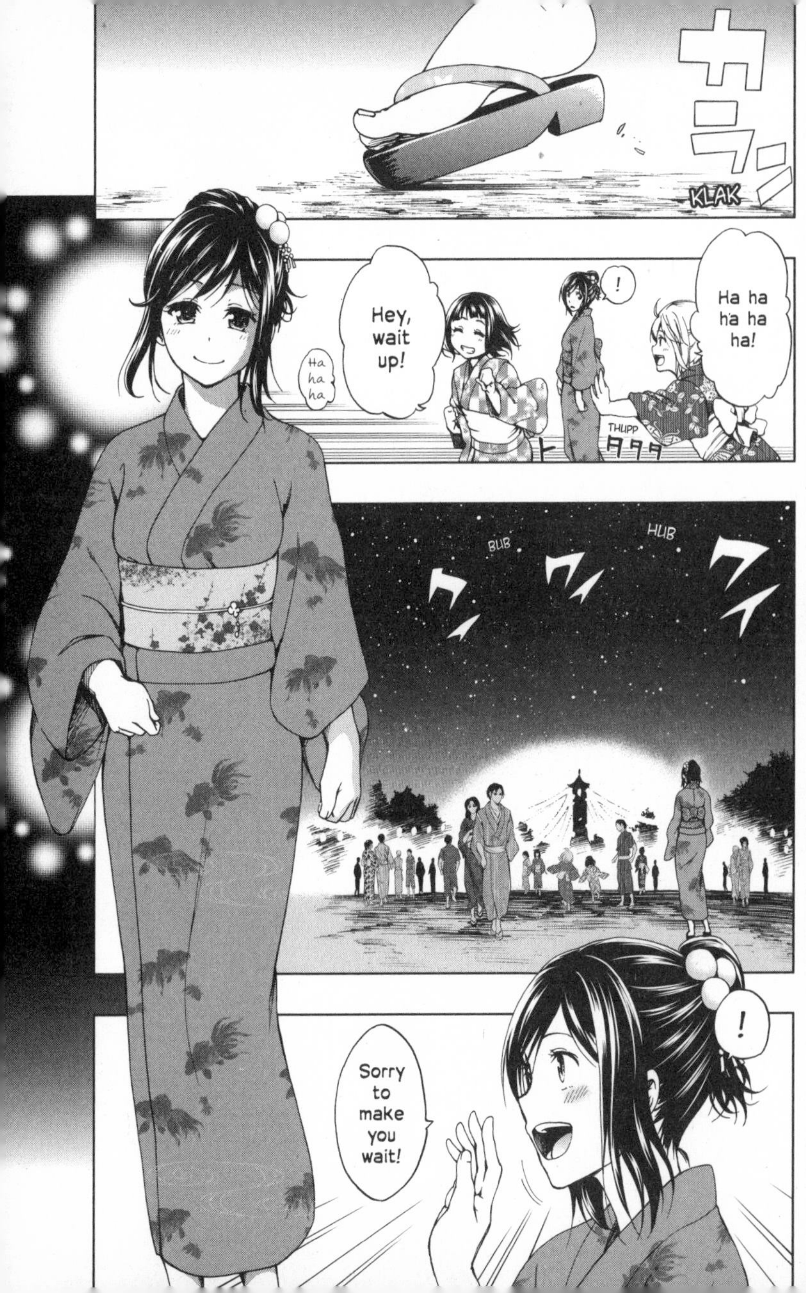
KLAK
Ha ha ha ha ha!
!
Hey, wait up!
Ha ha ha
THUPP
HUB
BUB
!
Sorry to make you wait!

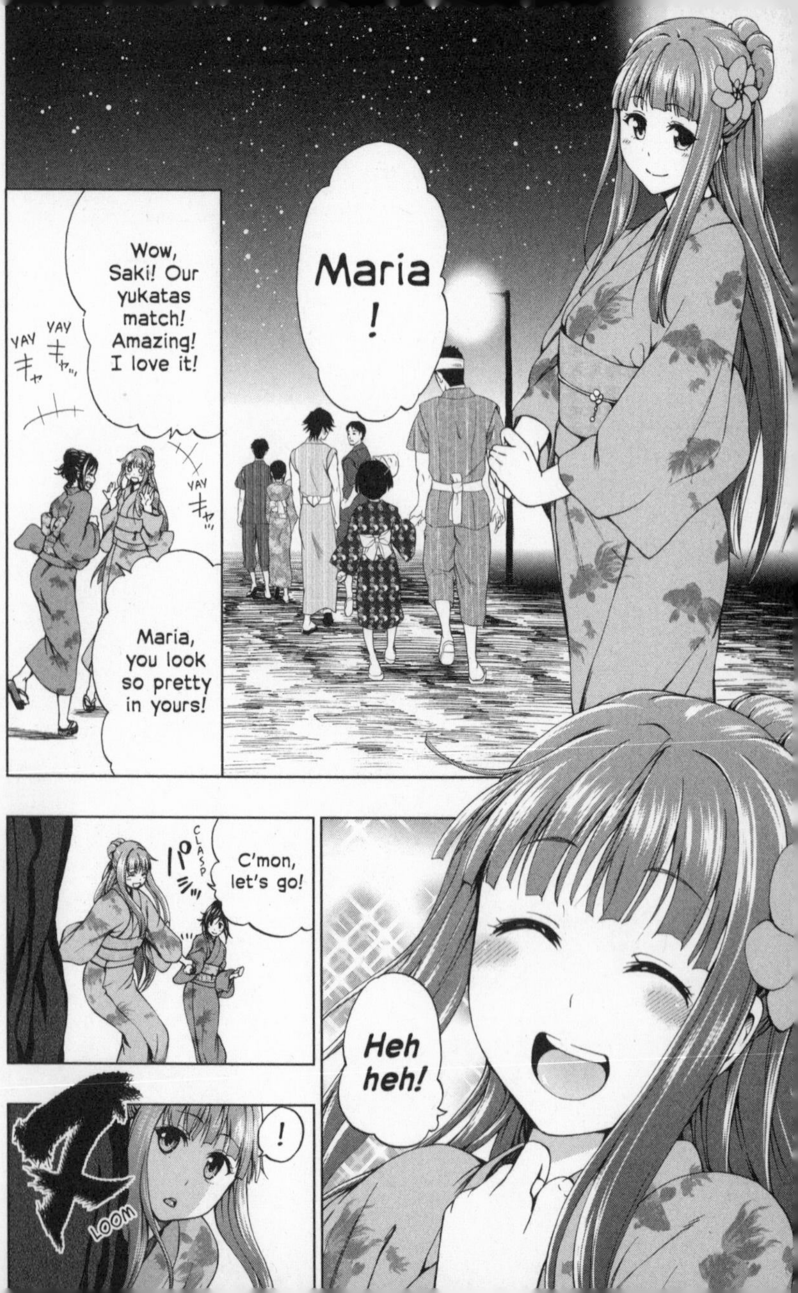
Maria !
Wow, Saki! Our yukatas match! Amazing! I love it!
YAY キャ
YAY キャ
YAY キャ
Maria, you look so pretty in yours!
Heh heh!
CLASP
C'mon, let's go!
!
LOOM

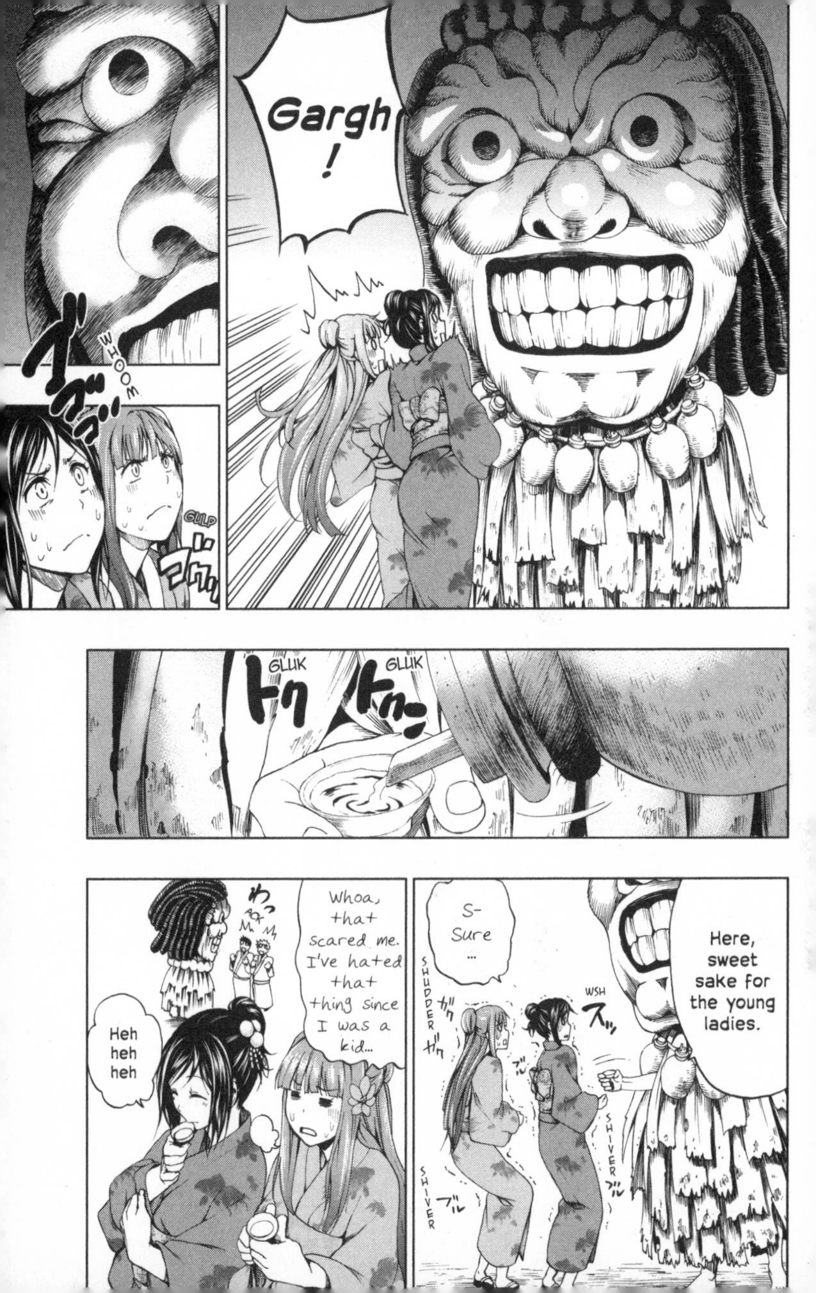
Gargh!
WHOOOM
GULP
GLUK
GLUK
Here, sweet sake for the young ladies.
S-Sure...
WSH
SHUDDER
SHIVER
SHIVER
Whoa, that scared me. I've hated that thing since I was a kid...
Heh heh heh

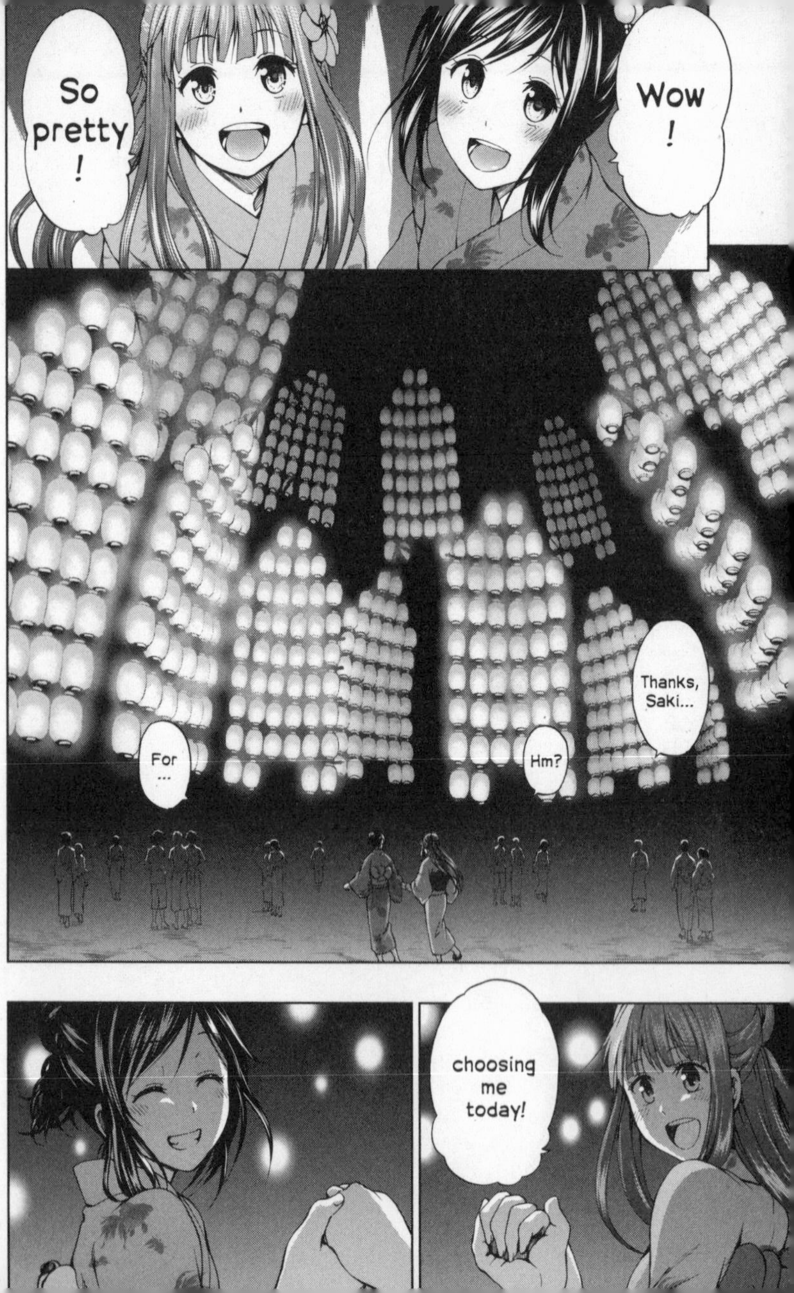
Wow!
So pretty!
Thanks, Saki...
Hm?
For...
choosing me today!

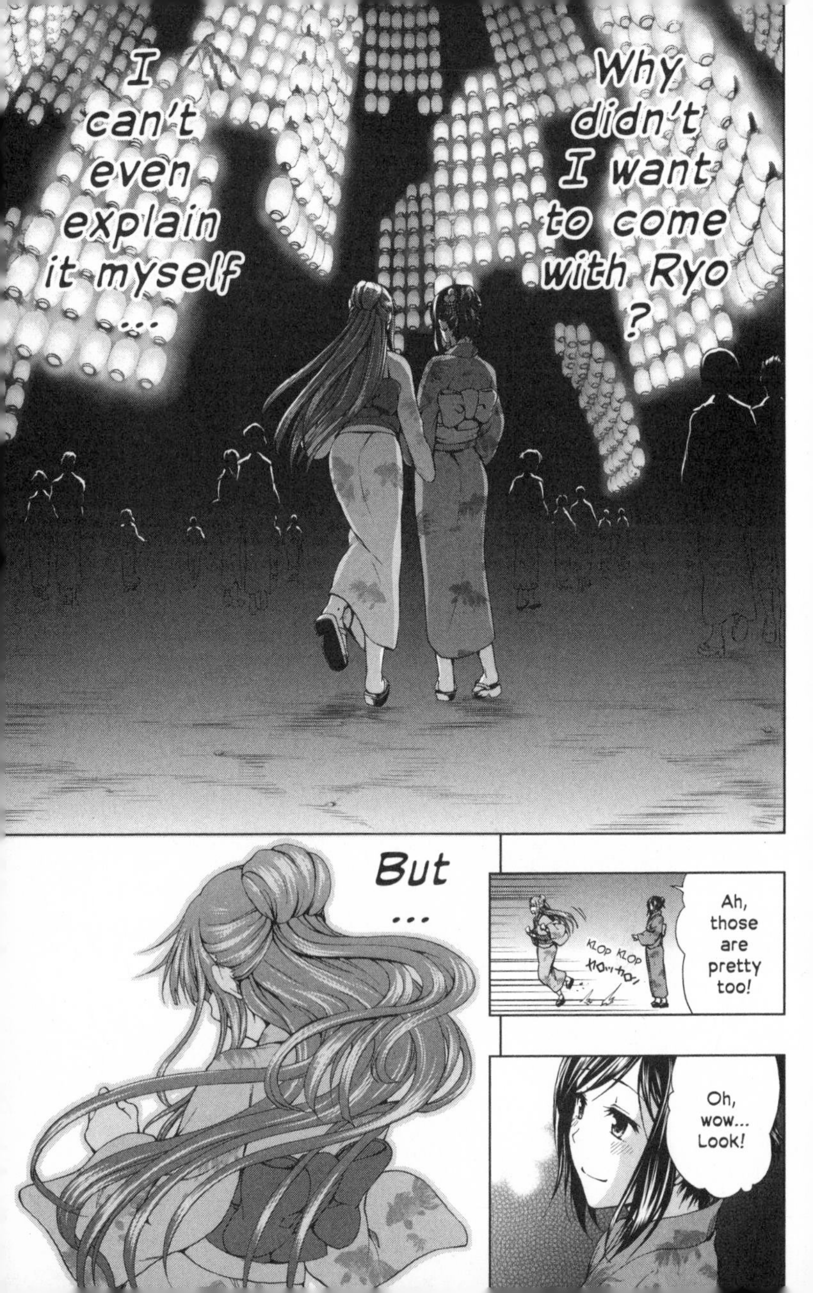
Why didn't I want to come with Ryo?
I can't even explain it myself...
Ah, those are pretty too!
KLOP KLOP
Oh, wow... Look!
But...

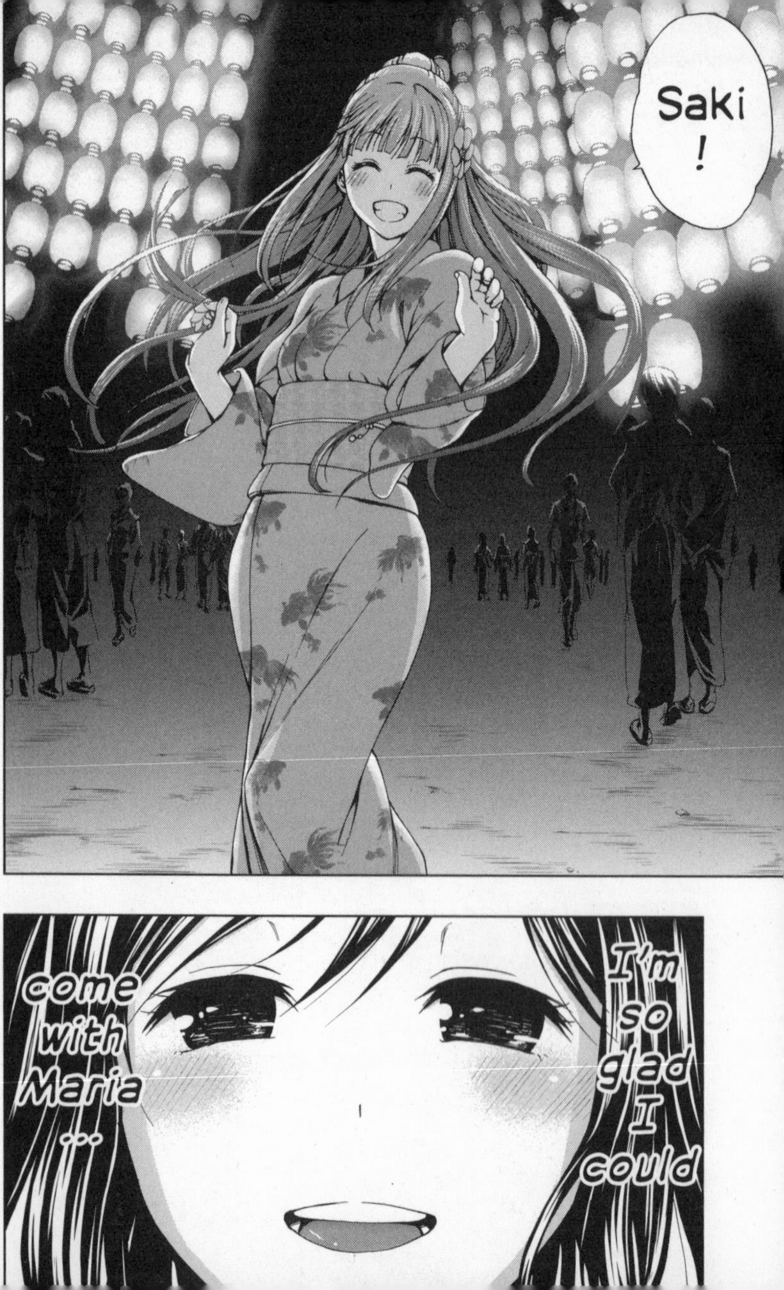
Saki
!
I'm so glad I could
come with Maria ...

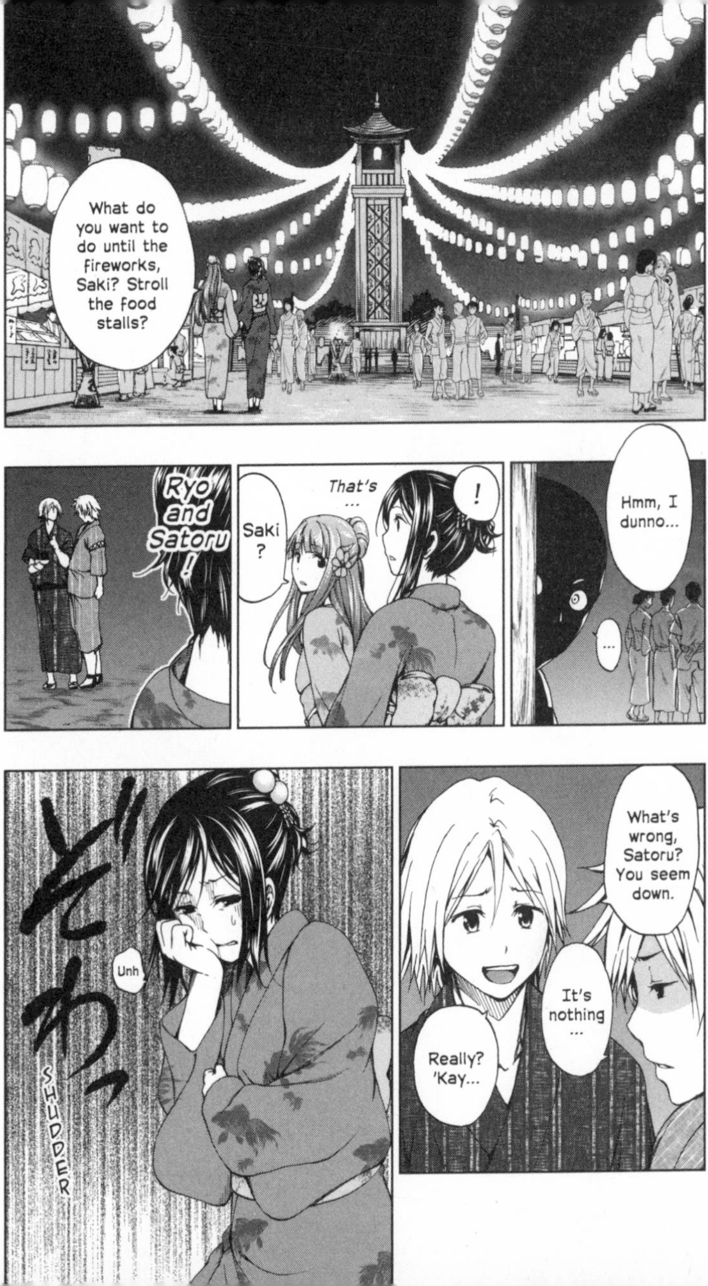
What do you want to do until the fireworks, Saki? Stroll the food stalls?
Hmm, I dunno...
...
!
That's ...
Saki ?
Ryo and Satoru !
What's wrong, Satoru? You seem down.
It's nothing ...
Really? 'Kay...
Unh
SHUDDER

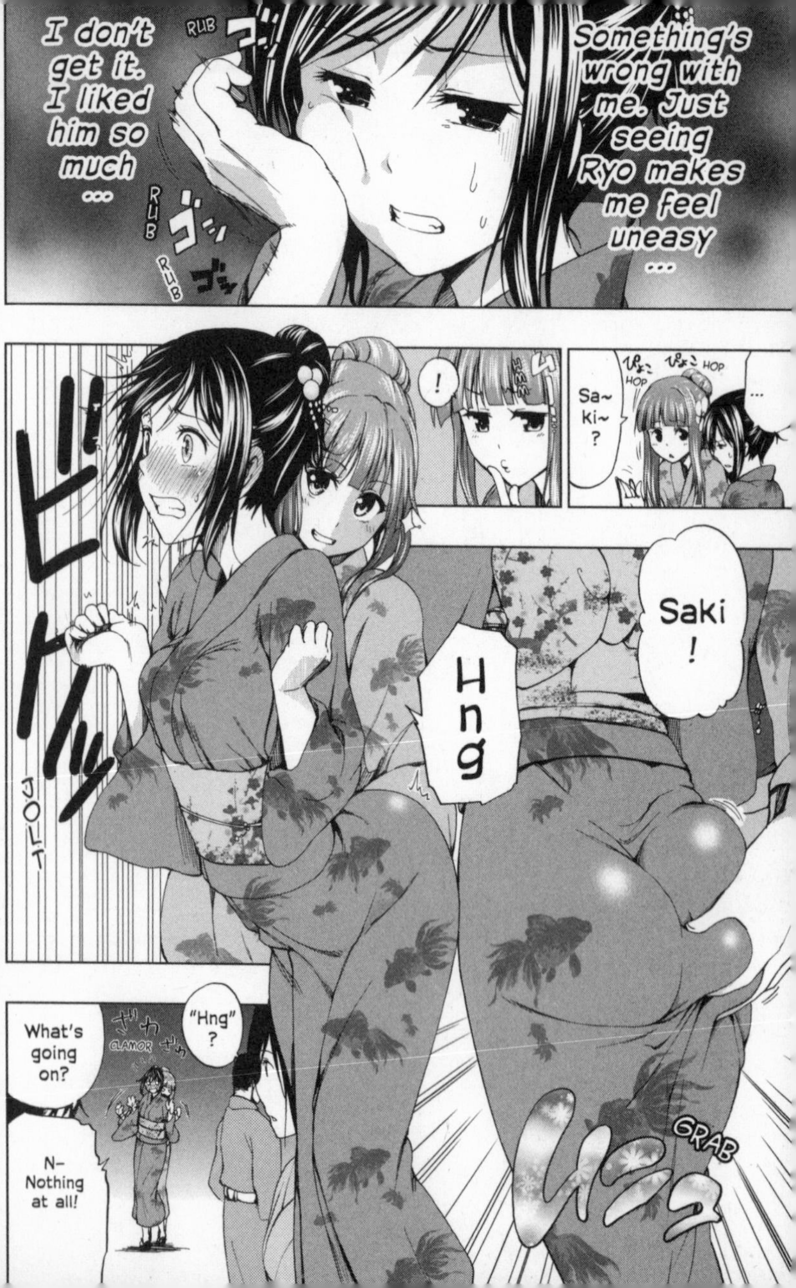

Something's wrong with me. Just seeing Ryo makes me feel uneasy ...
RUB
RUB
RUB
I don't get it. I liked him so much ...
...
ぴょこ HOP
ぴょこ HOP
Sa~ki~?
HMM
!
Saki!
Hng
JOLT
GRAB
"Hng"?
ざわ CLAMOR ざわ
What's going on?
N-Nothing at all!

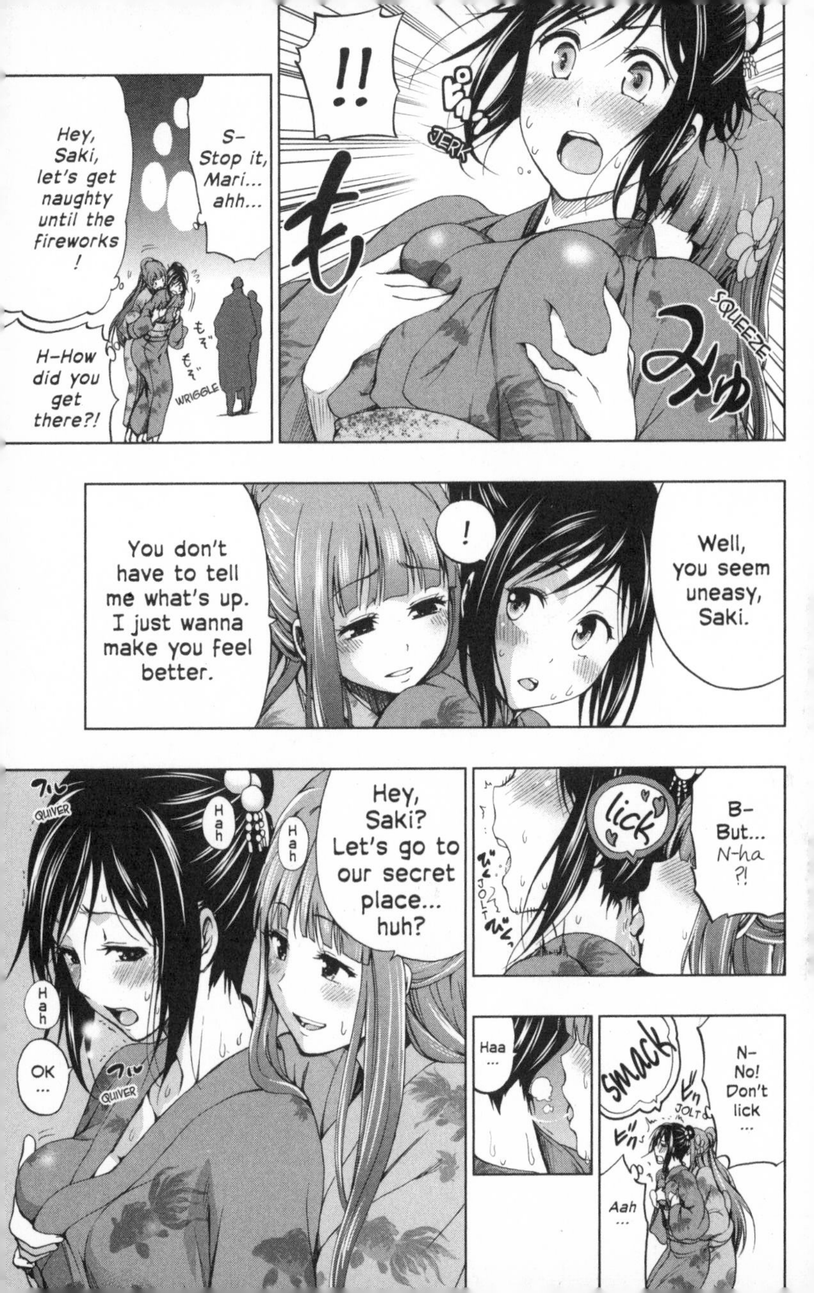
!!
JERK
SQUEEZE
みゅ
も
S- Stop it, Mari... ahh...
Hey, Saki, let's get naughty until the fireworks!
もぞもぞ
WRIGGLE
H-How did you get there?!
Well, you seem uneasy, Saki.
!
You don't have to tell me what's up. I just wanna make you feel better.
B- But... N-ha ?!
lick
JOLT
N- No! Don't lick ...
SMACK
JOLT
Haa ...
Aah ...
Hey, Saki? Let's go to our secret place... huh?
Hah
Hah
QUIVER
Hah
OK ...
QUIVER

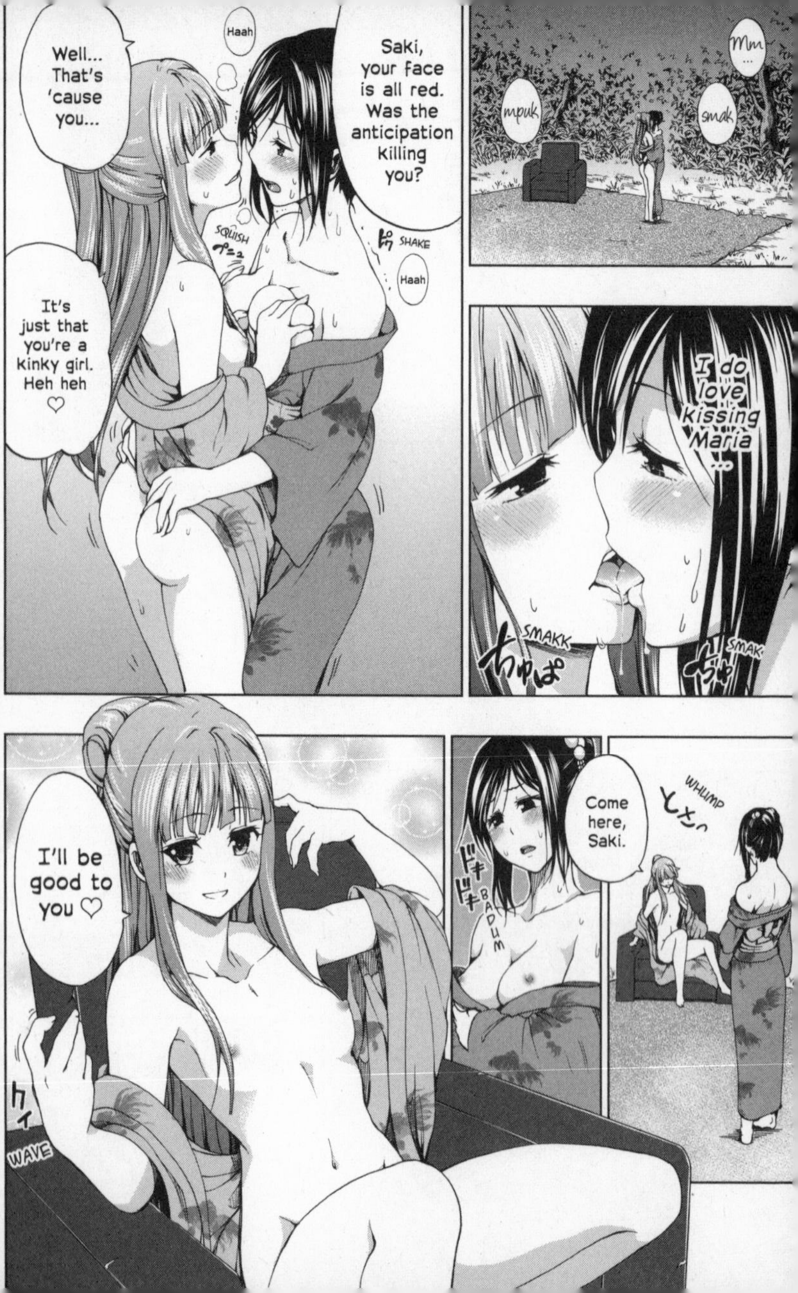
Mm ...
smak
mpuk
I do love kissing Maria ...
SMAK
SMAKK
Saki, your face is all red. Was the anticipation killing you?
Haah
Well... That's 'cause you...
SQUISH
SHAKE
Haah
It's just that you're a kinky girl. Heh heh ♡
WHUMP
Come here, Saki.
BADUM
I'll be good to you ♡
WAVE

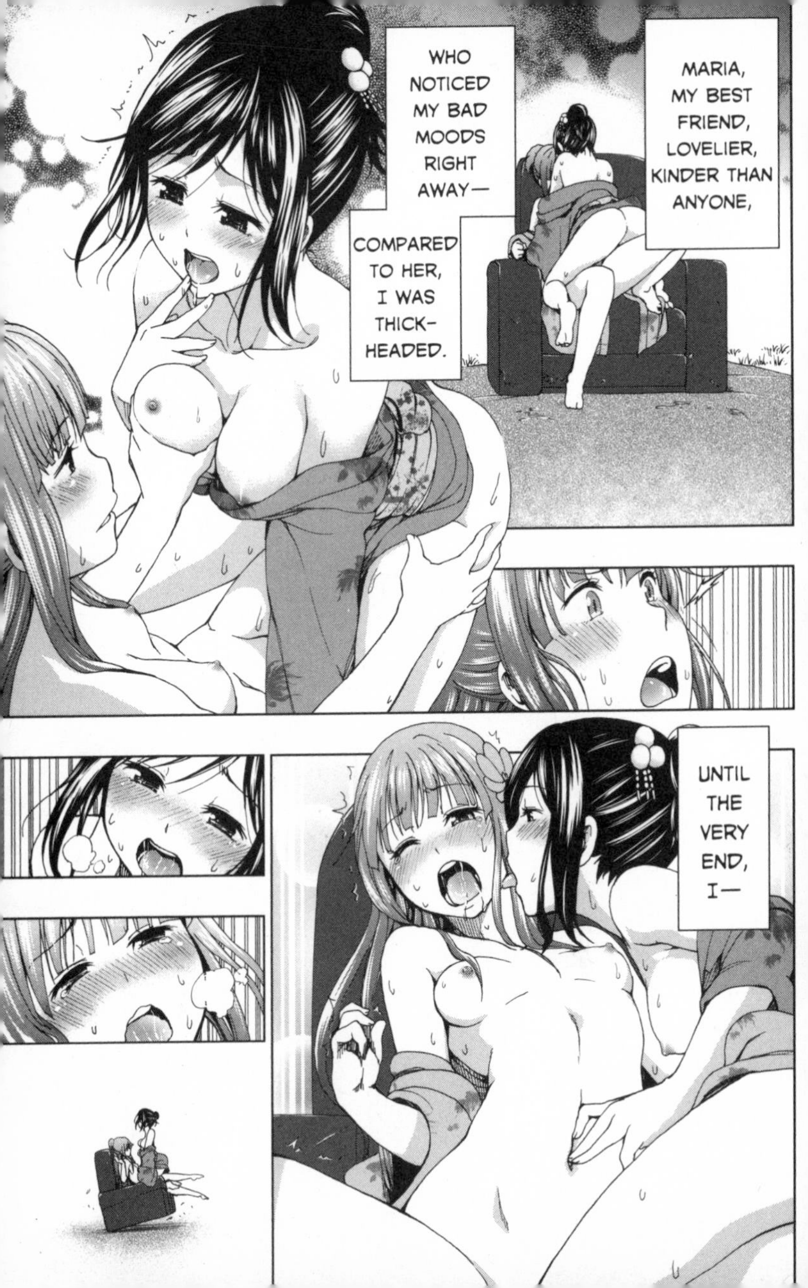
MARIA, MY BEST FRIEND, LOVELIER, KINDER THAN ANYONE,
WHO NOTICED MY BAD MOODS RIGHT AWAY—
COMPARED TO HER, I WAS THICK-HEADED.
UNTIL THE VERY END, I—

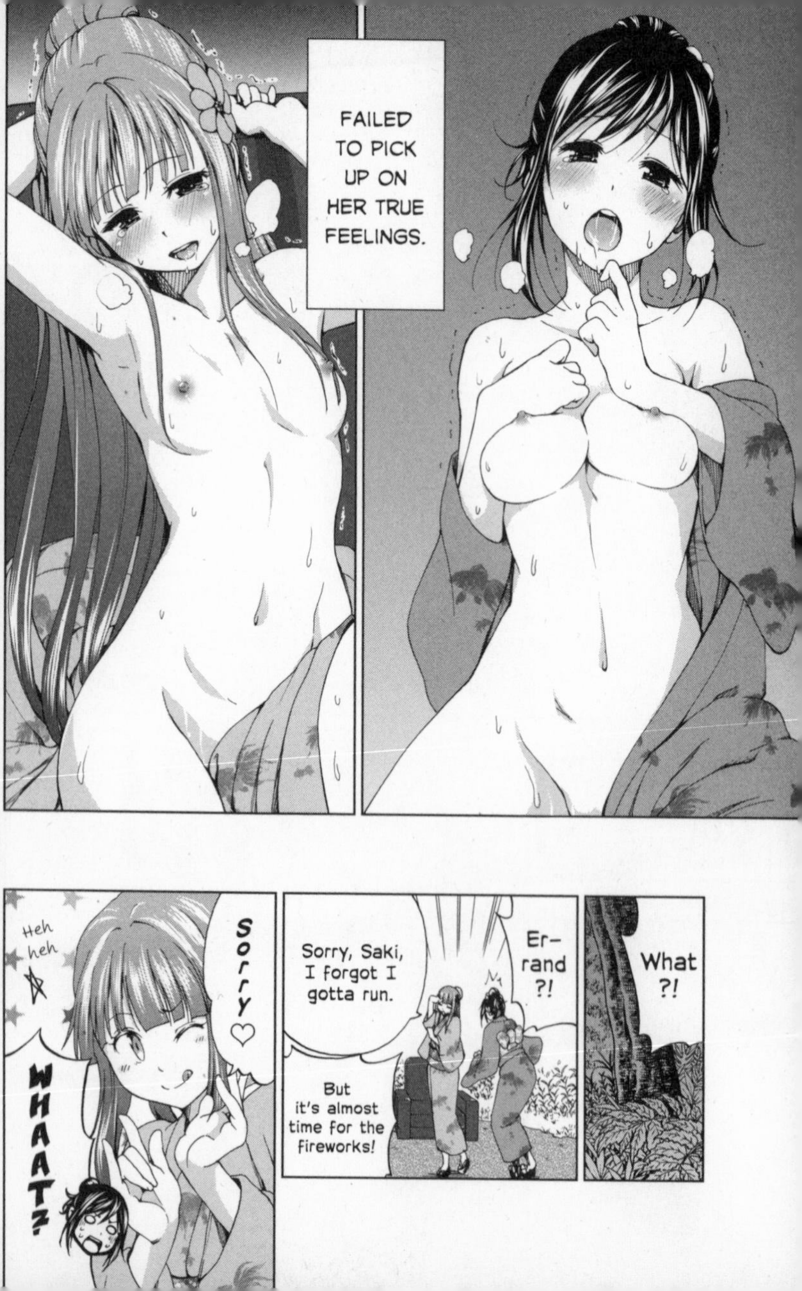
FAILED TO PICK UP ON HER TRUE FEELINGS.
What?!
Er-rand?!
Sorry, Saki, I forgot I gotta run.
But it's almost time for the fireworks!
Sorry ♡
Heh heh
WHAAAT?

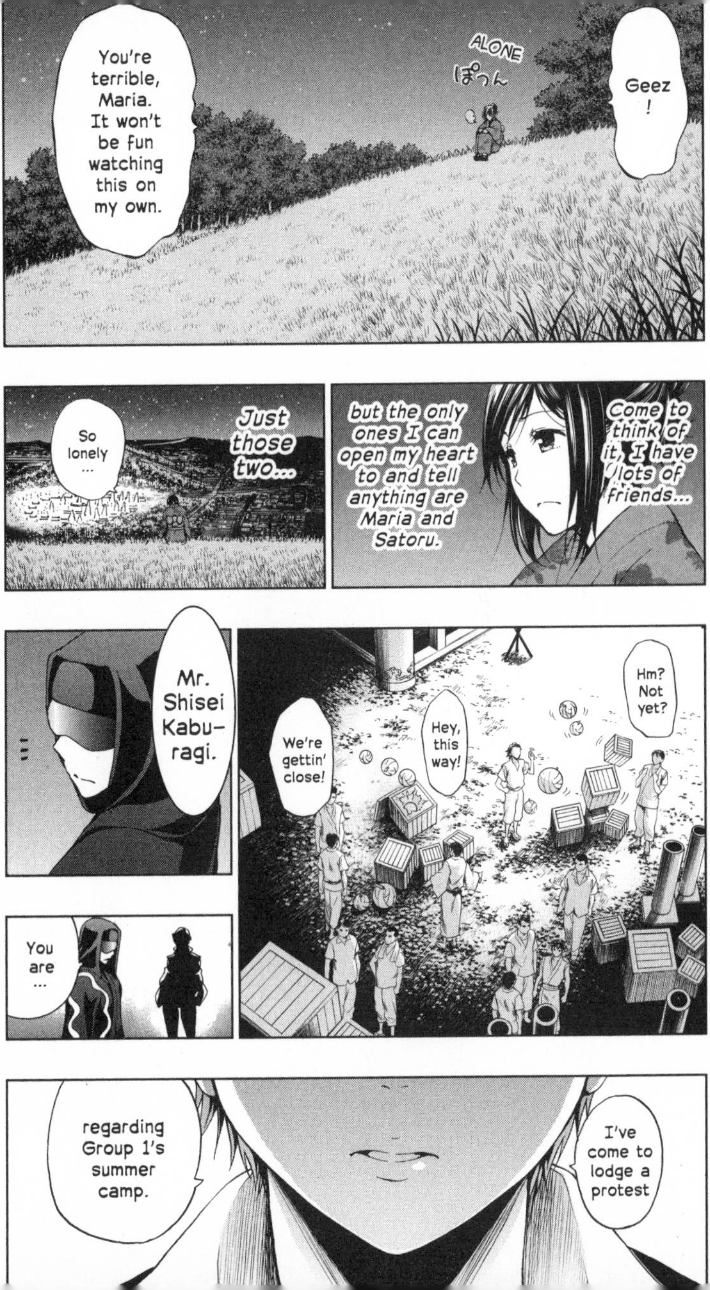
Geez!
ALONE
ぽつん
You're terrible, Maria. It won't be fun watching this on my own.
Come to think of it, I have lots of friends...
but the only ones I can open my heart to and tell anything are Maria and Satoru.
Just those two...
So lonely...
Hm? Not yet?
Hey, this way!
We're gettin' close!
Mr. Shisei Kaburagi.
You are...
I've come to lodge a protest
regarding Group 1's summer camp.

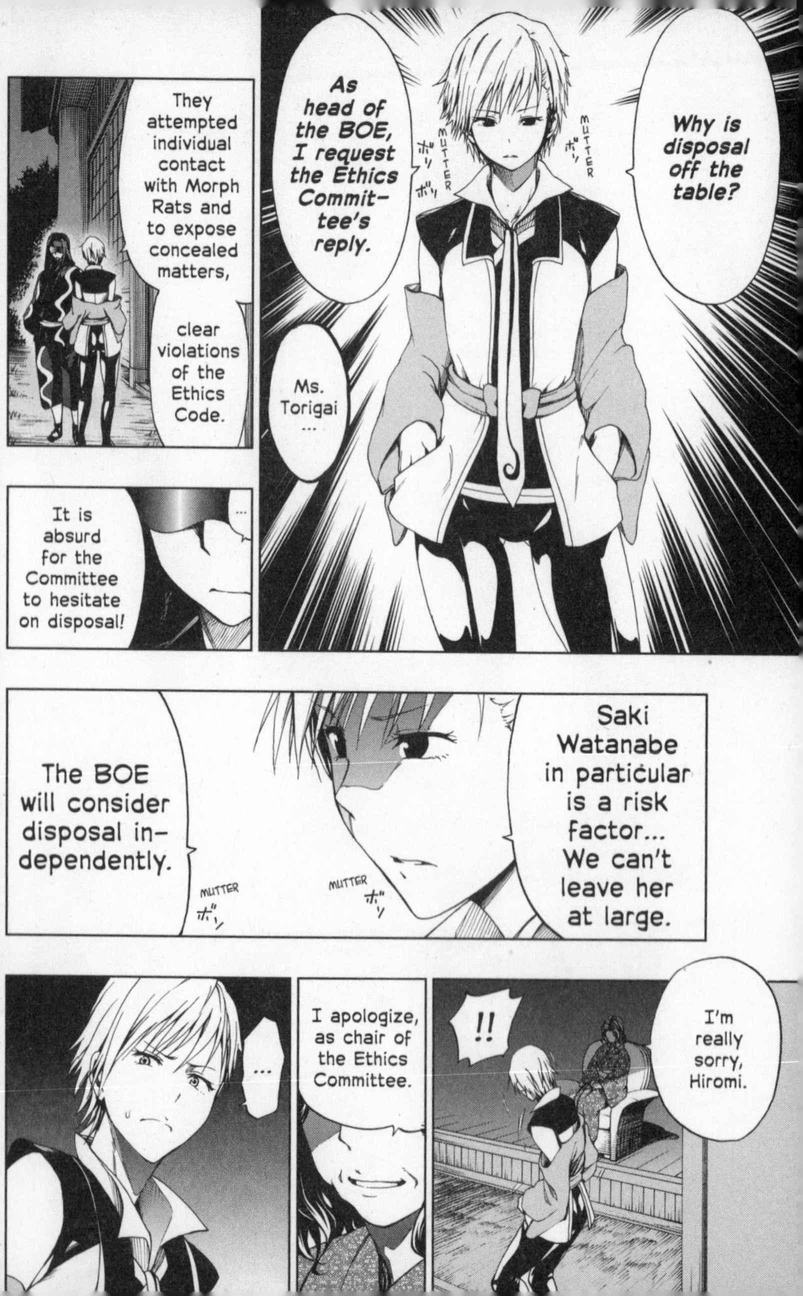

Why is disposal off the table?
MUTTER
ボソ
As head of the BOE, I request the Ethics Committee's reply.
MUTTER
ボソ ボソ
Ms. Torigai ...
They attempted individual contact with Morph Rats and to expose concealed matters,
clear violations of the Ethics Code.
...
It is absurd for the Committee to hesitate on disposal!
Saki Watanabe in particular is a risk factor... We can't leave her at large.
MUTTER
ボソ
MUTTER
ボソ
The BOE will consider disposal independently.
I'm really sorry, Hiromi.
!!
I apologize, as chair of the Ethics Committee.
...

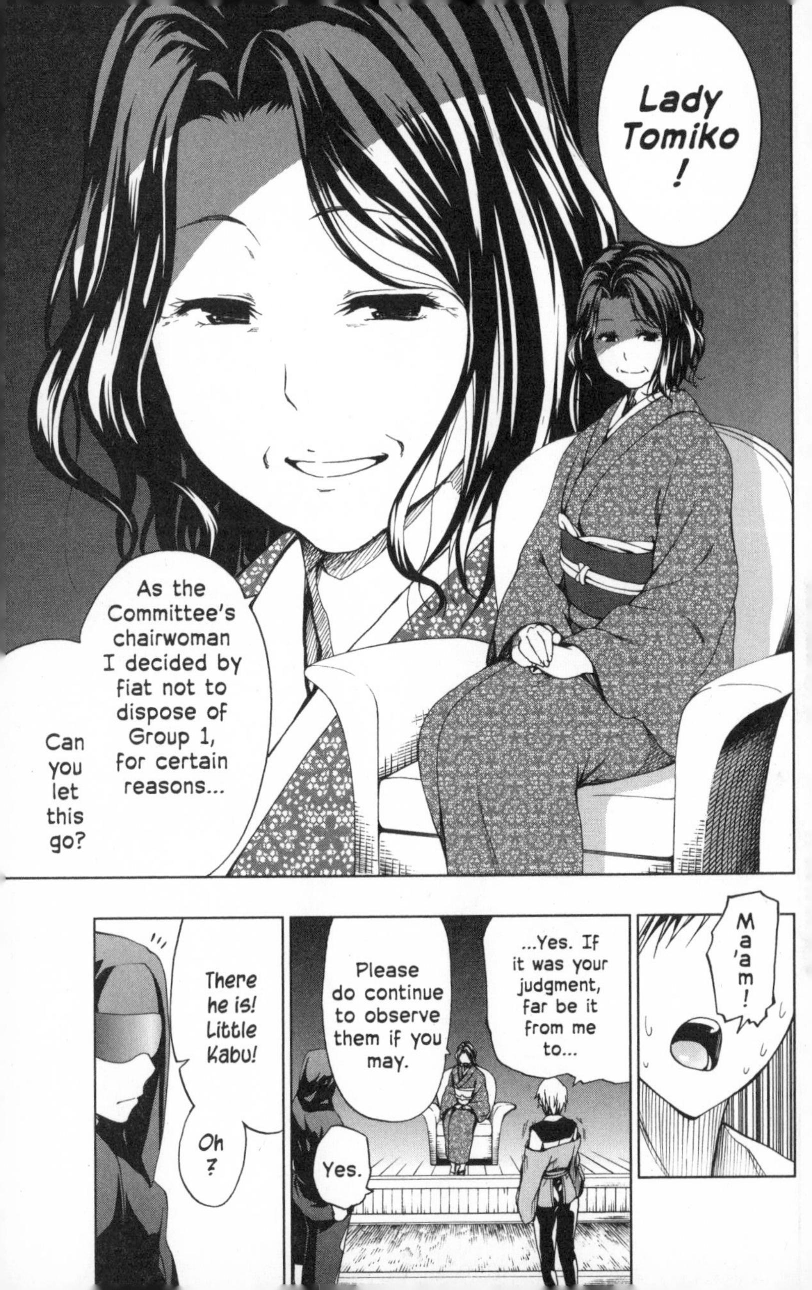
Lady Tomiko!
As the Committee's chairwoman I decided by fiat not to dispose of Group 1, for certain reasons...
Can you let this go?
Ma'am!
...Yes. If it was your judgment, far be it from me to...
Please do continue to observe them if you may.
Yes.
There he is! Little Kabu!
Oh?

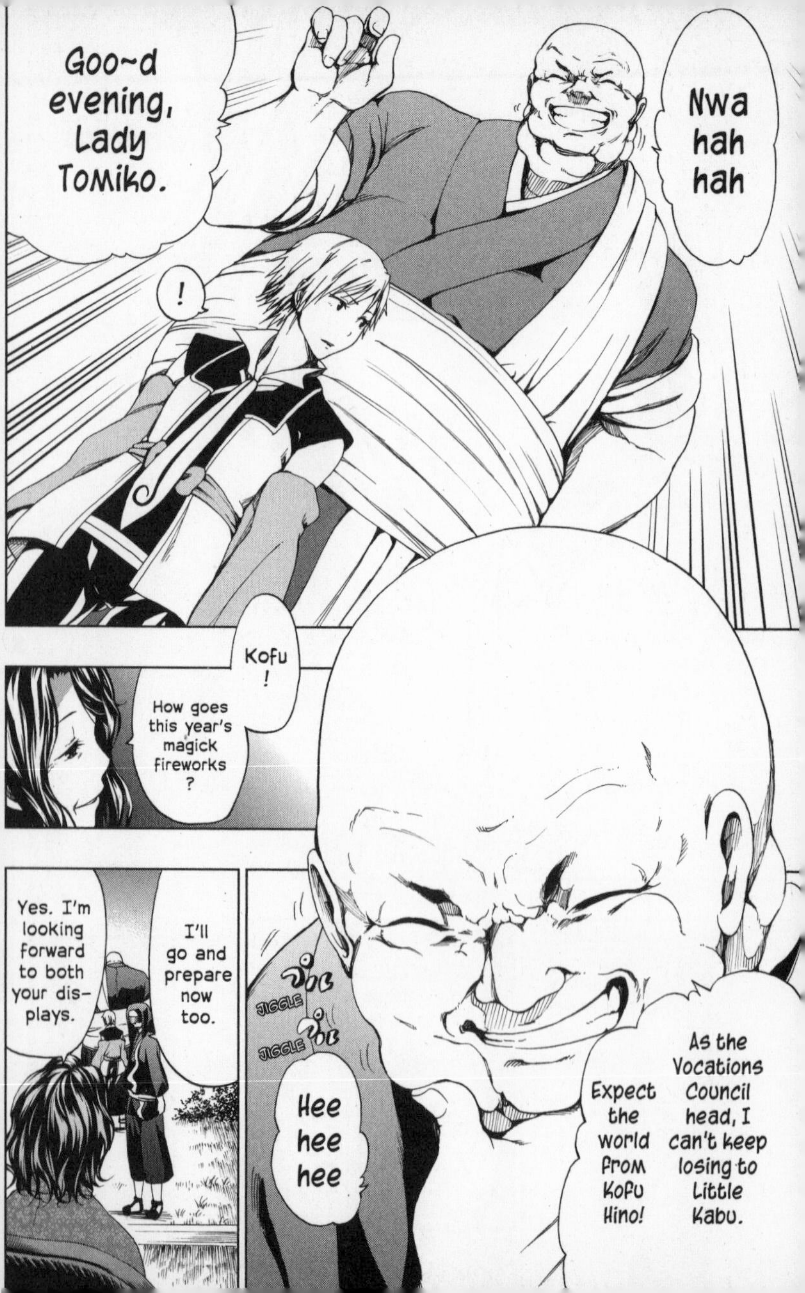
Nwa hah hah
Goo~d evening, Lady Tomiko.
!
As the Vocations Council head, I can't keep losing to Little Kabu.
Expect the world from Kofu Hino!
JIGGLE
JIGGLE
Hee hee hee
Kofu!
How goes this year's magick fireworks?
I'll go and prepare now too.
Yes. I'm looking forward to both your displays.

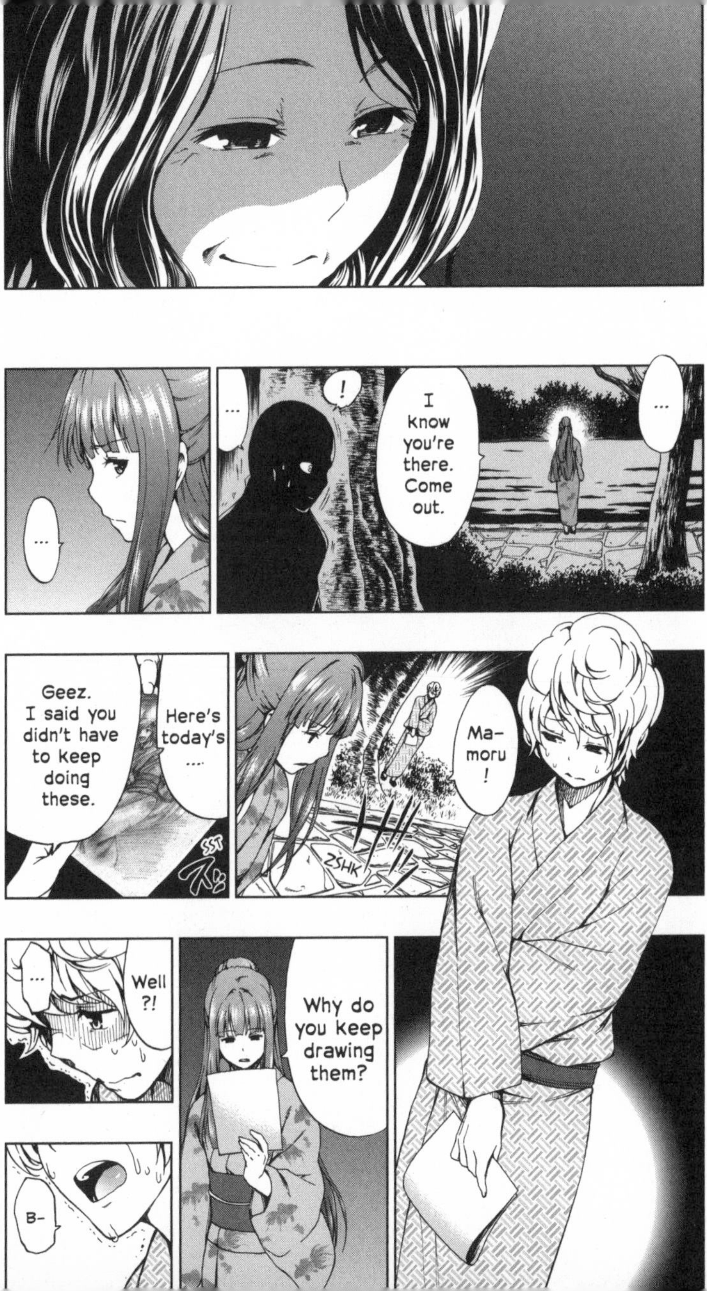
...
I know you're there. Come out.
!
...
...
Ma-moru!
ZSHK
Here's today's ....
Geez. I said you didn't have to keep doing these.
SST
Why do you keep drawing them?
Well?!
...
B-

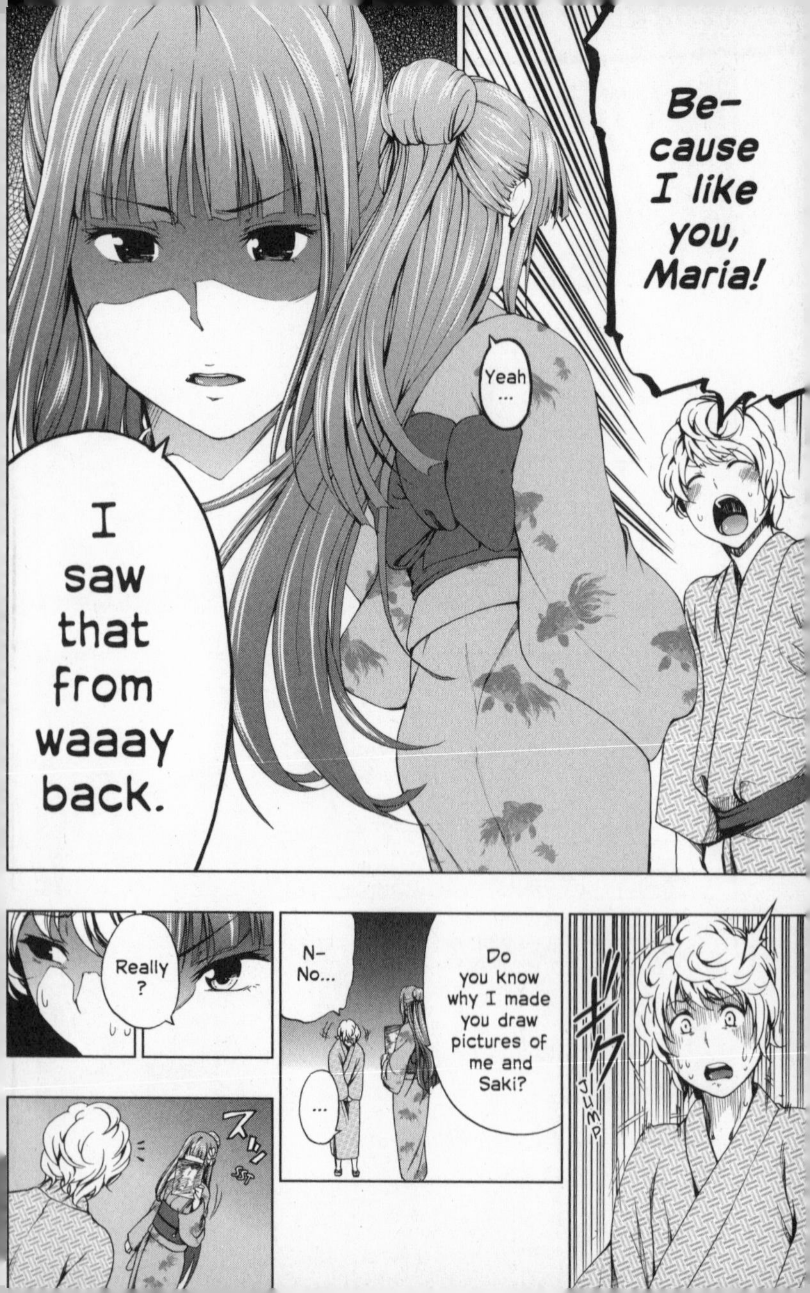
Be-cause I like you, Maria!
Yeah ...
I saw that from waaay back.
JUMP
Do you know why I made you draw pictures of me and Saki?
N- No...
...
Really ?
SST

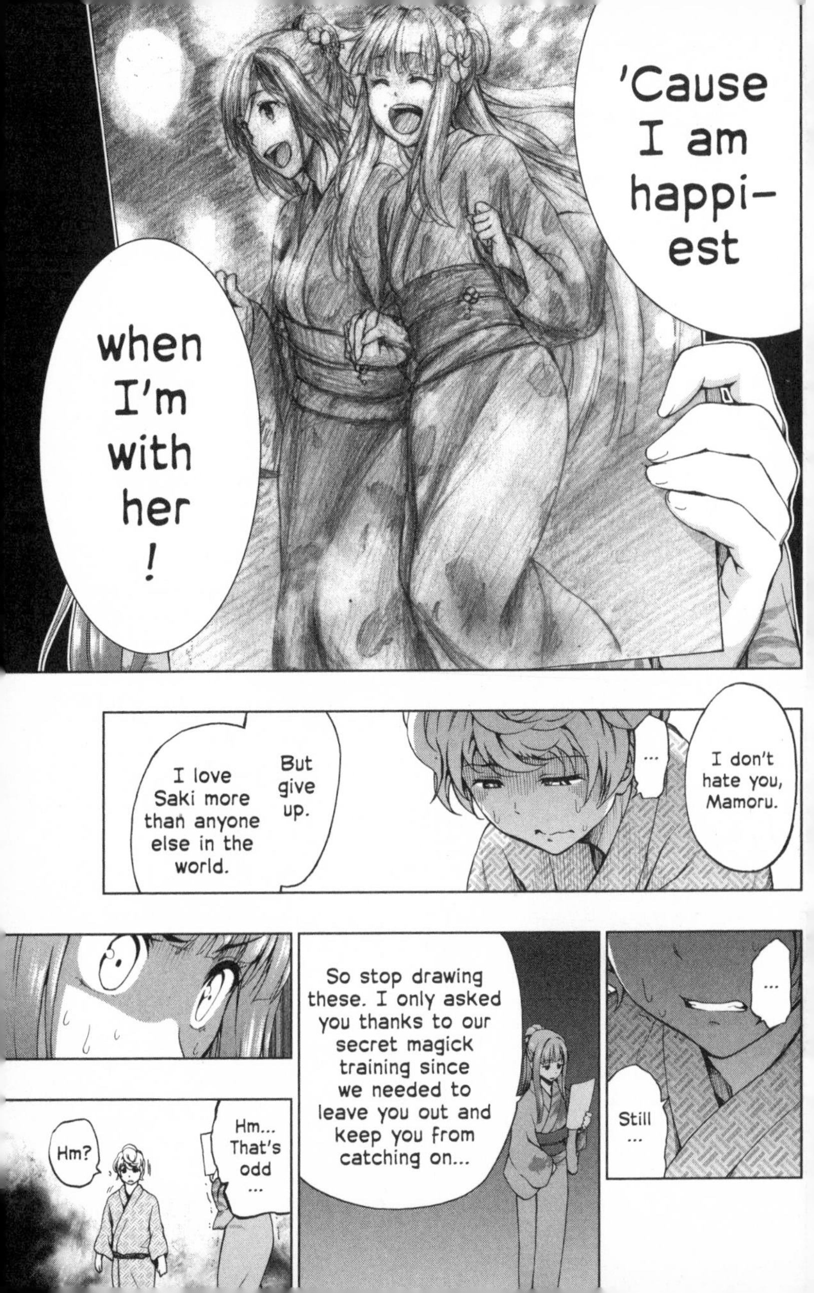
'Cause I am happi- est
when I'm with her !
I don't hate you, Mamoru.
...
But give up.
I love Saki more than anyone else in the world.
...
Still ...
So stop drawing these. I only asked you thanks to our secret magick training since we needed to leave you out and keep you from catching on...
Hm... That's odd ...
Hm?

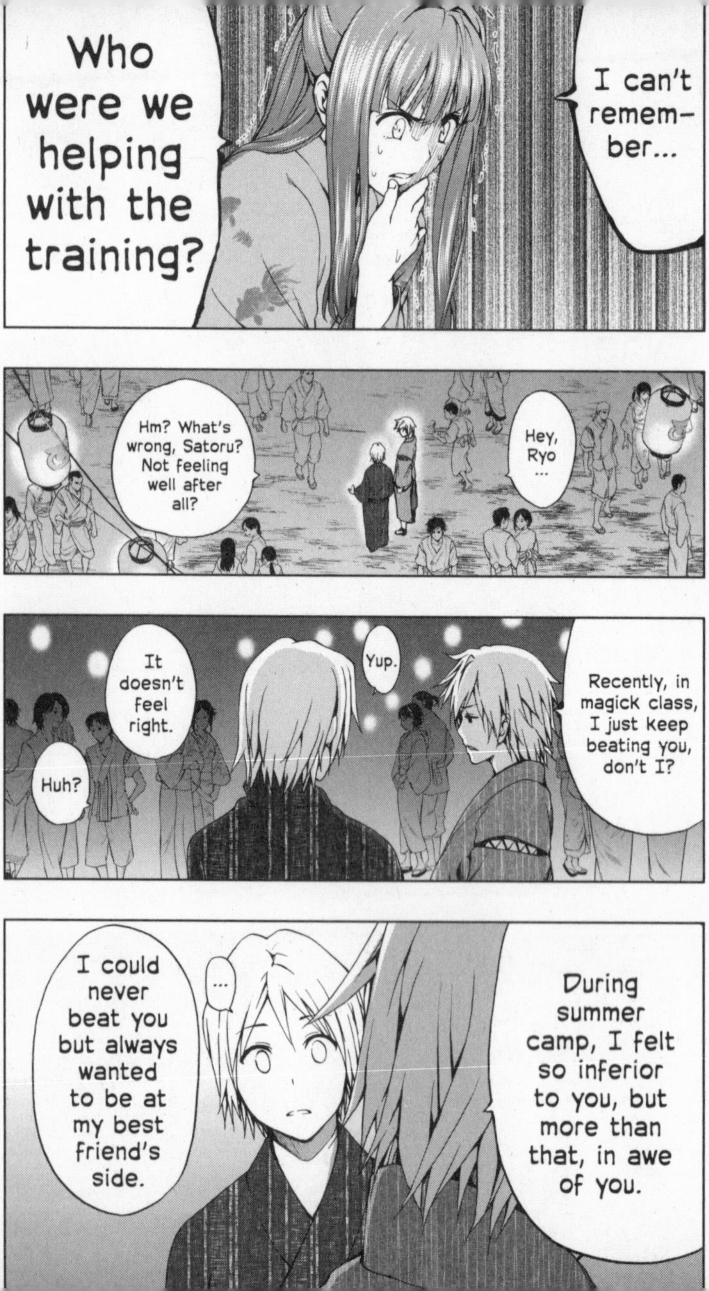
I can't remember...
Who were we helping with the training?
Hey, Ryo...
Hm? What's wrong, Satoru? Not feeling well after all?
Recently, in magick class, I just keep beating you, don't I?
Yup.
It doesn't feel right.
Huh?
During summer camp, I felt so inferior to you, but more than that, in awe of you.
...
I could never beat you but always wanted to be at my best friend's side.

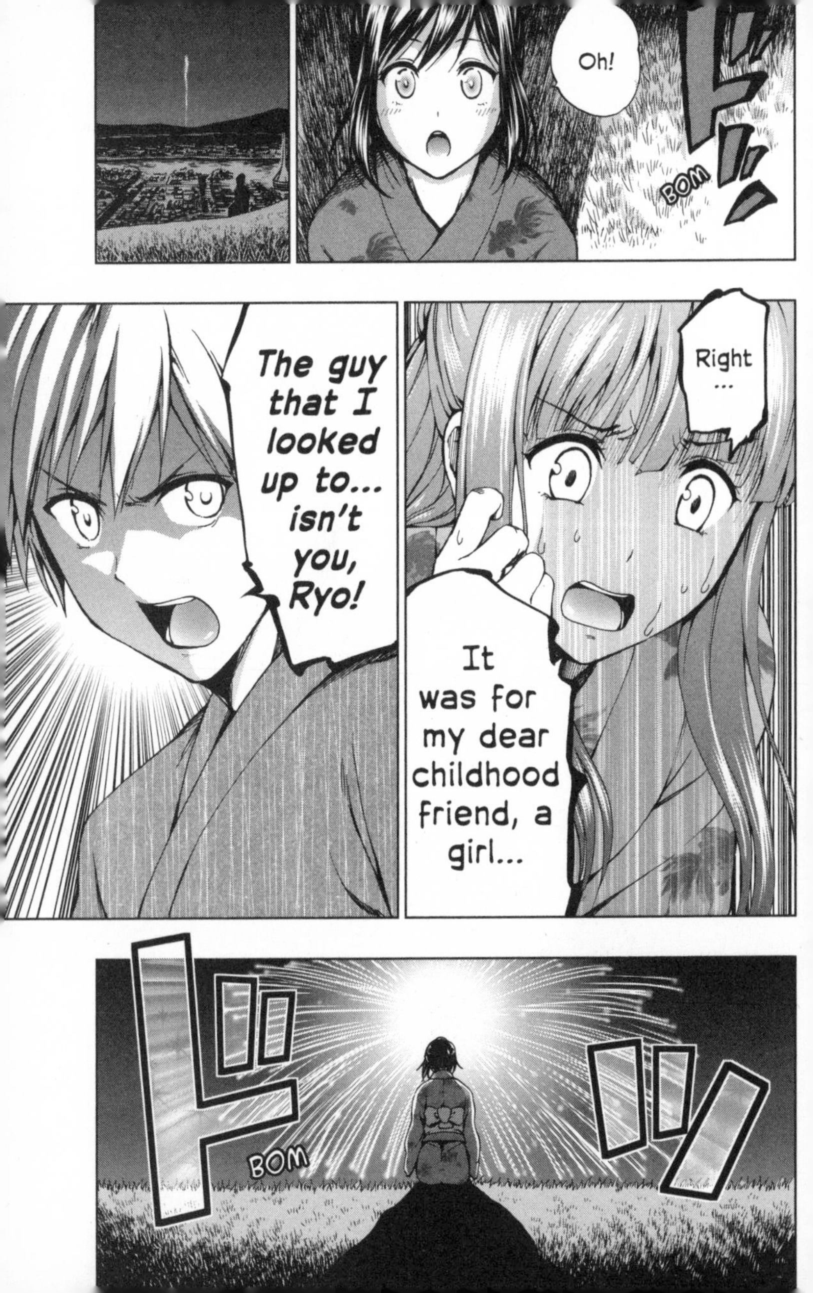

Oh!
BOM
Right ...
It was for my dear childhood friend, a girl...
The guy that I looked up to... isn't you, Ryo!
BOM

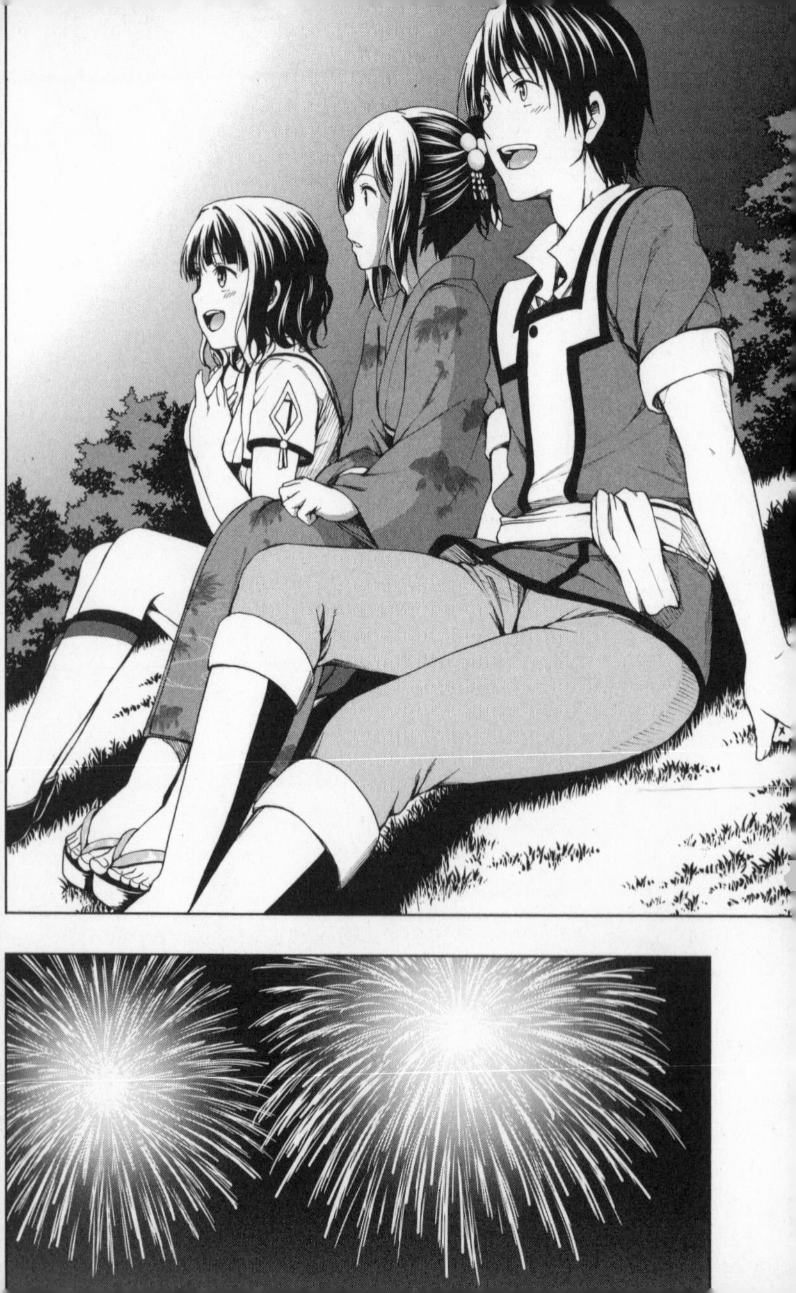

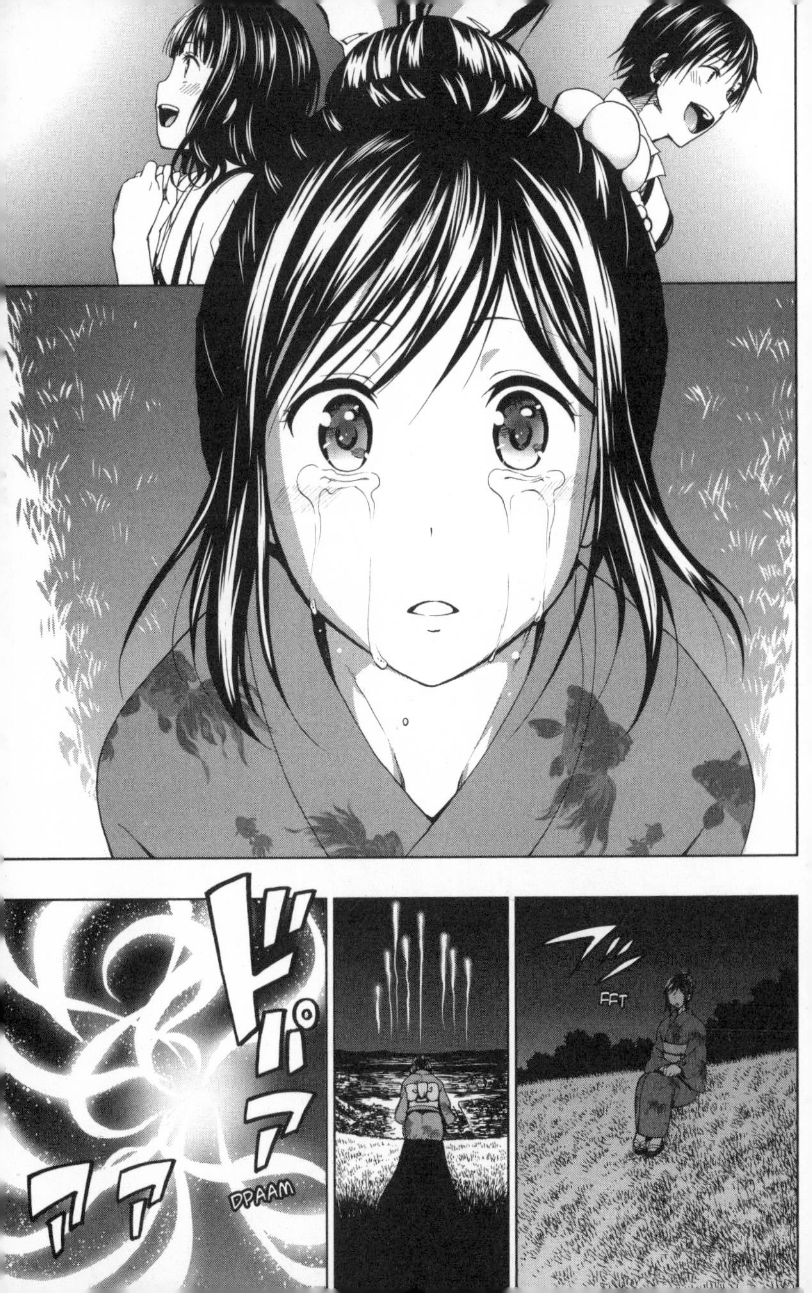
フッ
FFT
ドパァァァ
DPAAM

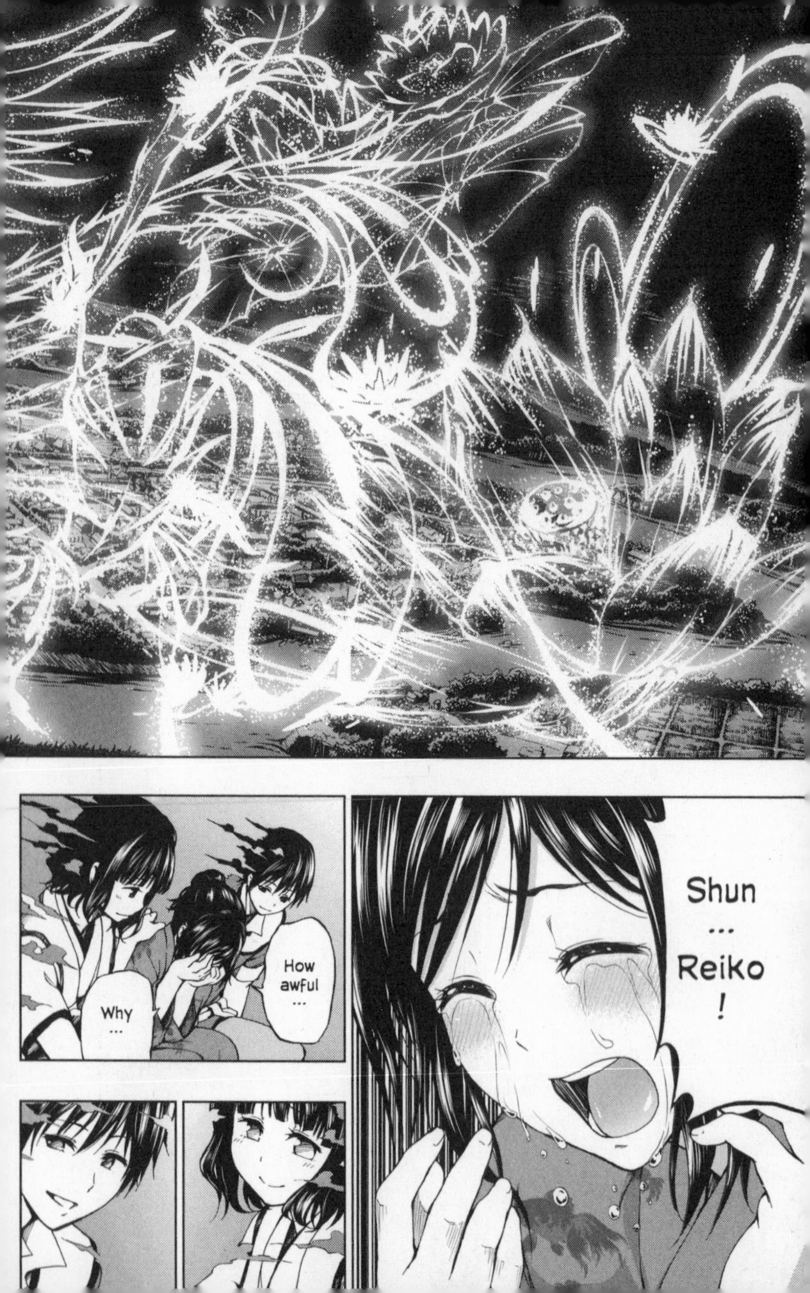
Shun ... Reiko !
How awful ...
Why ...

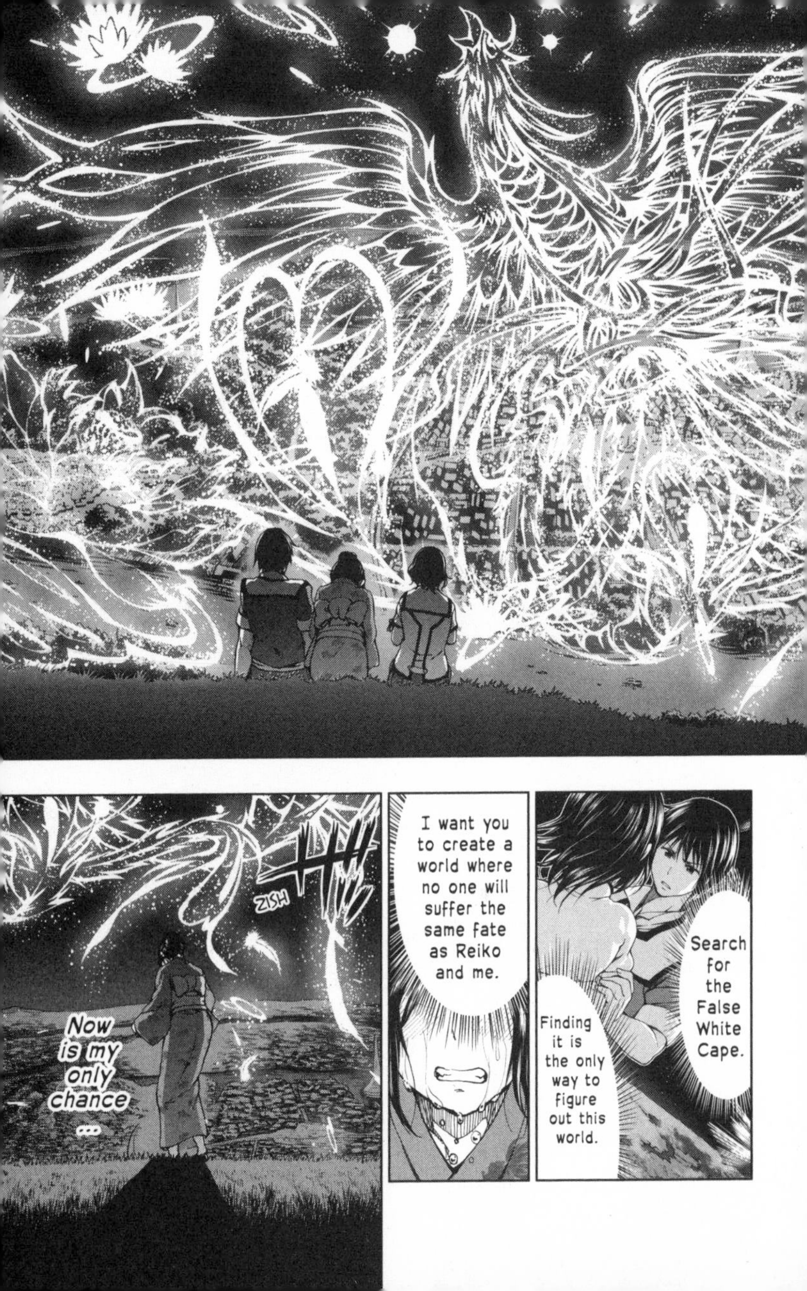
Search for the False White Cape.
Finding it is the only way to figure out this world.
I want you to create a world where no one will suffer the same fate as Reiko and me.
ZISH
Now is my only chance ...

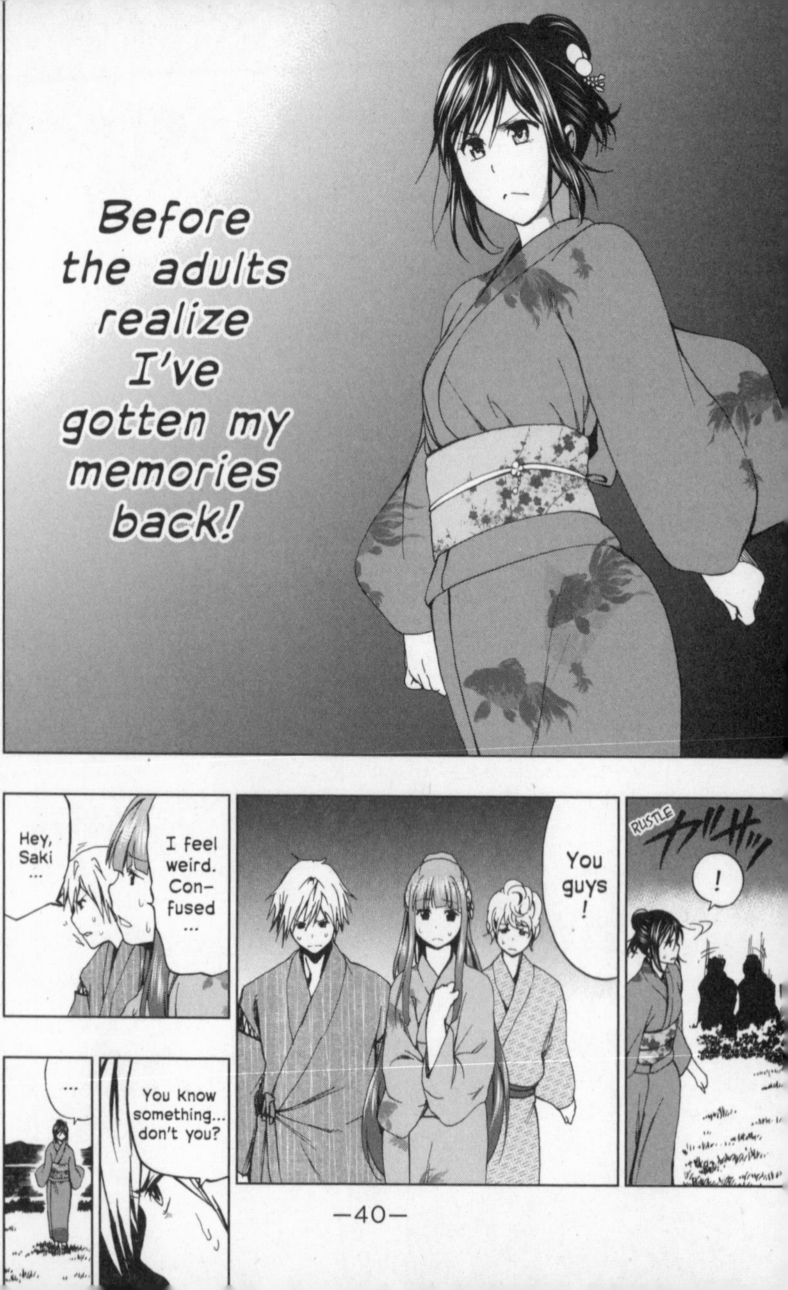
Before the adults realize I've gotten my memories back!
RUSTLE
!
You guys!
Hey, Saki...
I feel weird. Confused...
You know something... don't you?
...

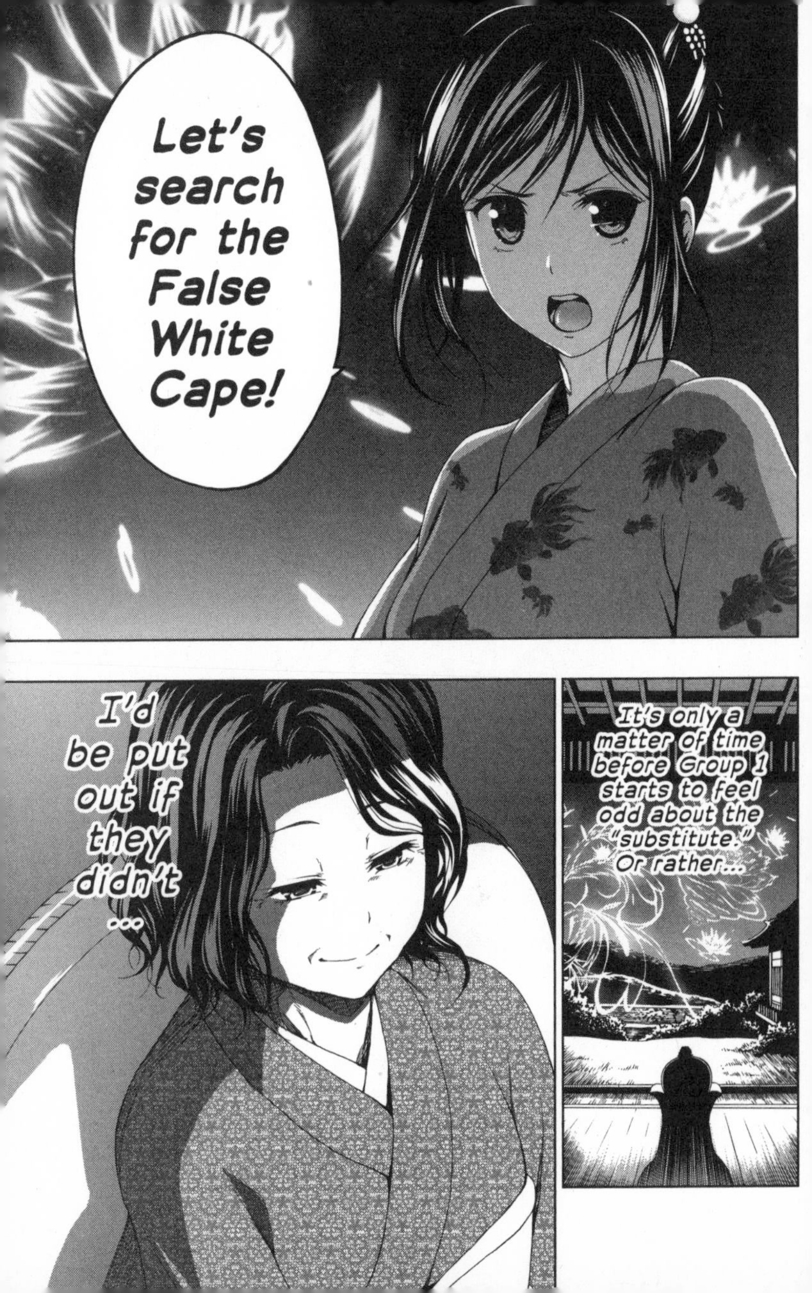
Let's search for the False White Cape!
It's only a matter of time before Group 1 starts to feel odd about the "substitute." Or rather...
I'd be put out if they didn't...

... Yeah.

Let's go.

ZSHK

ZSHK

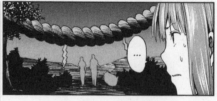

...

...

SHAKE

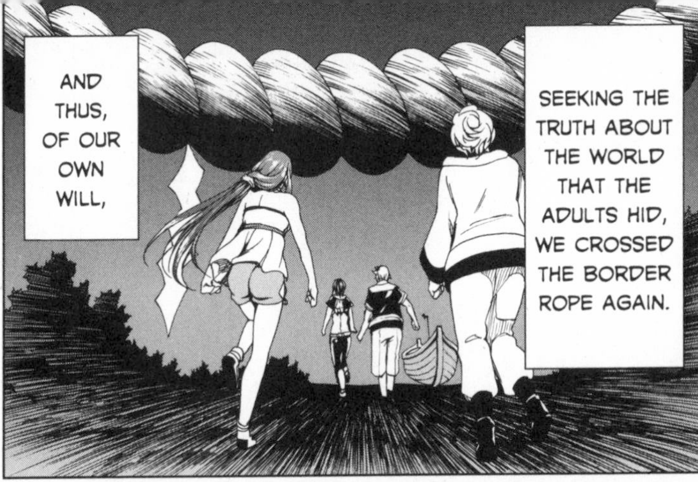
SEEKING THE TRUTH ABOUT THE WORLD THAT THE ADULTS HID, WE CROSSED THE BORDER ROPE AGAIN.
AND THUS, OF OUR OWN WILL,
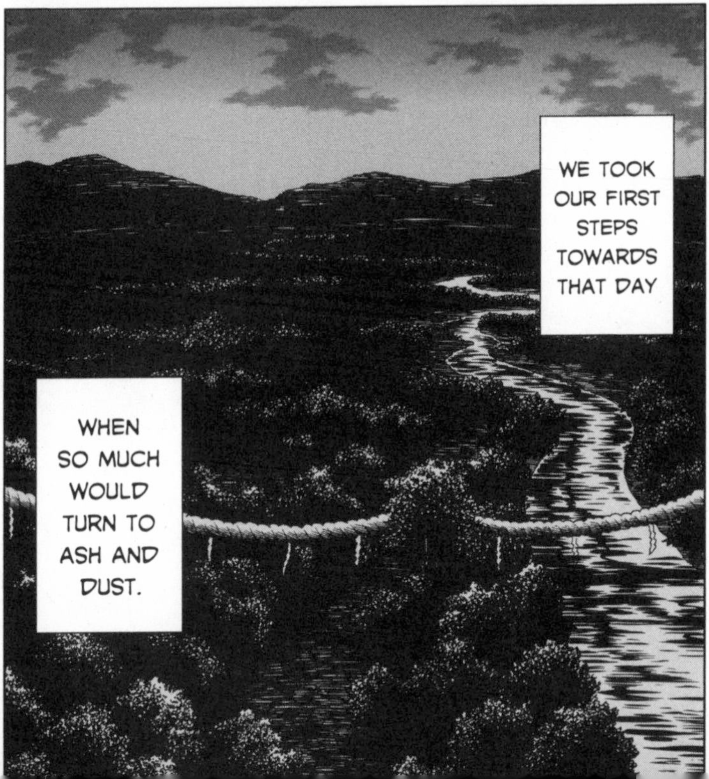
WE TOOK OUR FIRST STEPS TOWARDS THAT DAY
WHEN SO MUCH WOULD TURN TO ASH AND DUST.

FROM
THE
NEW
WORLD

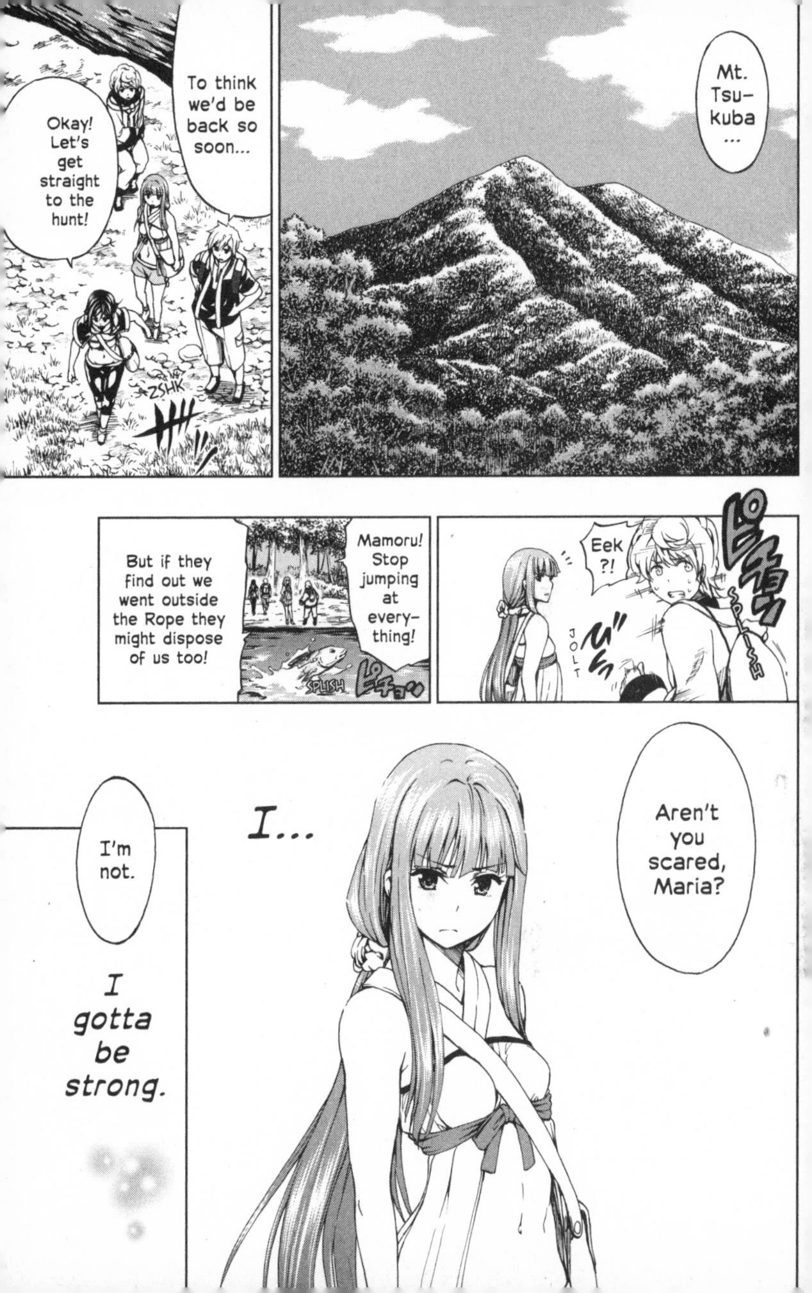
Mt. Tsu-kuba...
To think we'd be back so soon...
Okay! Let's get straight to the hunt!
ZSHK
Eek ?!
SPLISH
JOLT
Mamoru! Stop jumping at every-thing!
But if they find out we went outside the Rope they might dispose of us too!
SPLISH
Aren't you scared, Maria?
I...
I'm not.
I gotta be strong.

Chapter 10
False White Cape

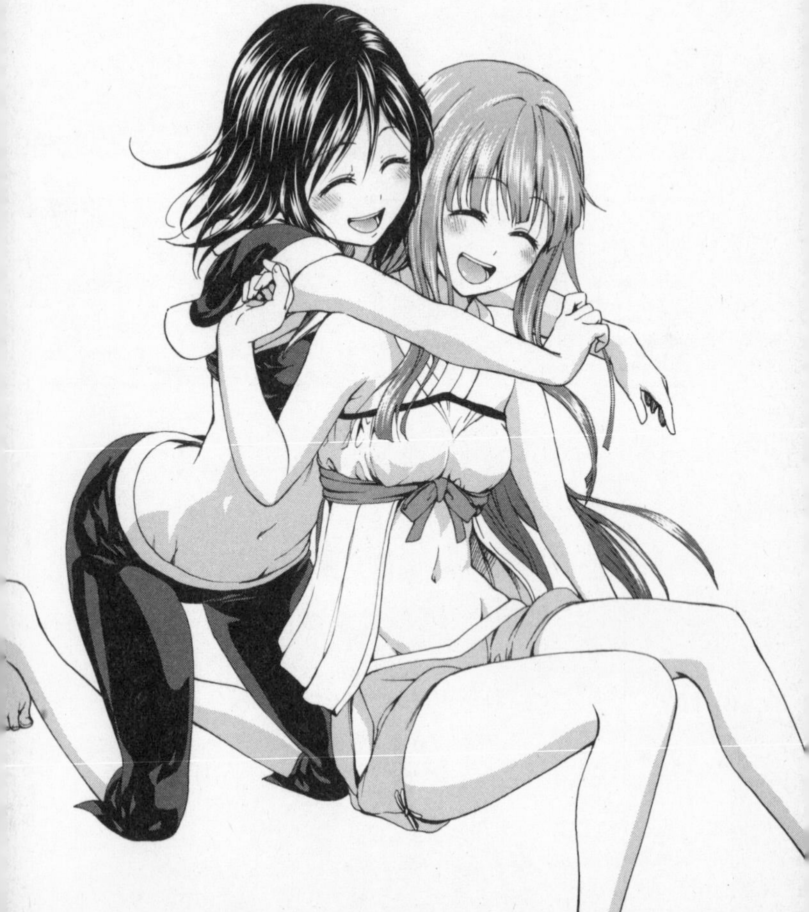

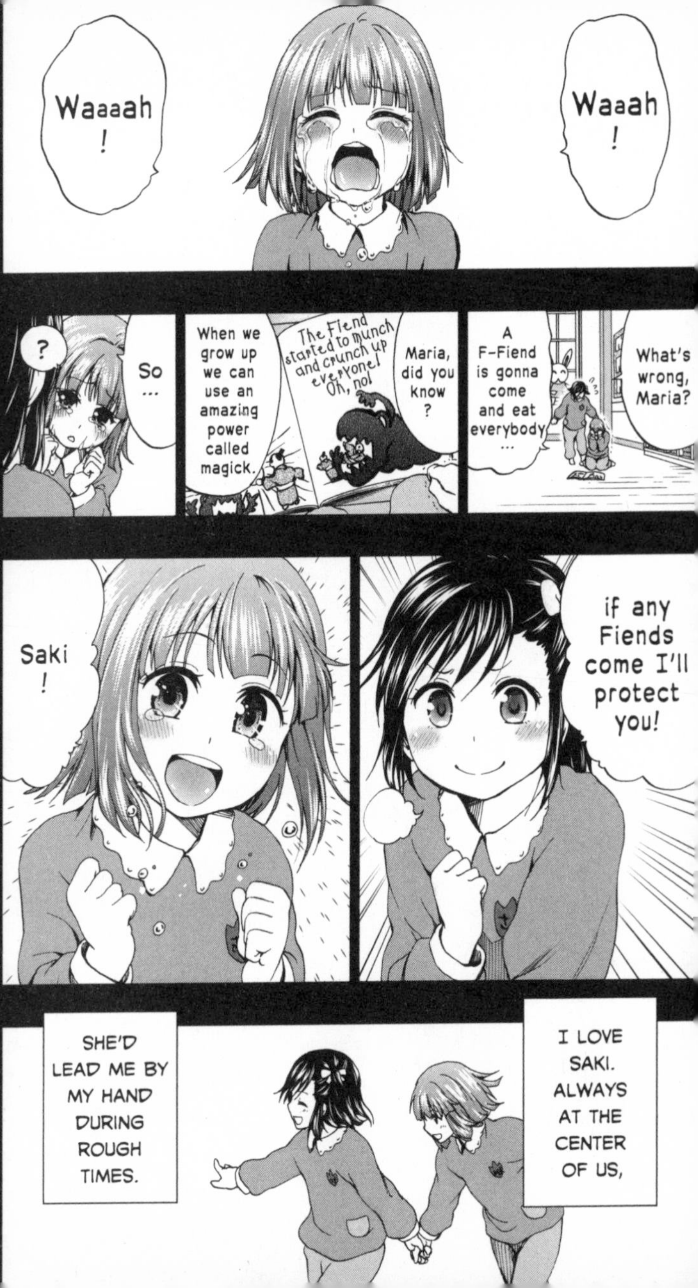
Waaah!
Waaaah!
What's wrong, Maria?
A F-Fiend is gonna come and eat everybody...
Maria, did you know?
The Fiend started to munch and crunch up everyone! Oh, no!
When we grow up we can use an amazing power called magick.
?
So...
if any Fiends come I'll protect you!
Saki!
I LOVE SAKI. ALWAYS AT THE CENTER OF US,
SHE'D LEAD ME BY MY HAND DURING ROUGH TIMES.

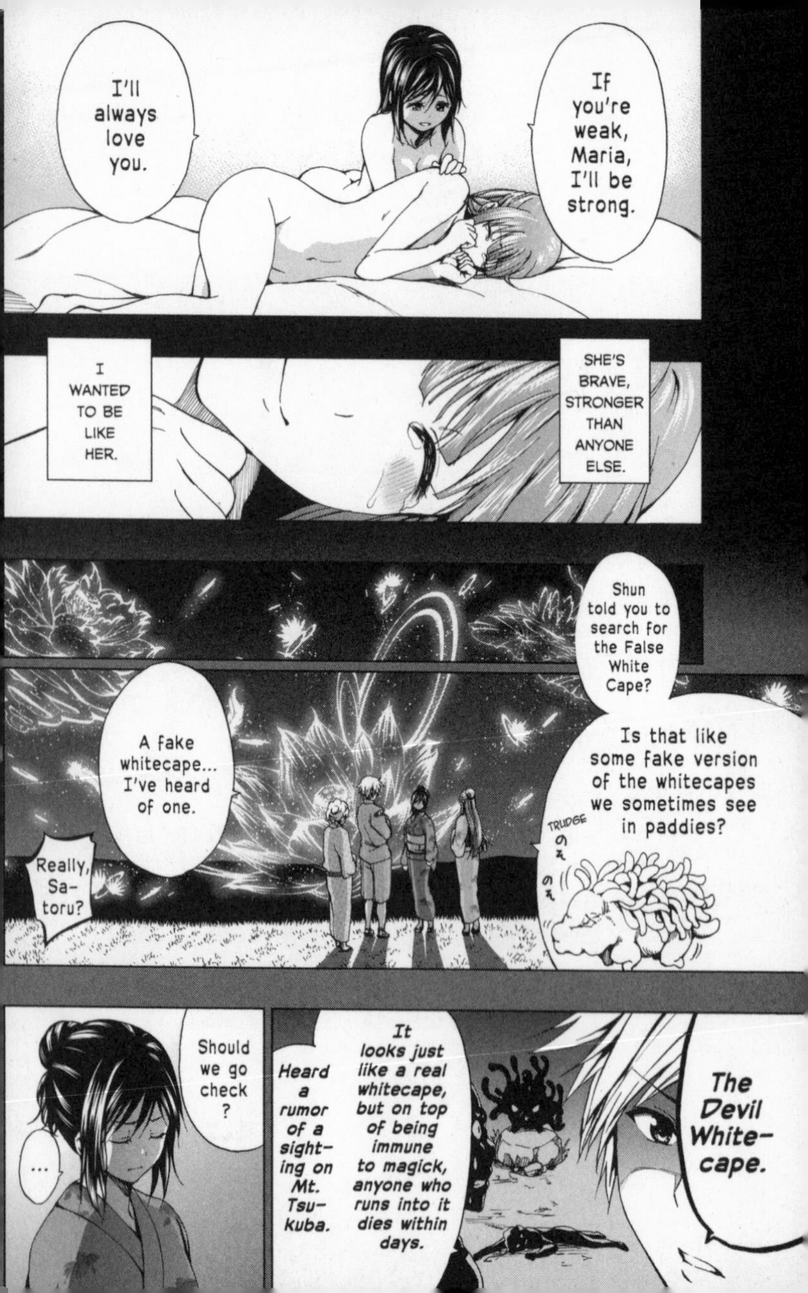
If you're weak, Maria, I'll be strong.
I'll always love you.
SHE'S BRAVE, STRONGER THAN ANYONE ELSE.
I WANTED TO BE LIKE HER.
Shun told you to search for the False White Cape?
Is that like some fake version of the whitecapes we sometimes see in paddies?
TRUDGE
のそ
のそ
A fake whitecape... I've heard of one.
Really, Sa-toru?
The Devil White-cape.
It looks just like a real whitecape, but on top of being immune to magick, anyone who runs into it dies within days.
Heard a rumor of a sight-ing on Mt. Tsu-kuba.
Should we go check?
...

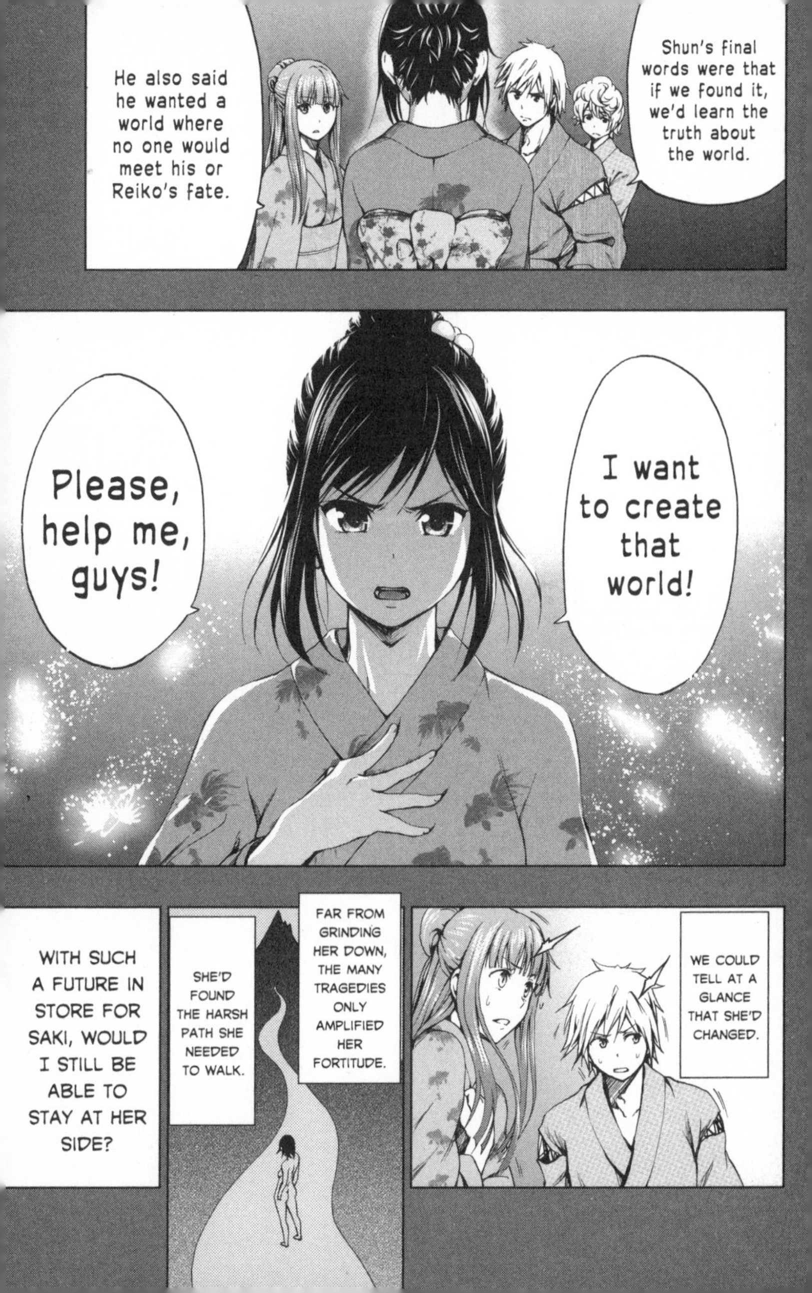
Shun's final words were that if we found it, we'd learn the truth about the world.
He also said he wanted a world where no one would meet his or Reiko's fate.
I want to create that world!
Please, help me, guys!
WE COULD TELL AT A GLANCE THAT SHE'D CHANGED.
FAR FROM GRINDING HER DOWN, THE MANY TRAGEDIES ONLY AMPLIFIED HER FORTITUDE.
SHE'D FOUND THE HARSH PATH SHE NEEDED TO WALK.
WITH SUCH A FUTURE IN STORE FOR SAKI, WOULD I STILL BE ABLE TO STAY AT HER SIDE?

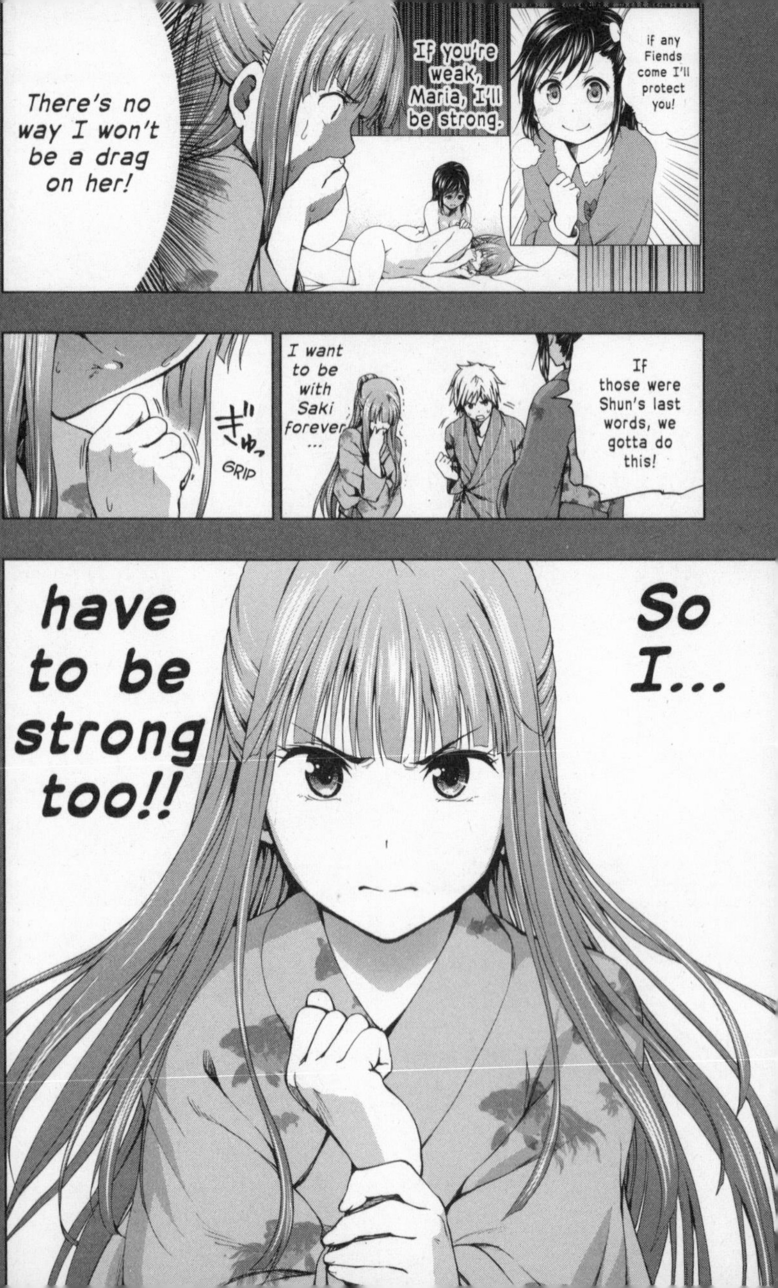
if any Fiends come I'll protect you!
If you're weak, Maria, I'll be strong.
There's no way I won't be a drag on her!
If those were Shun's last words, we gotta do this!
I want to be with Saki forever...
ぎゅっ
GRIP
So I...
have to be strong too!!

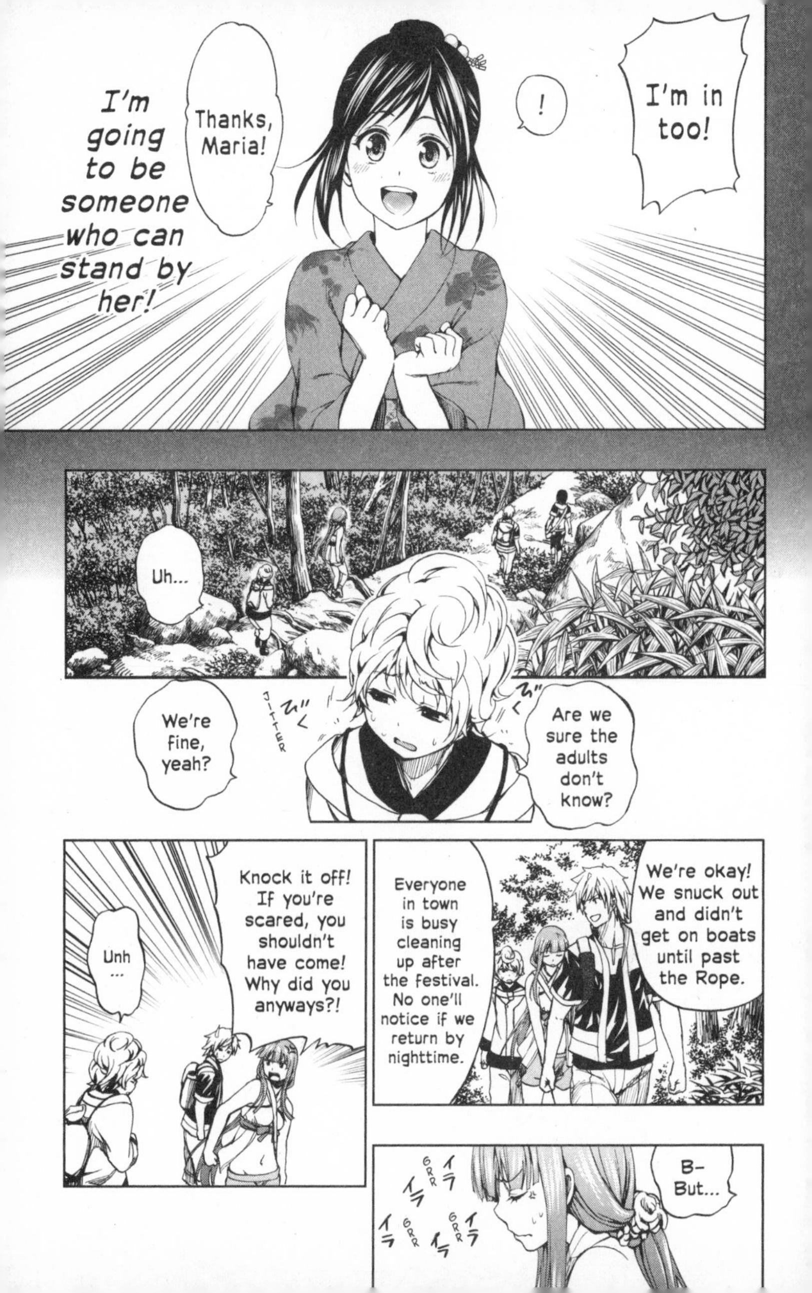
I'm in too!
!
Thanks, Maria!
I'm going to be someone who can stand by her!
Uh...
Are we sure the adults don't know?
JITTER
We're fine, yeah?
We're okay! We snuck out and didn't get on boats until past the Rope.
Everyone in town is busy cleaning up after the festival. No one'll notice if we return by nighttime.
B- But...
GRR GRR GRR
Knock it off! If you're scared, you shouldn't have come! Why did you anyways?!
Unh ...

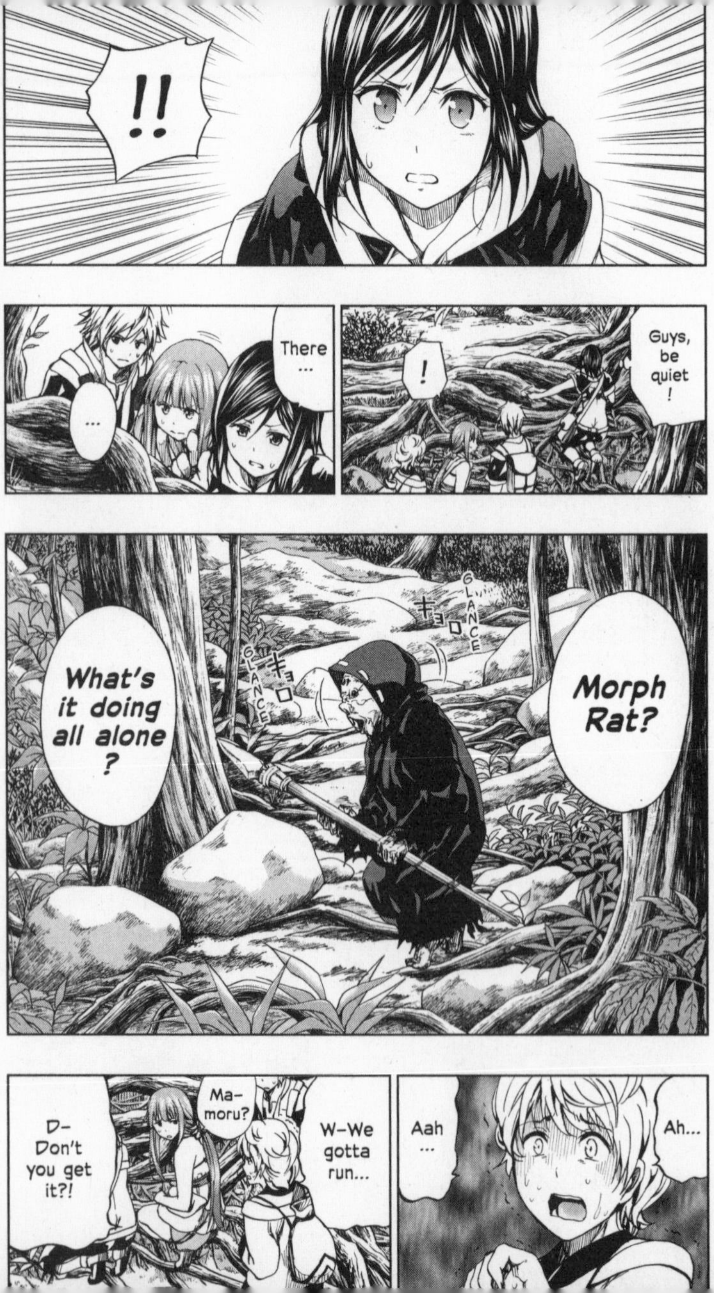
!!
Guys, be quiet!
!
There...
...
Morph Rat?
GLANCE
キョロ
GLANCE
キョロ
What's it doing all alone?
Ah...
Aah...
W-We gotta run...
Ma-moru?
D-Don't you get it?!

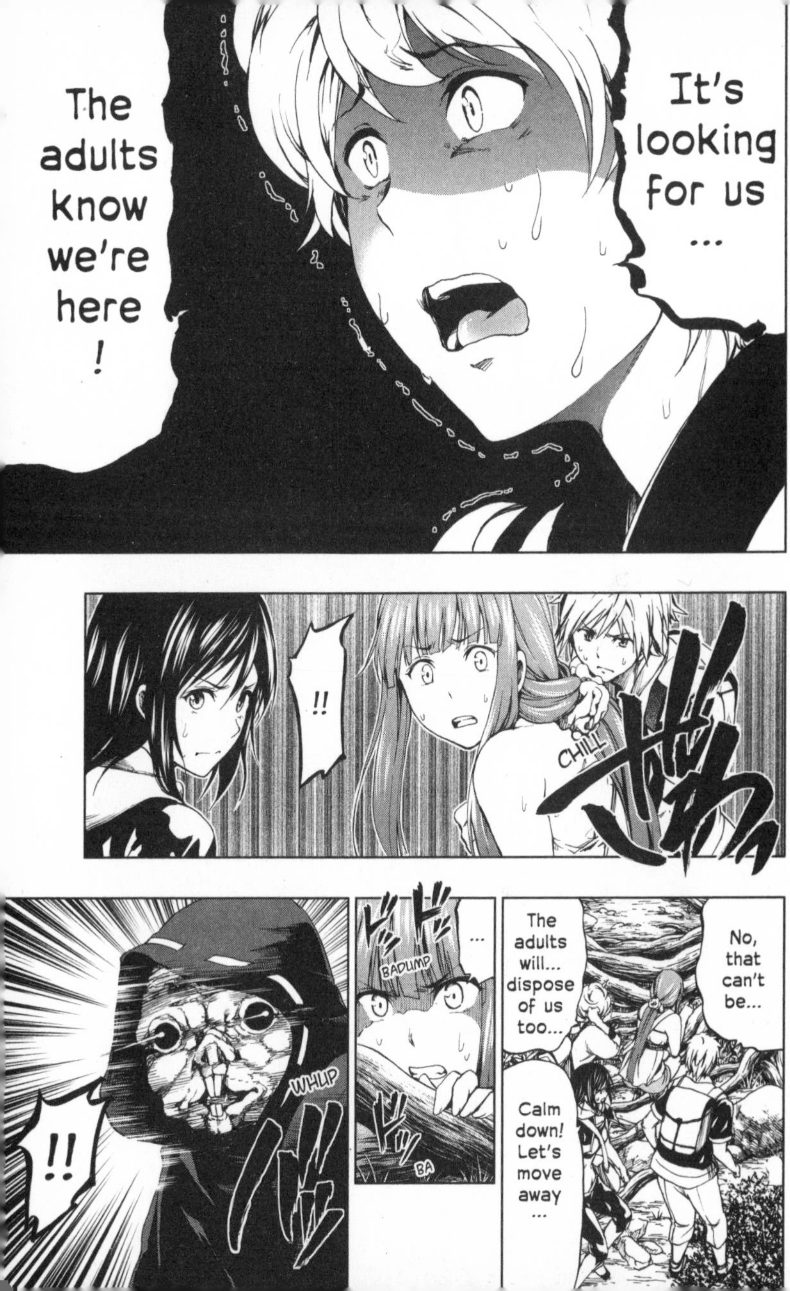
It's looking for us ...
The adults know we're here !
CHILL
!!
No, that can't be...
The adults will... dispose of us too...
Calm down! Let's move away ...
...
BADUMP
BA
WHUP
!!

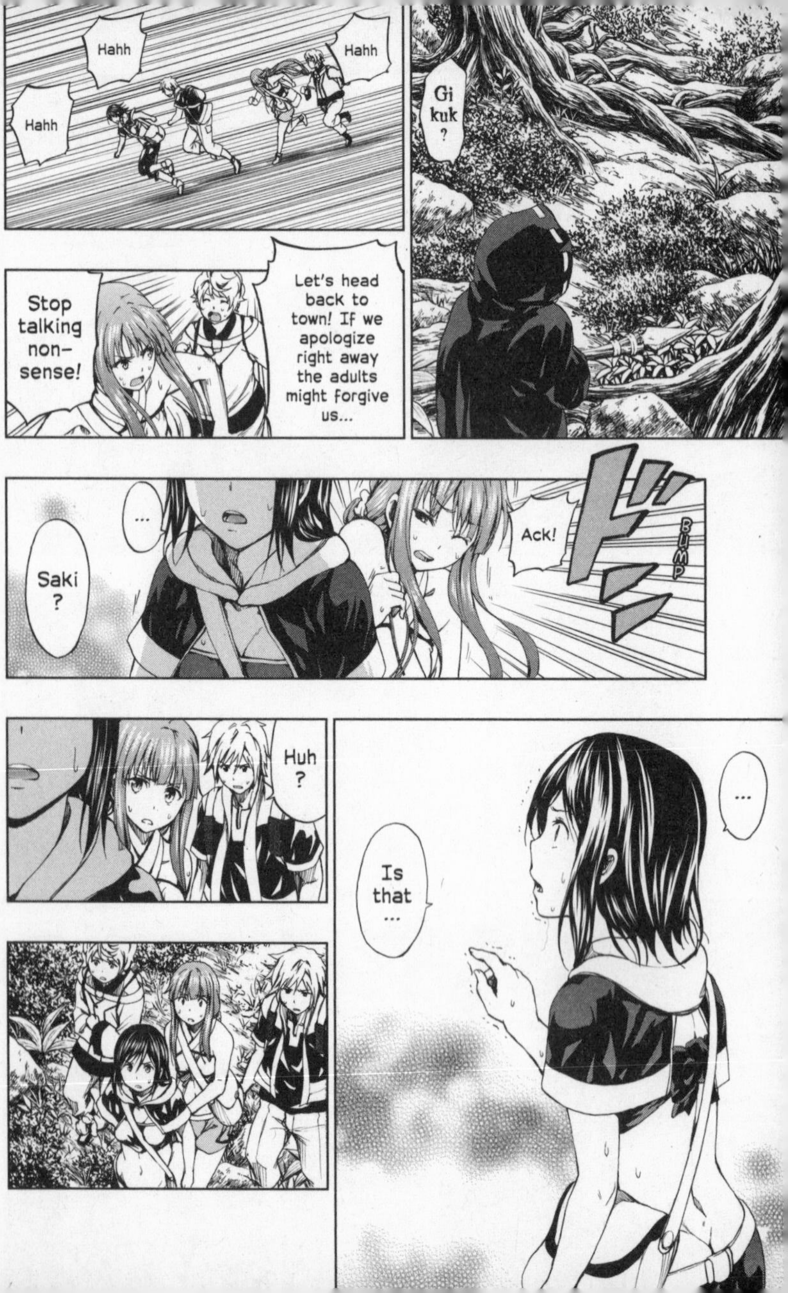
Gi kuk ?
Hahh
Hahh
Hahh
Let's head back to town! If we apologize right away the adults might forgive us...
Stop talking non-sense!
BUMP
Ack!
...
Saki ?
...
Is that ...
Huh ?

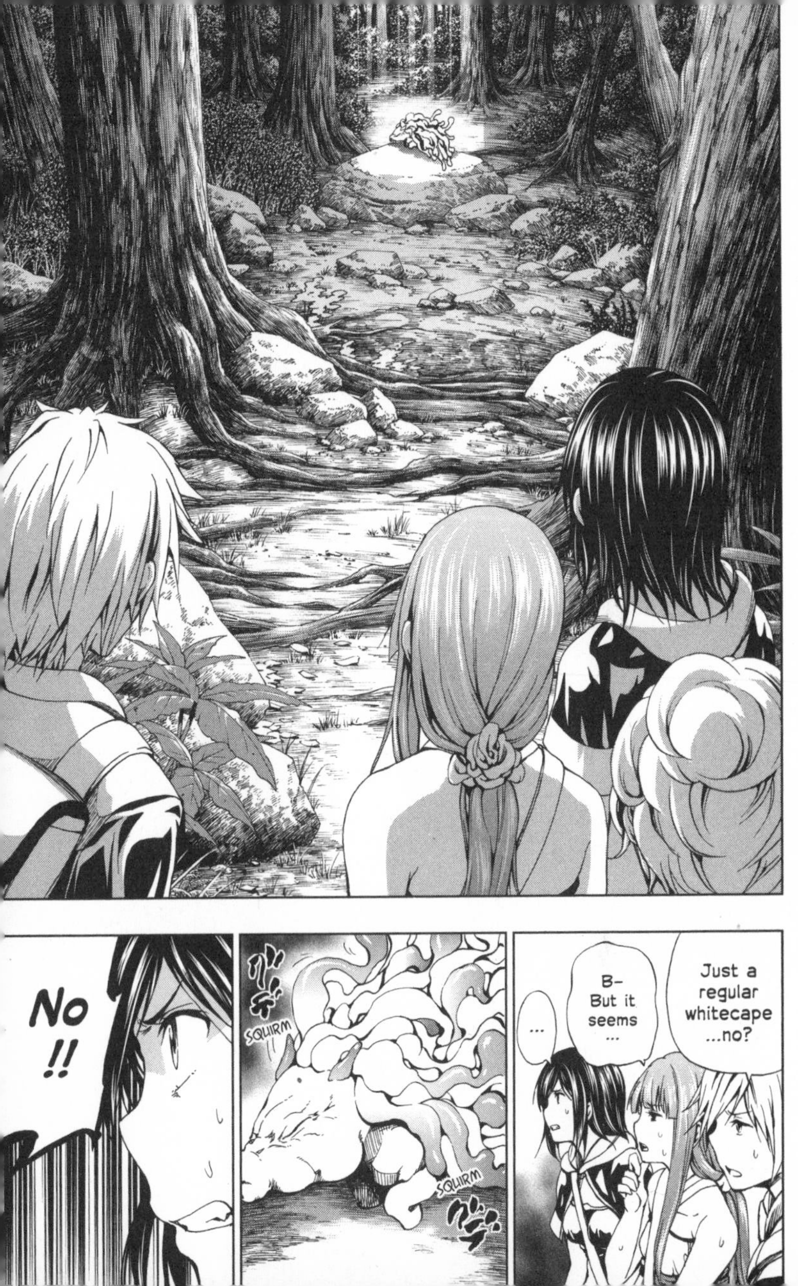
Just a regular whitecape ...no?
B– But it seems ...
...
SQUIRM
SQUIRM
No !!

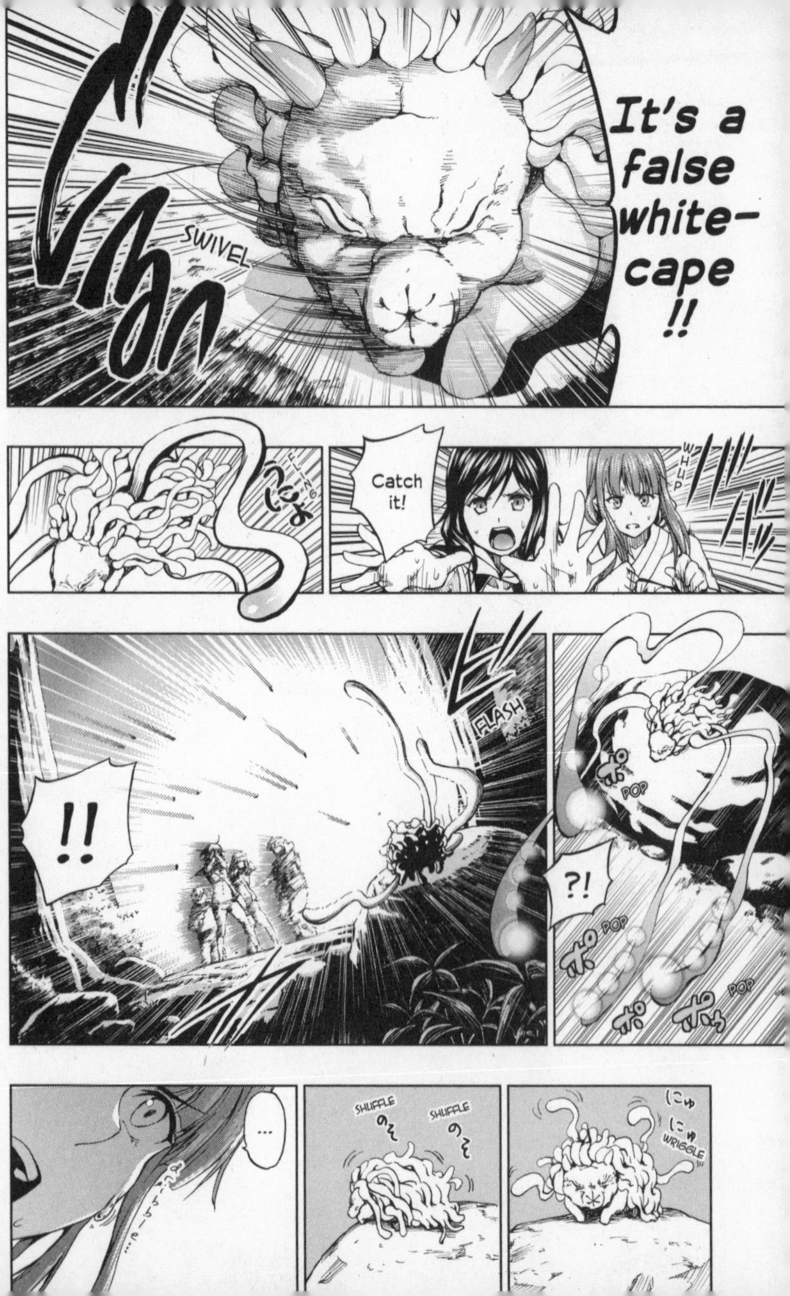
It's a false white-cape !!
SWIVEL
WHUP
Catch it!
FLING
?!
POP
POP
POP
FLASH
!!
WRIGGLE
SHUFFLE
SHUFFLE
...

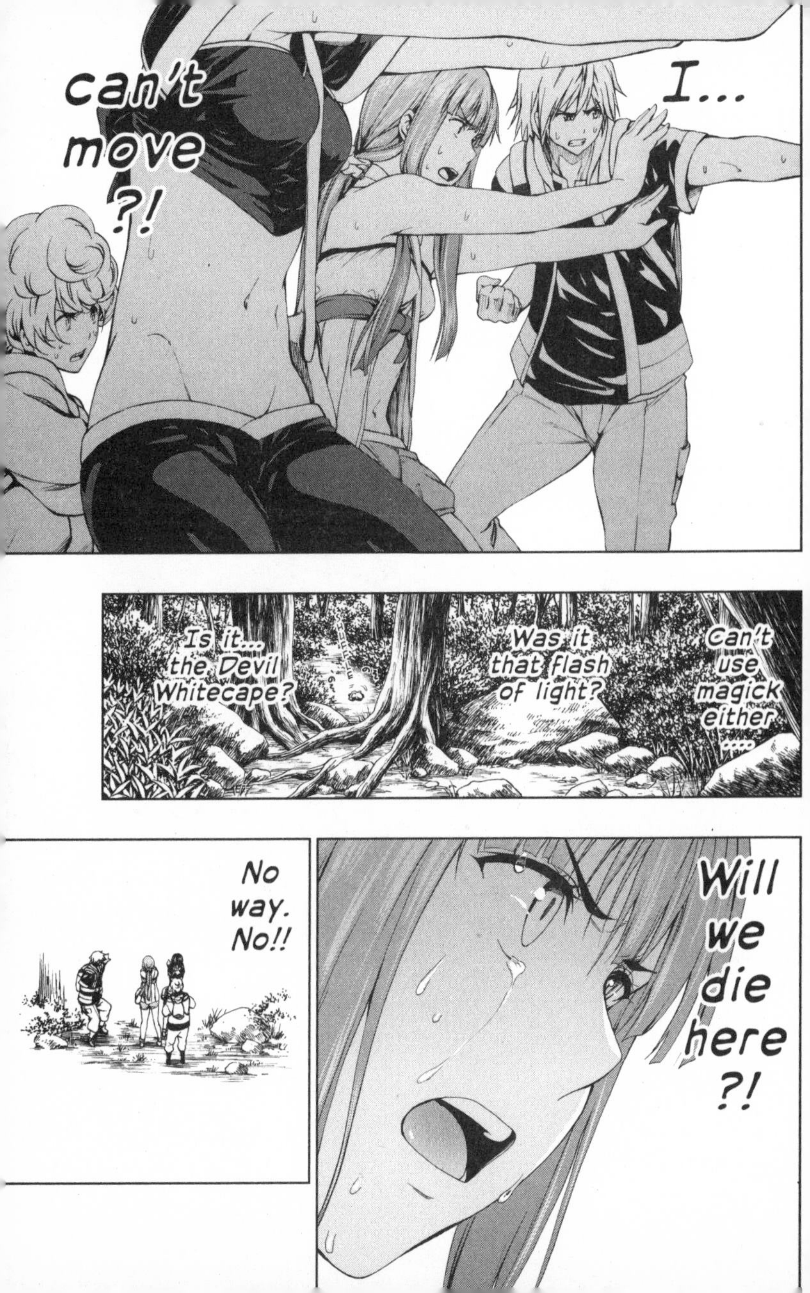
I...
can't move ?!
Can't use magick either ....
Was it that flash of light?
Is it... the Devil Whitecape?
Will we die here ?!
No way. No!!

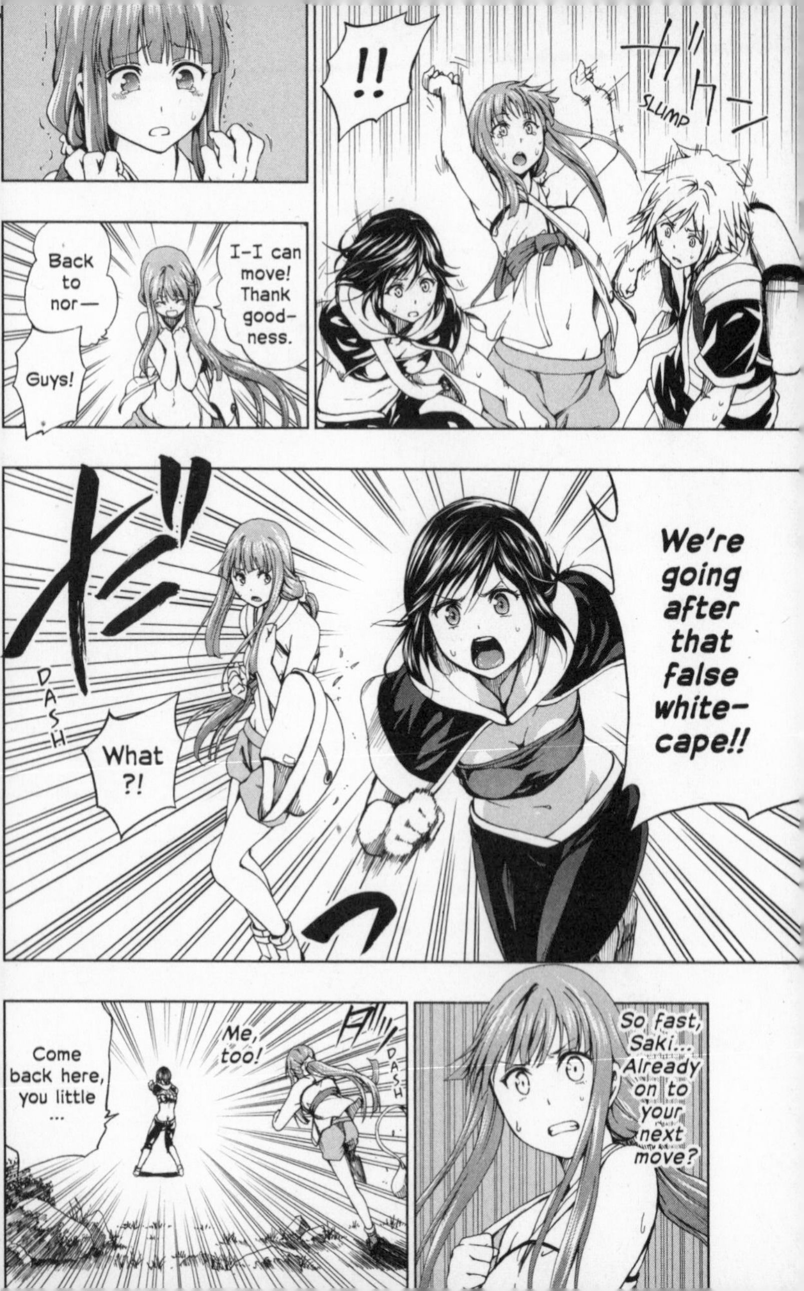
!!
SLUMP
I-I can move! Thank goodness.
Back to nor—
Guys!
We're going after that false white-cape!!
DASH
What?!
So fast, Saki... Already on to your next move?
Me, too!
DASH
Come back here, you little ...

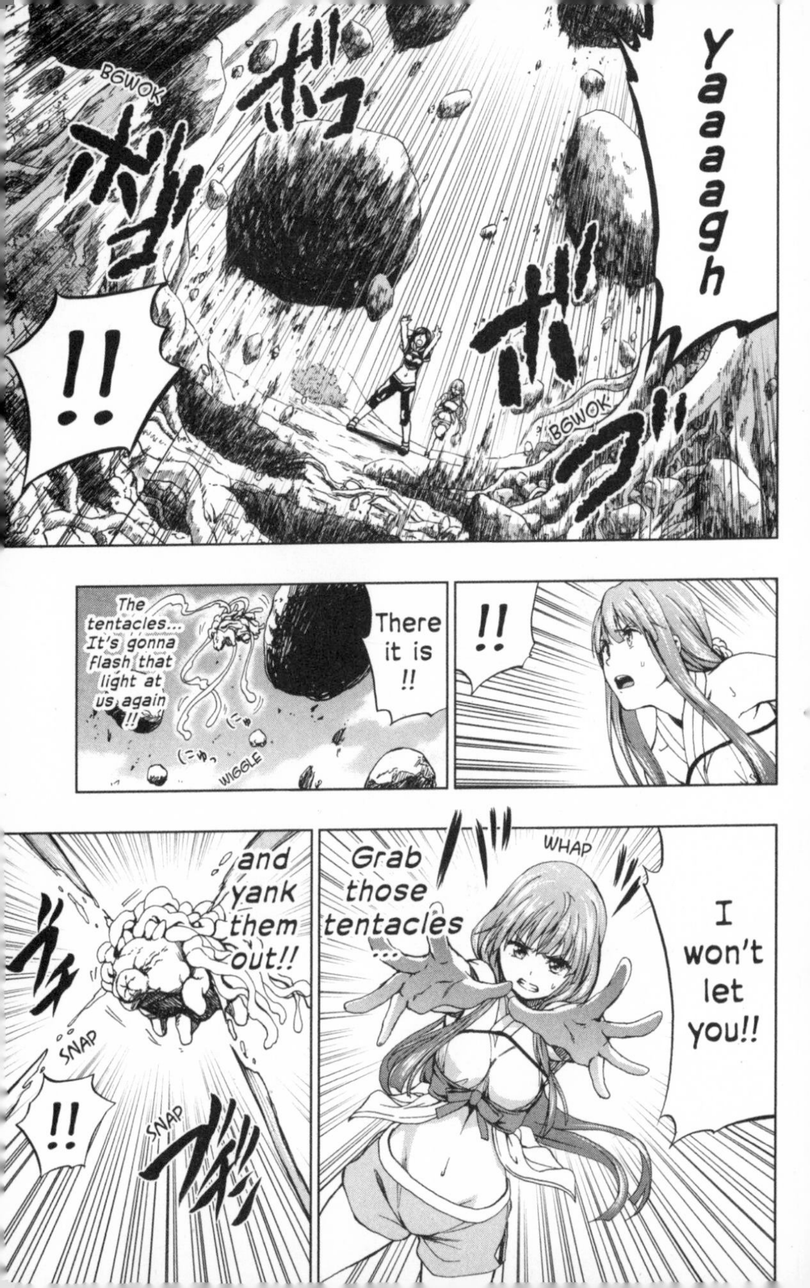
Yaaaagh
BGWOK
BGWOK
!!
!!
There it is !!
The tentacles... It's gonna flash that light at us again!!
WIGGLE
I won't let you!!
WHAP
Grab those tentacles...
and yank them out!!
SNAP
!!
SNAP

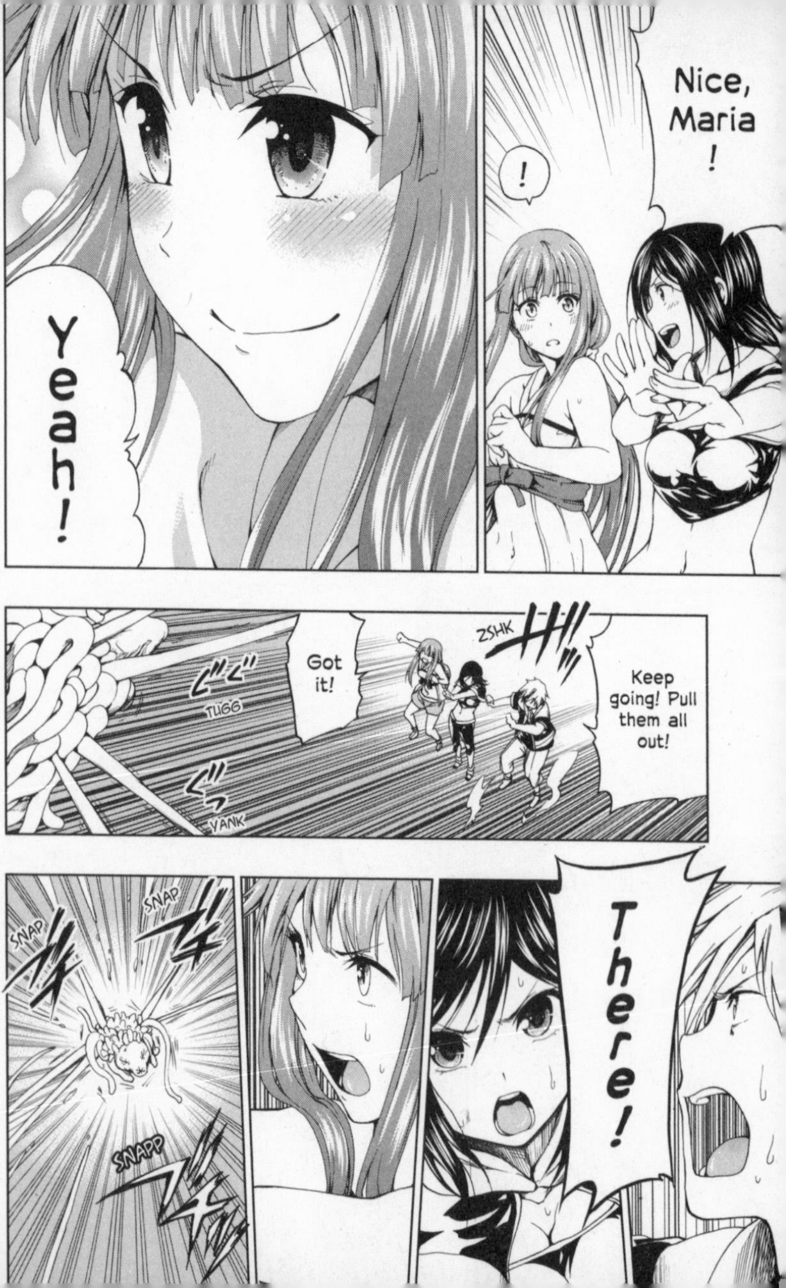
Nice, Maria!
!
Yeah!
ZSHK
Keep going! Pull them all out!
Got it!
TUGG
YANK
There!
SNAP
SNAP
SNAPP

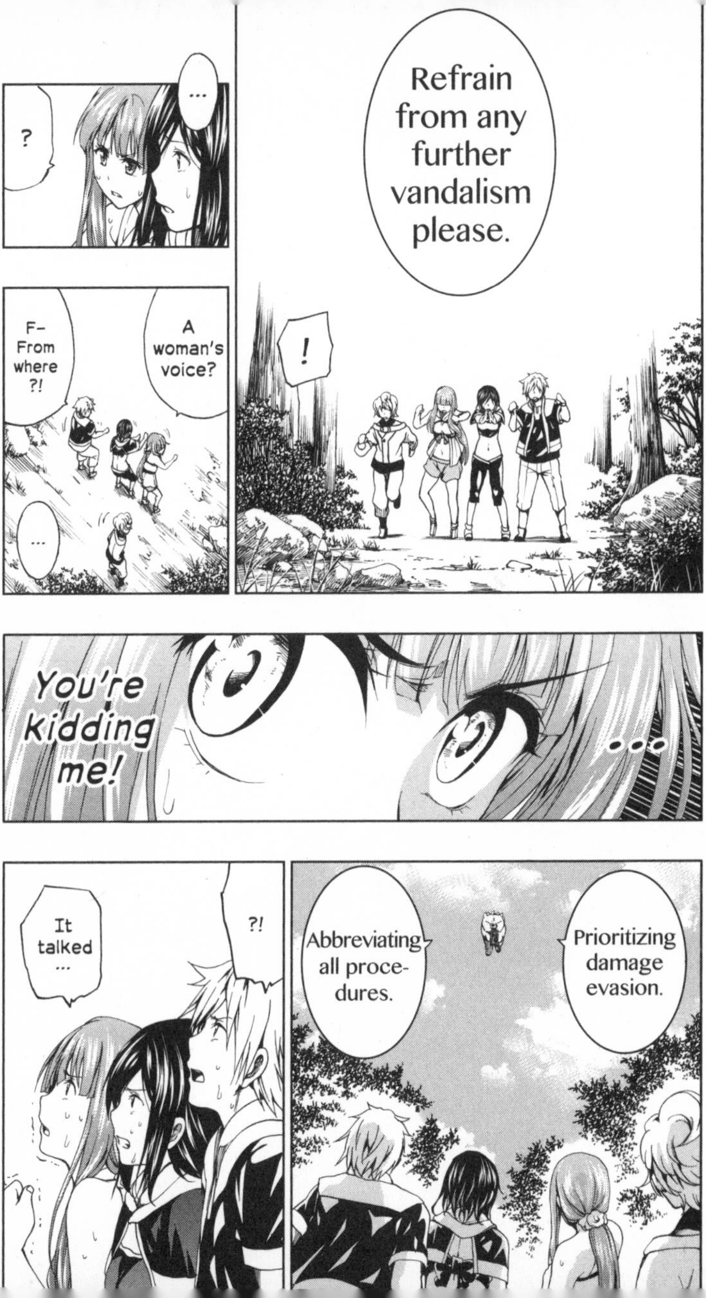
Refrain from any further vandalism please.
!
...
?
A woman's voice?
F- From where ?!
...
...
You're kidding me!
Prioritizing damage evasion.
Abbreviating all procedures.
?!
It talked ...

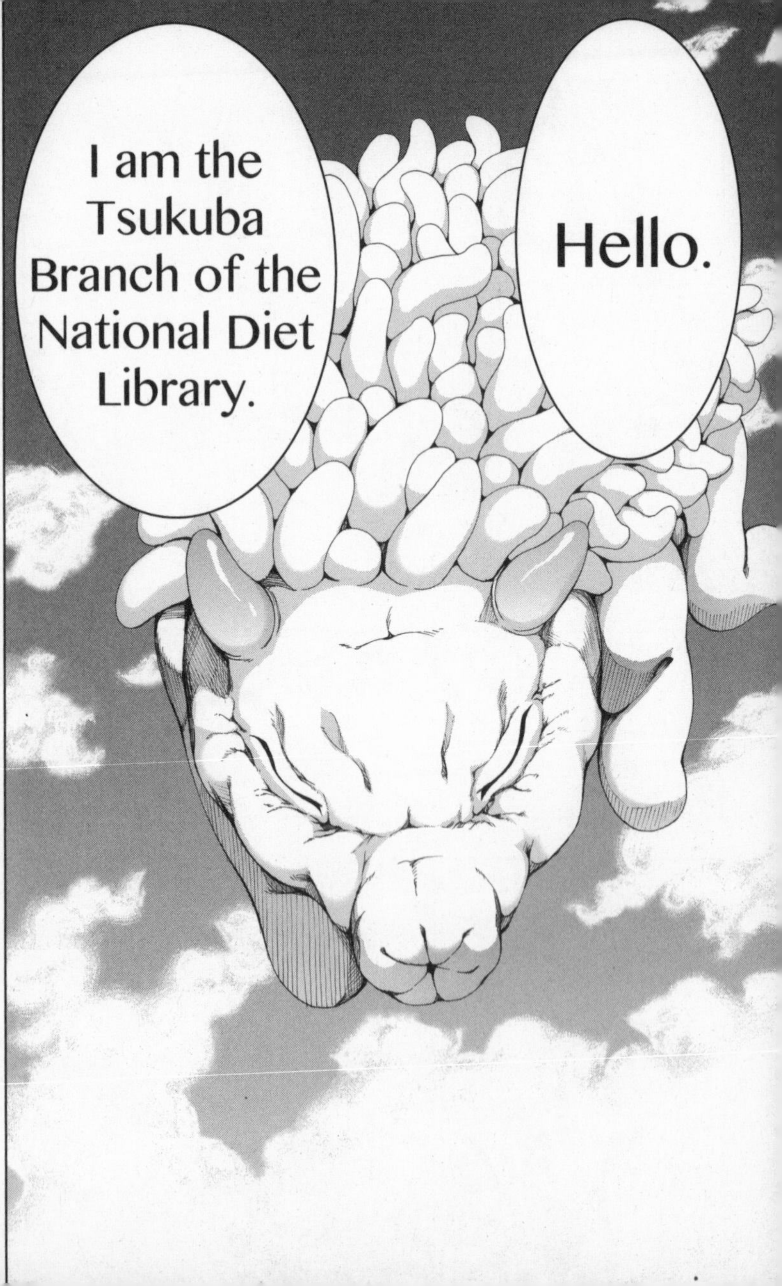
Hello.
I am the Tsukuba Branch of the National Diet Library.

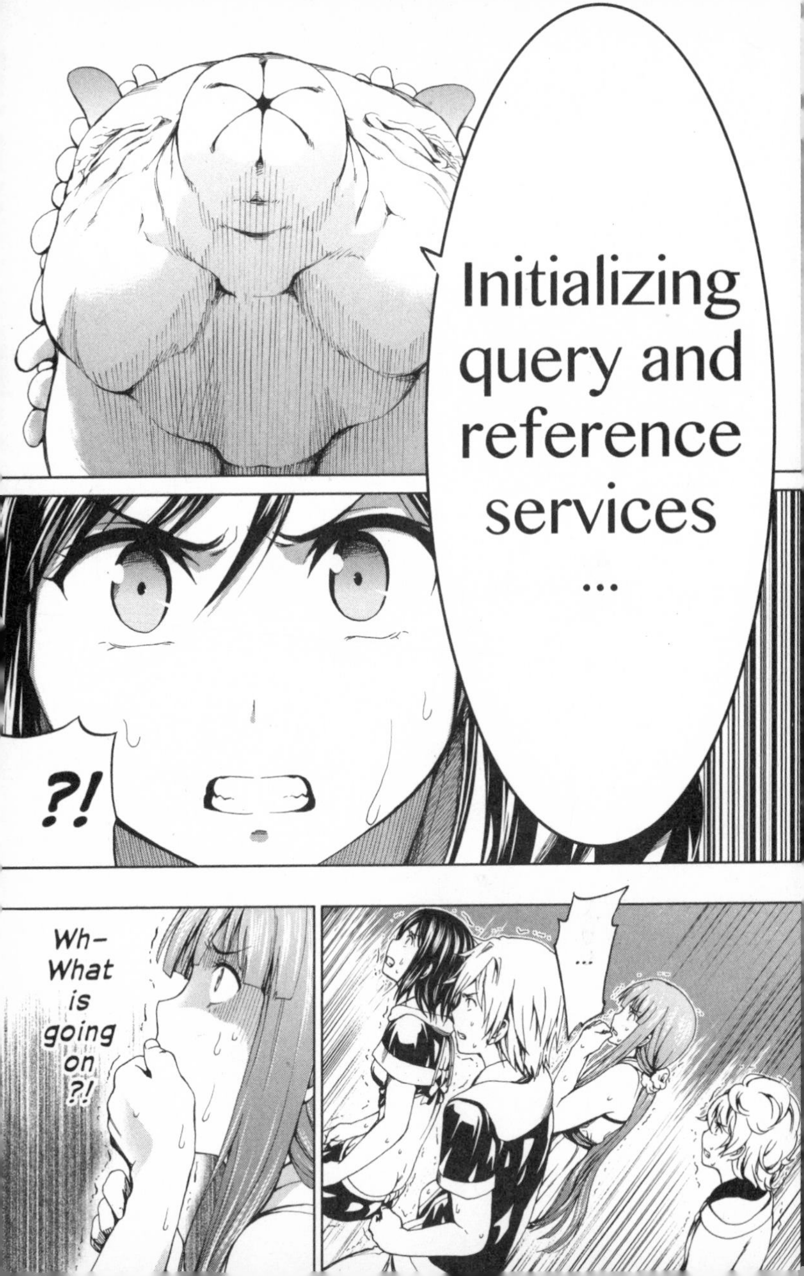
Initializing query and reference services ...
?!
...
Wh- What is going on ?!

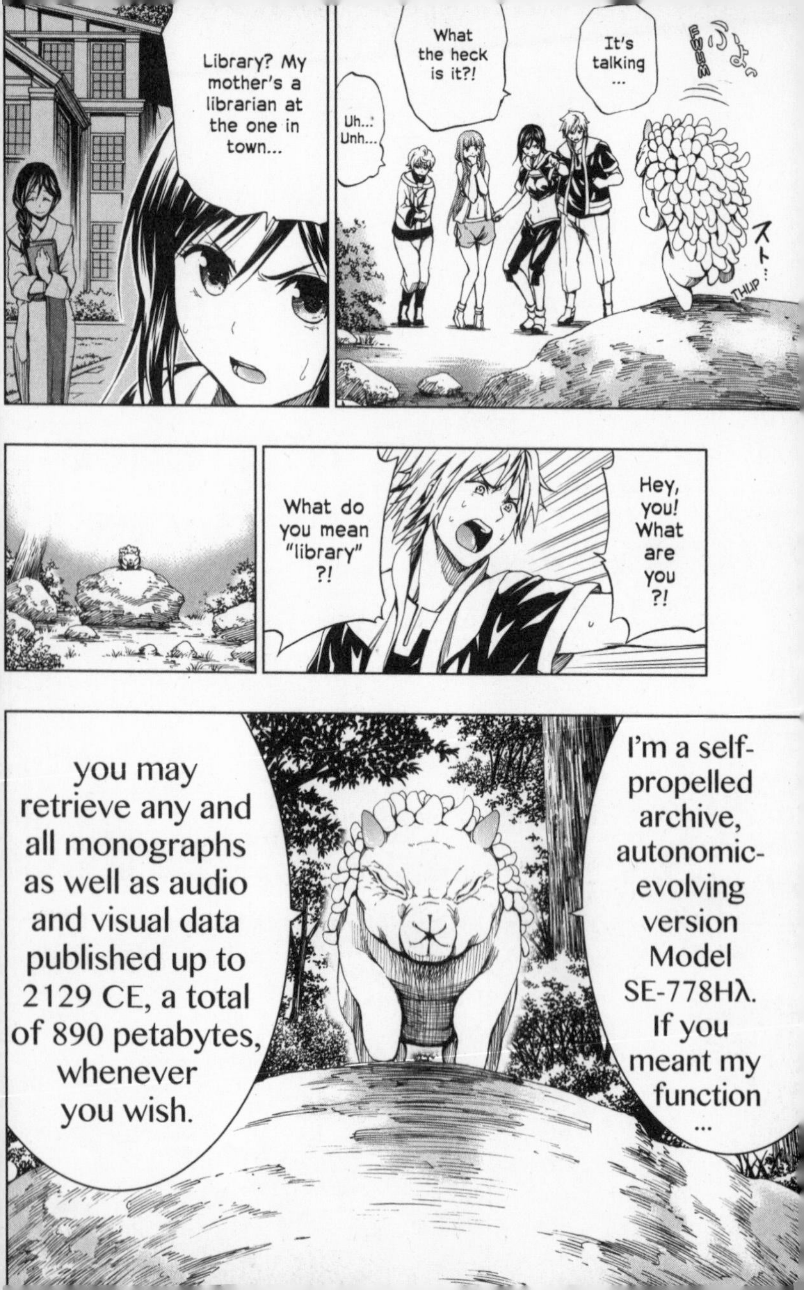
ふよっ FWUM
It's talking ...
What the heck is it?!
Uh...! Unh...
スト… THUP
Library? My mother's a librarian at the one in town...
Hey, you! What are you ?!
What do you mean "library" ?!
I'm a self-propelled archive, autonomic-evolving version Model SE-778Hλ. If you meant my function ...
you may retrieve any and all monographs as well as audio and visual data published up to 2129 CE, a total of 890 petabytes, whenever you wish.

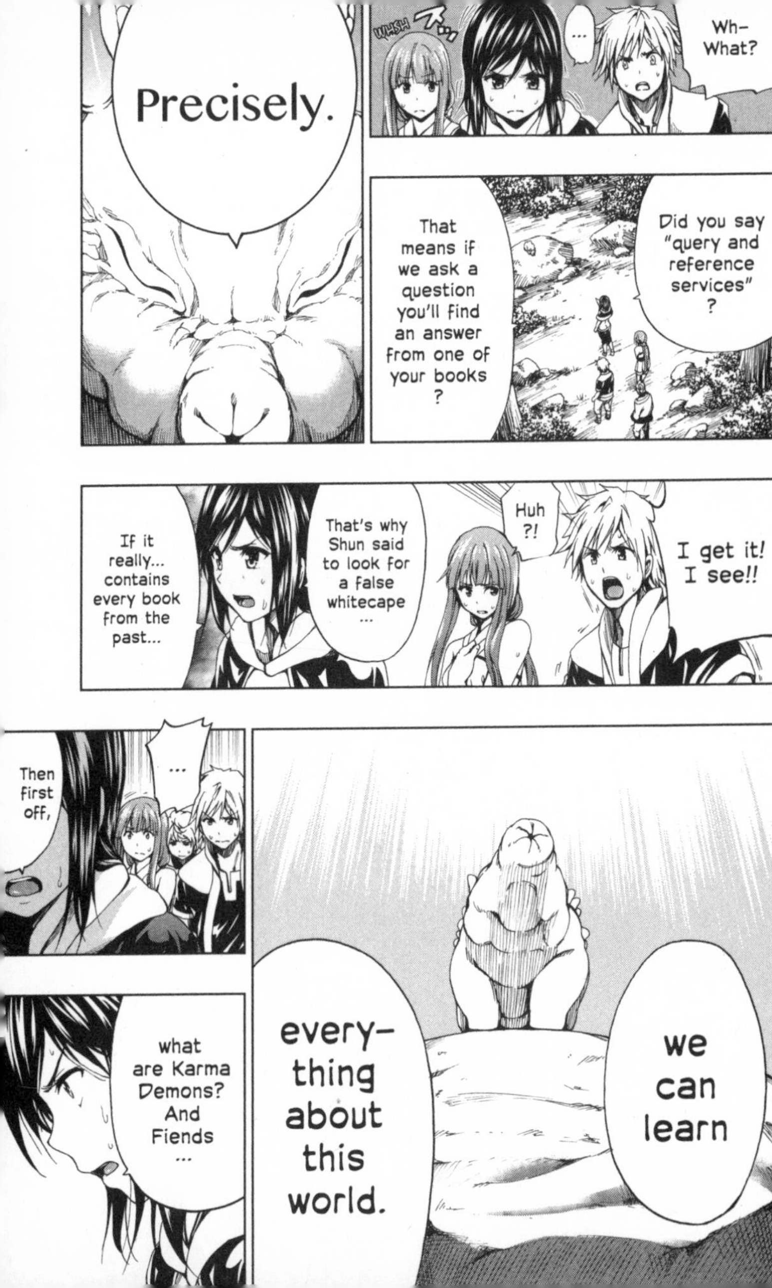
Wh– What?
...
WHSH
Did you say "query and reference services" ?
That means if we ask a question you'll find an answer from one of your books ?
Precisely.
I get it! I see!!
Huh ?!
That's why Shun said to look for a false whitecape ...
If it really... contains every book from the past...
we can learn
every- thing about this world.
Then first off,
...
what are Karma Demons? And Fiends ...

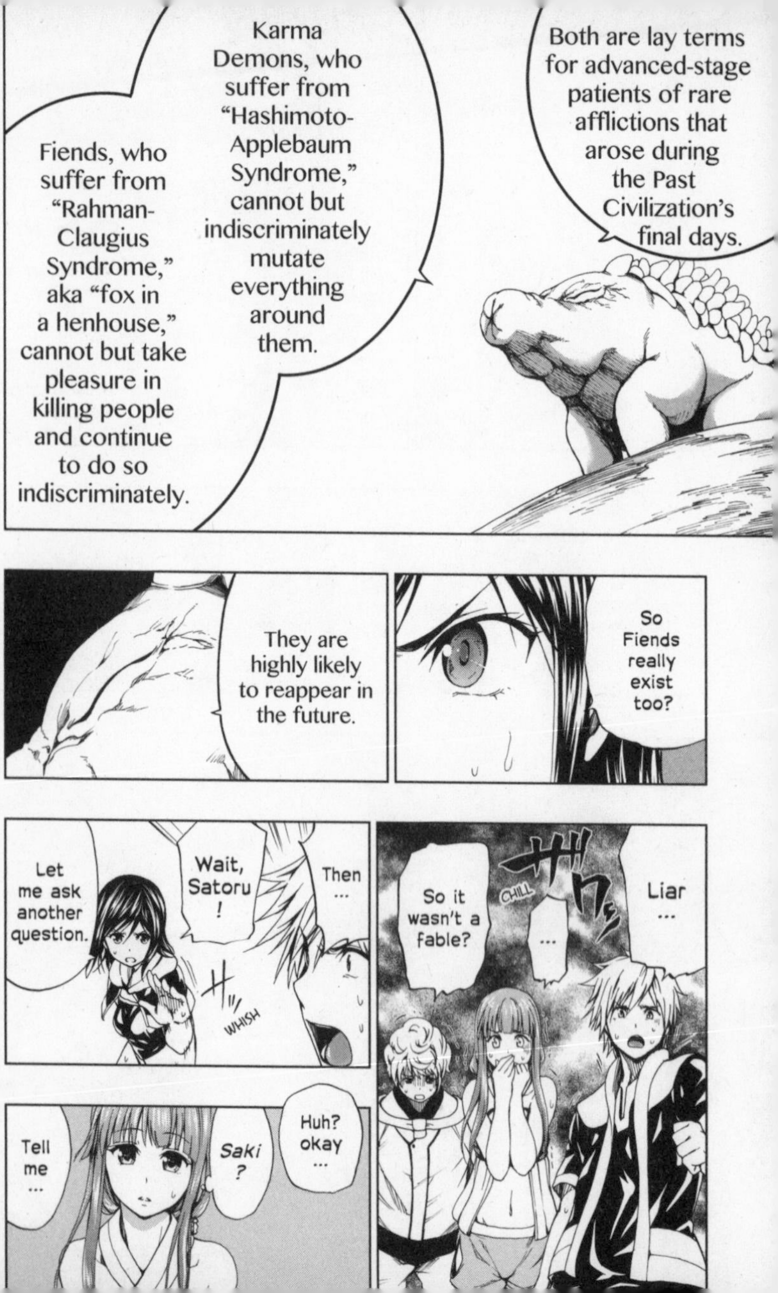
Both are lay terms for advanced-stage patients of rare afflictions that arose during the Past Civilization's final days.
Karma Demons, who suffer from "Hashimoto-Applebaum Syndrome," cannot but indiscriminately mutate everything around them.
Fiends, who suffer from "Rahman-Claugius Syndrome," aka "fox in a henhouse," cannot but take pleasure in killing people and continue to do so indiscriminately.
So Fiends really exist too?
They are highly likely to reappear in the future.
Liar ...
CHILL
...
So it wasn't a fable?
Then ...
Wait, Satoru !
Let me ask another question.
WHISH
Huh? okay ...
Saki ?
Tell me ...

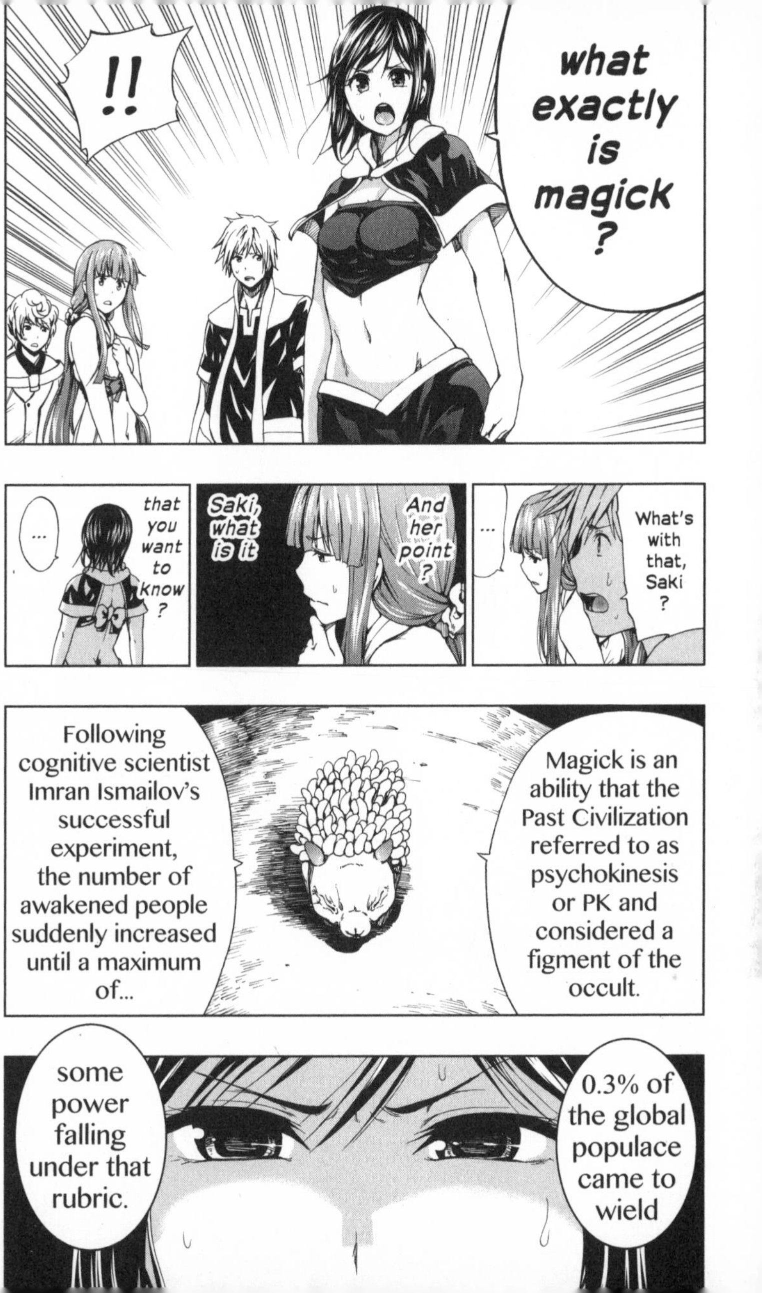
what exactly is magick ?
!!
What's with that, Saki ?
...
And her point ?
Saki, what is it
that you want to know ?
...
Magick is an ability that the Past Civilization referred to as psychokinesis or PK and considered a figment of the occult.
Following cognitive scientist Imran Ismailov's successful experiment, the number of awakened people suddenly increased until a maximum of...
0.3% of the global populace came to wield
some power falling under that rubric.

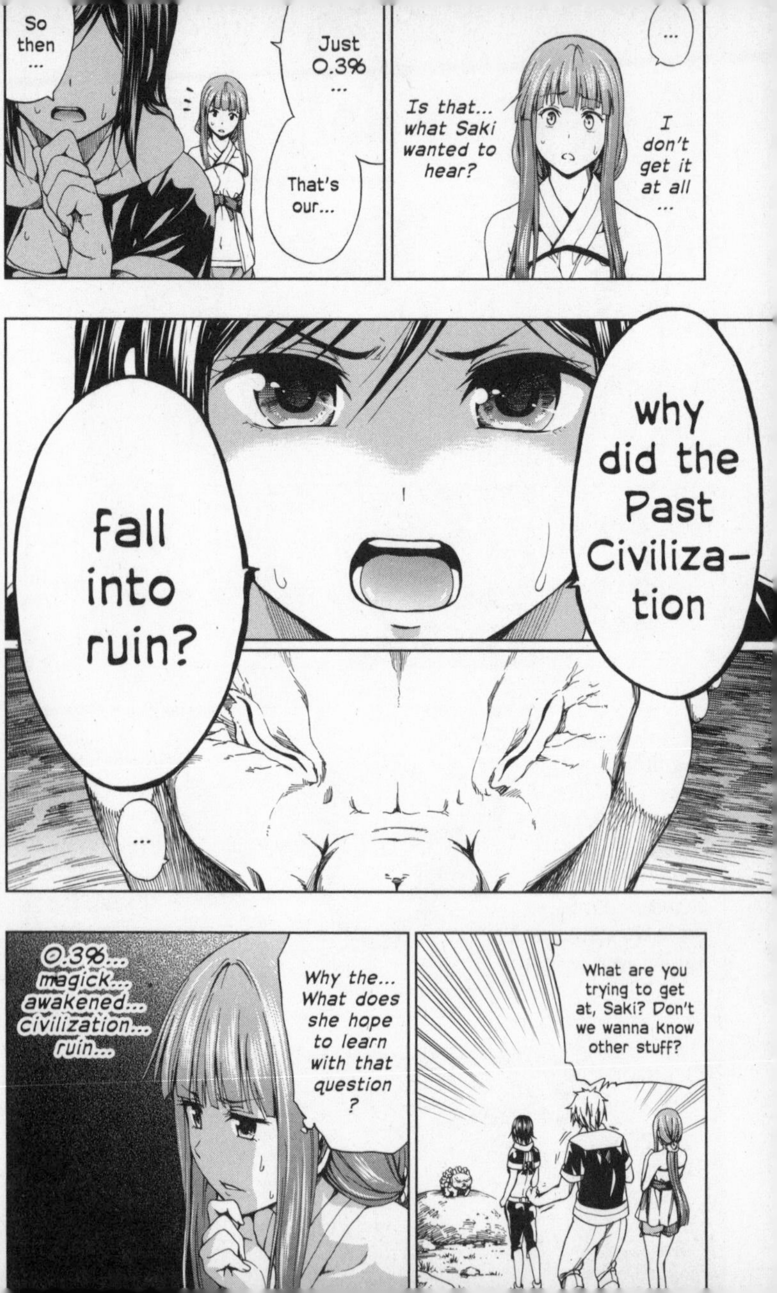
...
I don't get it at all ...
Is that... what Saki wanted to hear?
Just 0.3% ...
That's our...
So then ...
why did the Past Civiliza-tion
fall into ruin?
...
What are you trying to get at, Saki? Don't we wanna know other stuff?
Why the... What does she hope to learn with that question?
0.3%... magick... awakened... civilization... ruin...

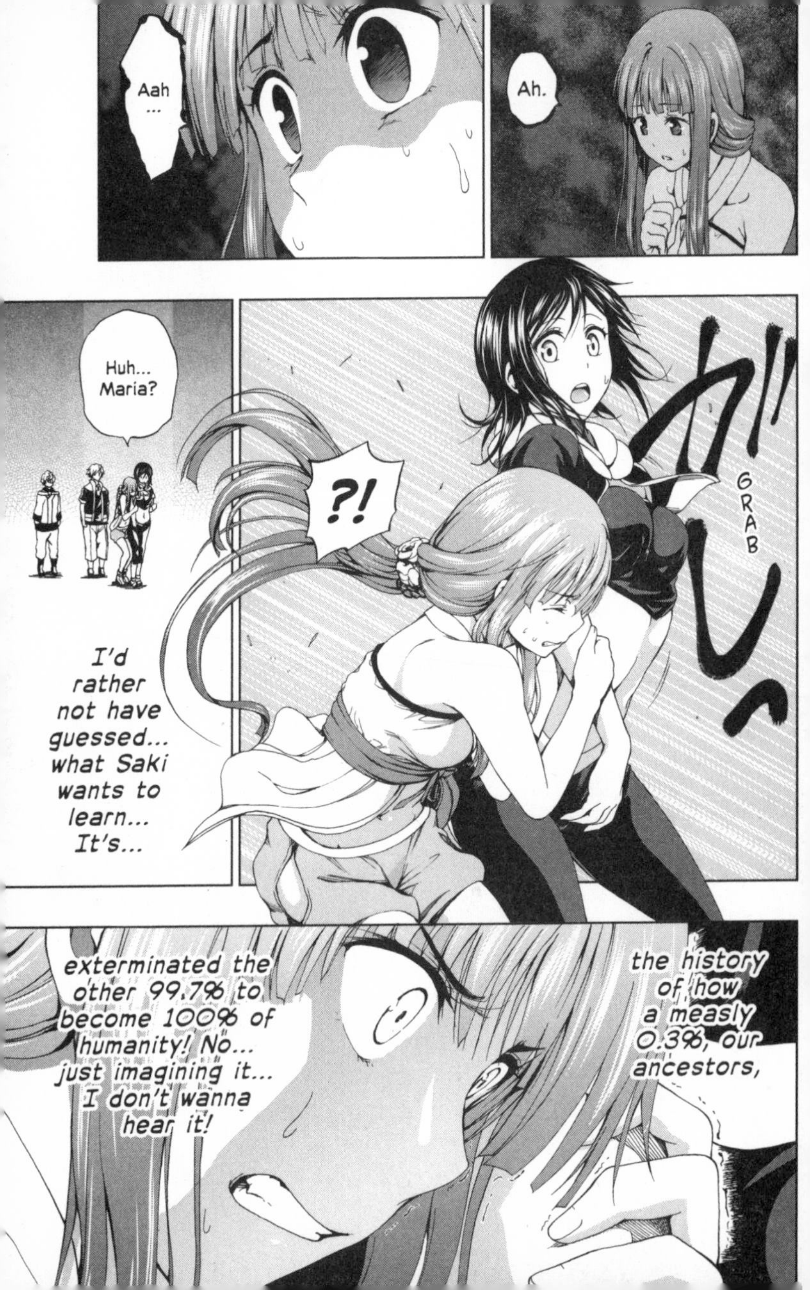
Ah.
Aah ...
GRAB
?!
Huh... Maria?
I'd rather not have guessed... what Saki wants to learn... It's...
the history of how a measly 0.3%, our ancestors,
exterminated the other 99.7% to become 100% of humanity! No... just imagining it... I don't wanna hear it!

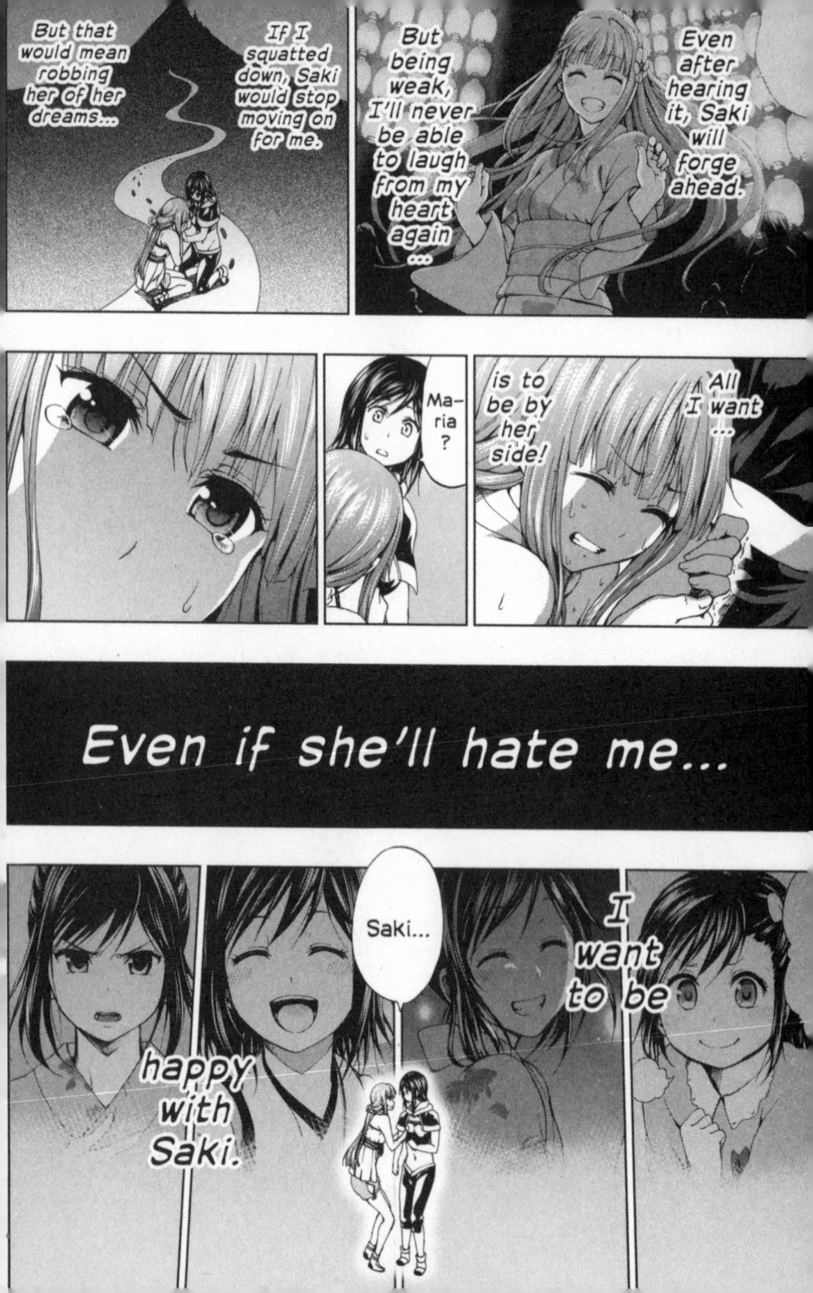
Even after hearing it, Saki will forge ahead.
But being weak, I'll never be able to laugh from my heart again...
If I squatted down, Saki would stop moving on for me.
But that would mean robbing her of her dreams...
All I want...
is to be by her side!
Ma-ria?
Even if she'll hate me...
I want to be
Saki...
happy with Saki.

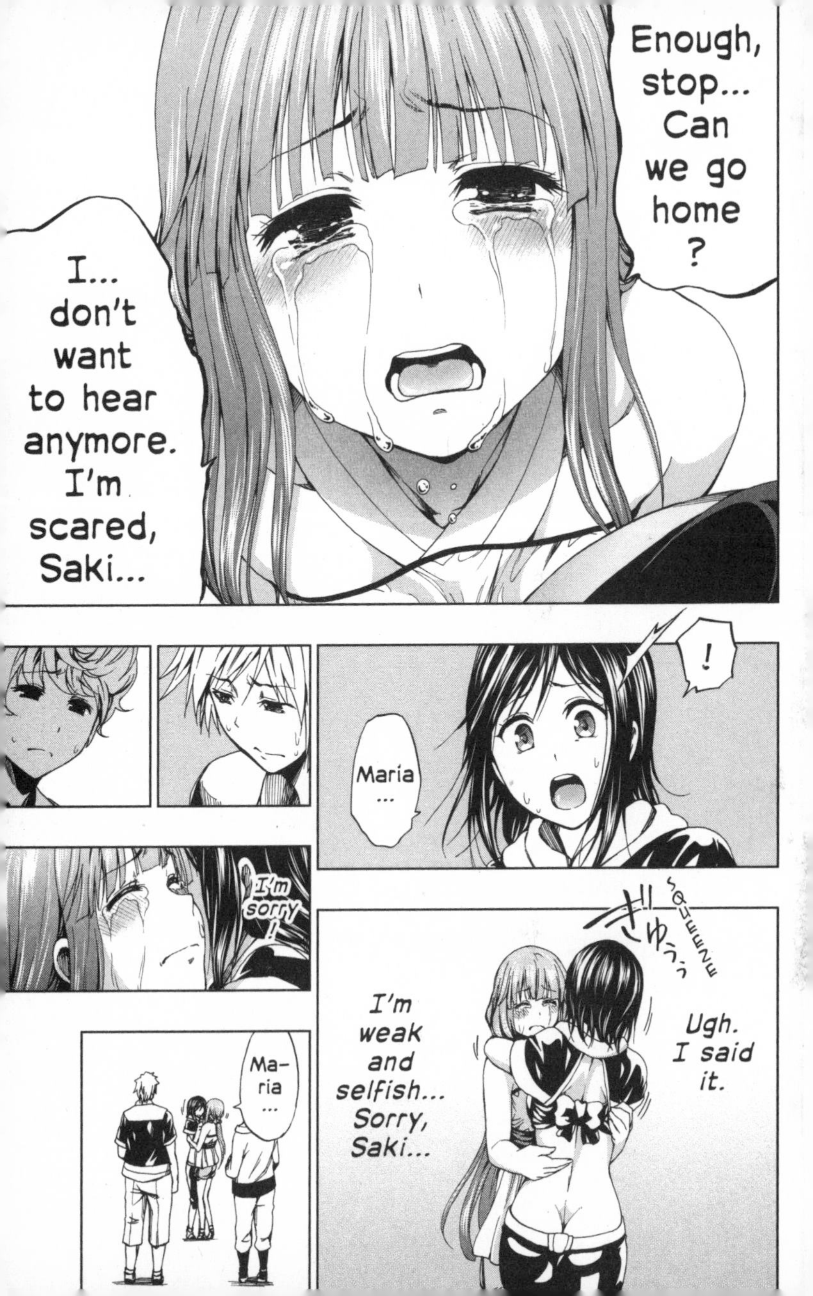
Enough, stop... Can we go home?
I... don't want to hear anymore. I'm scared, Saki...
!
Maria...
ぎゅうう
SQUEEZE
Ugh. I said it.
I'm weak and selfish... Sorry, Saki...
I'm sorry!
Ma-ria...

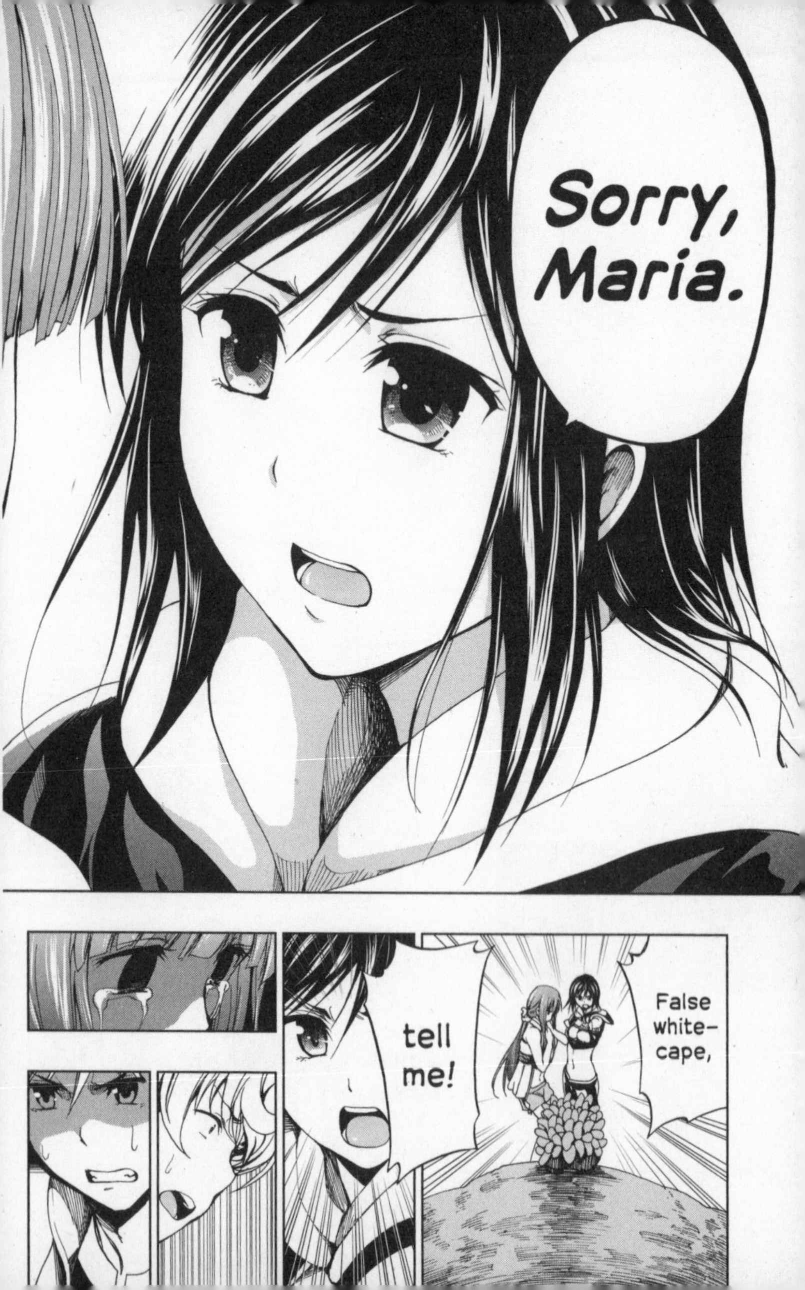
Sorry, Maria.
False white-cape,
tell me!

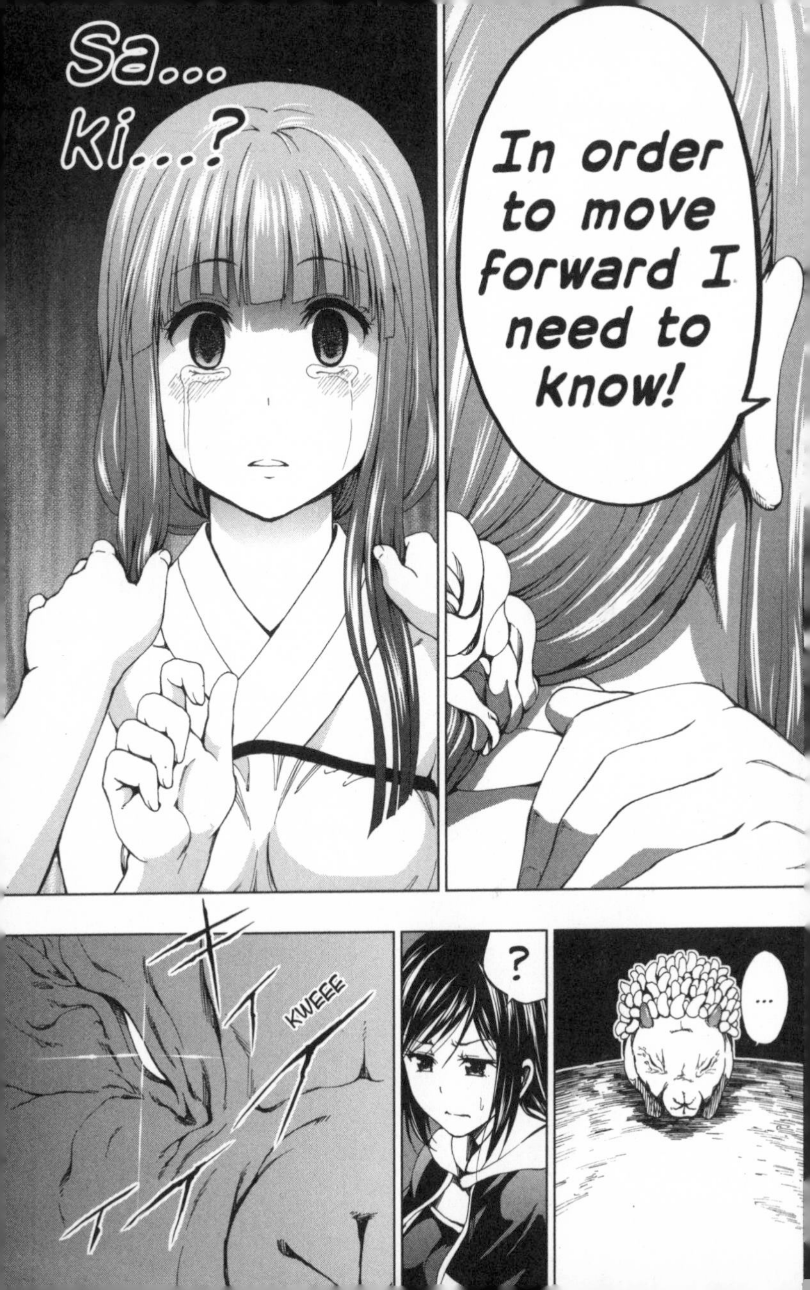
In order to move forward I need to know!
Sa... ki...?
...
?
KWEEE

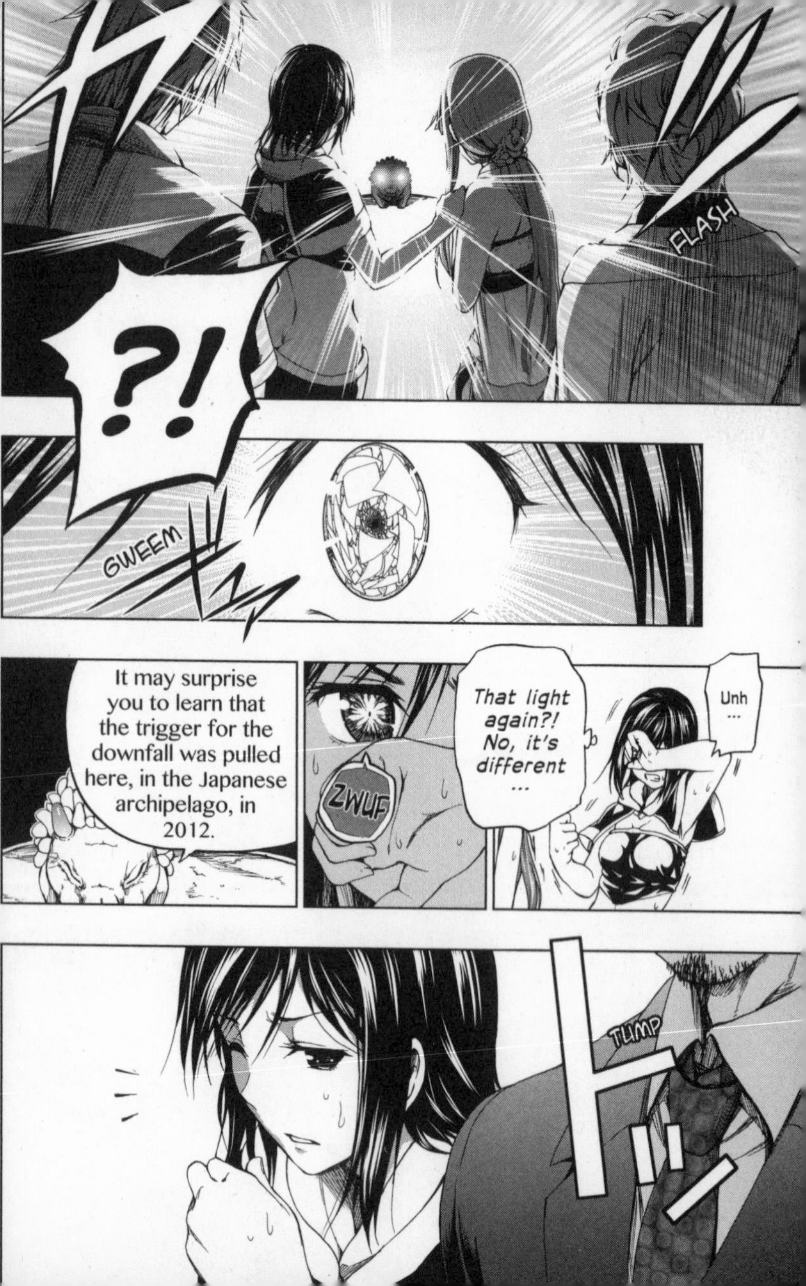
FLASH
?!
GWEEM
Unh ...
That light again?! No, it's different ...
ZWUF
It may surprise you to learn that the trigger for the downfall was pulled here, in the Japanese archipelago, in 2012.
TUMP

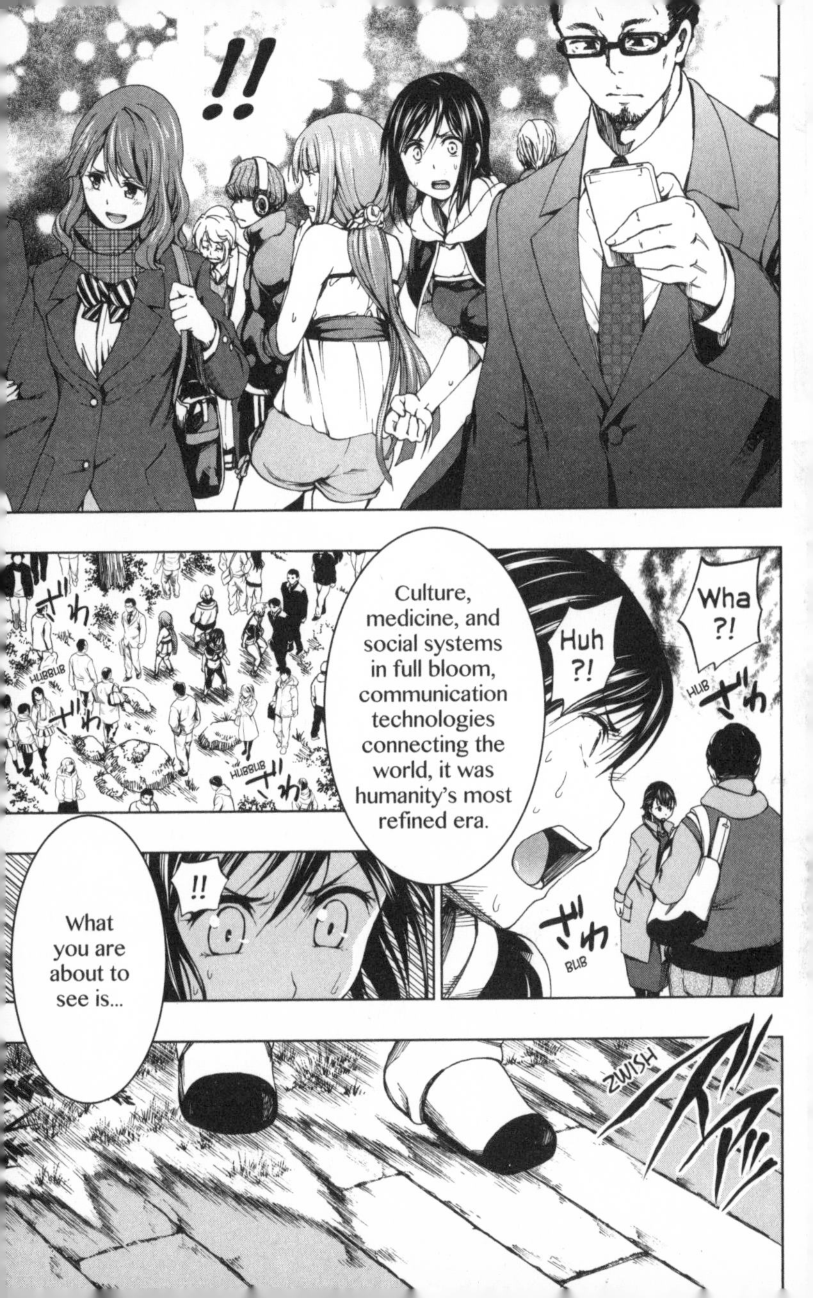
!!
Wha ?!
Huh ?!
HUB ざわ
Culture, medicine, and social systems in full bloom, communication technologies connecting the world, it was humanity's most refined era.
ざわ
HUBBUB
ざわ
HUBBUB ざわ
ざわ BUB
!!
What you are about to see is...
ZWISH

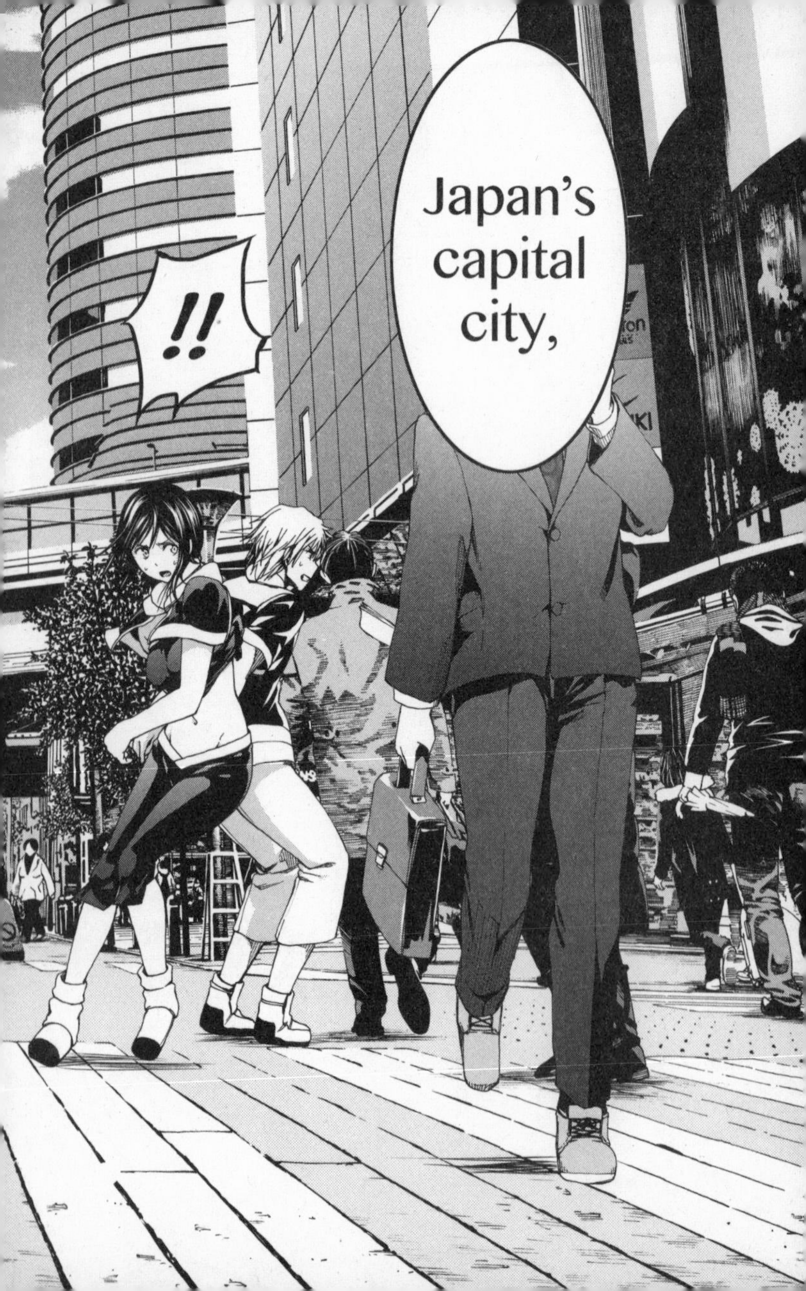
Japan's capital city,
!!

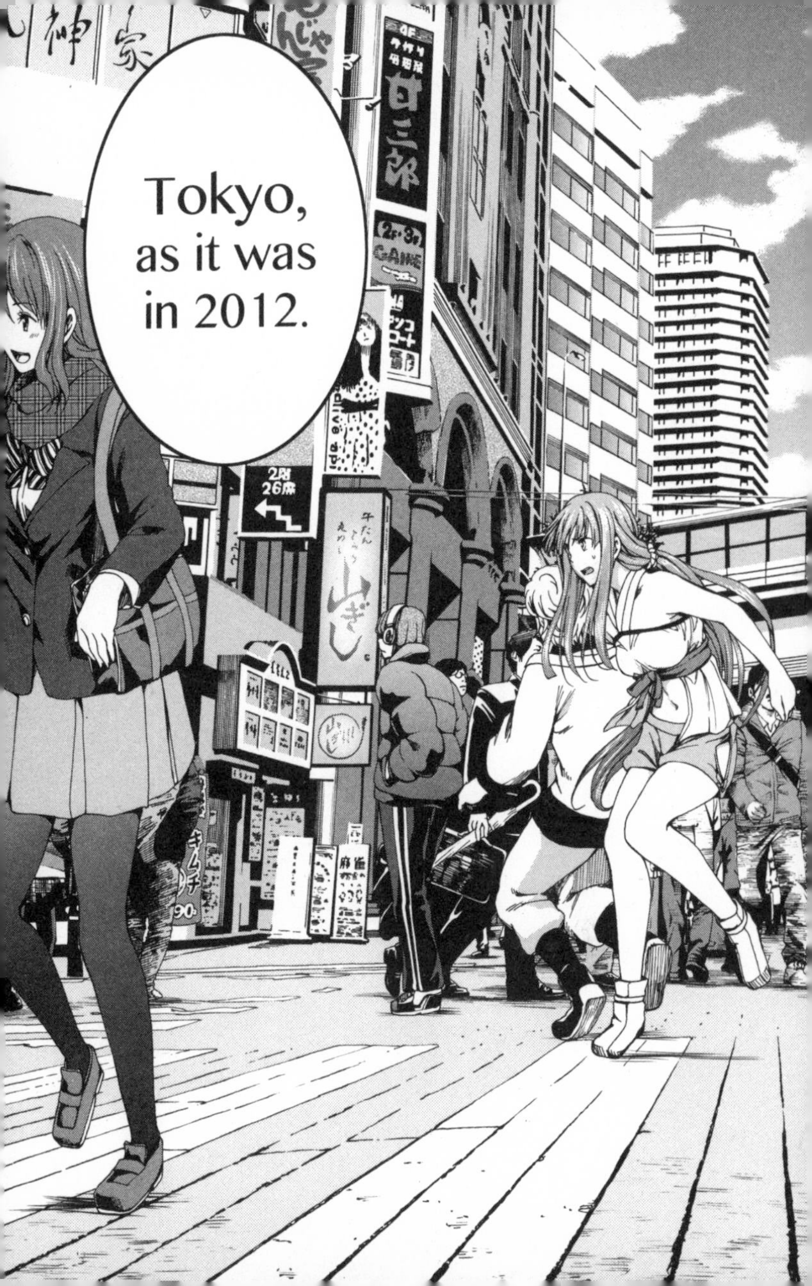
Tokyo, as it was in 2012.

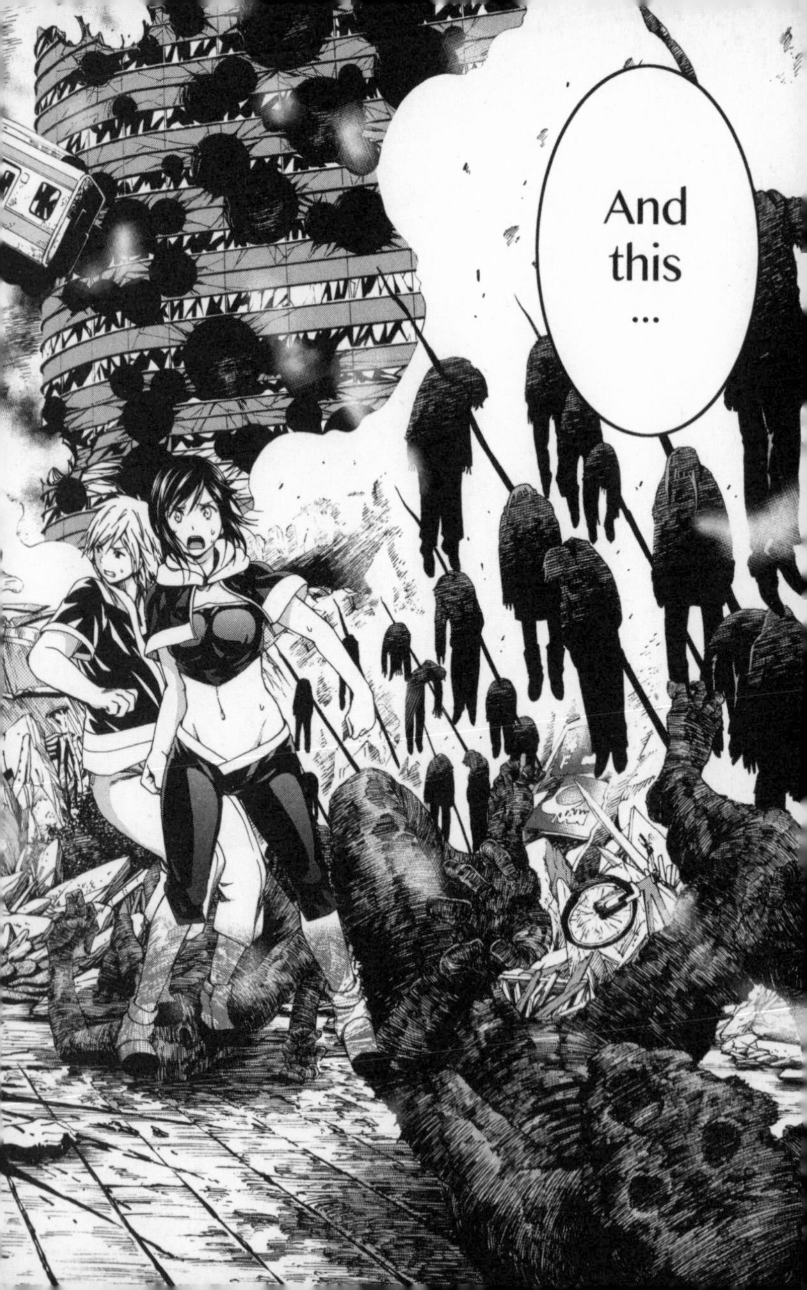
And this ...

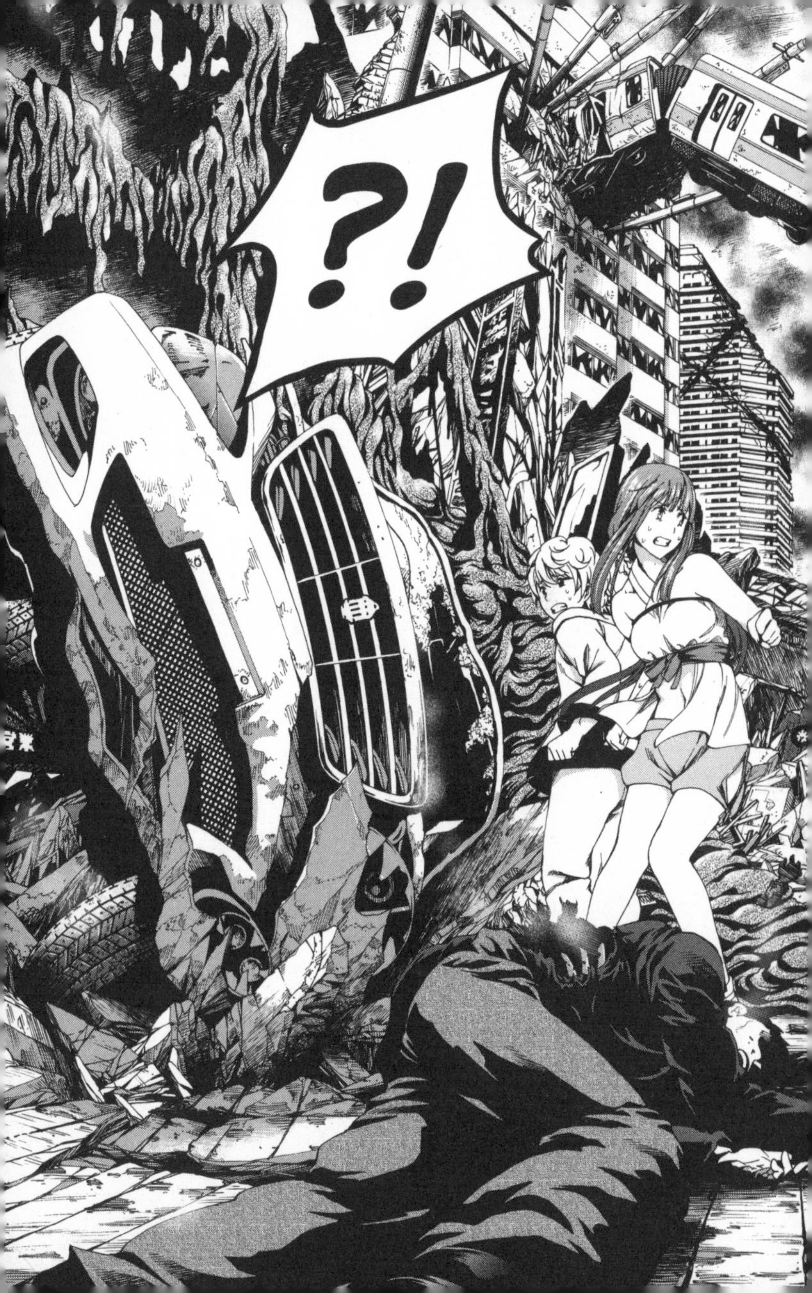
?!

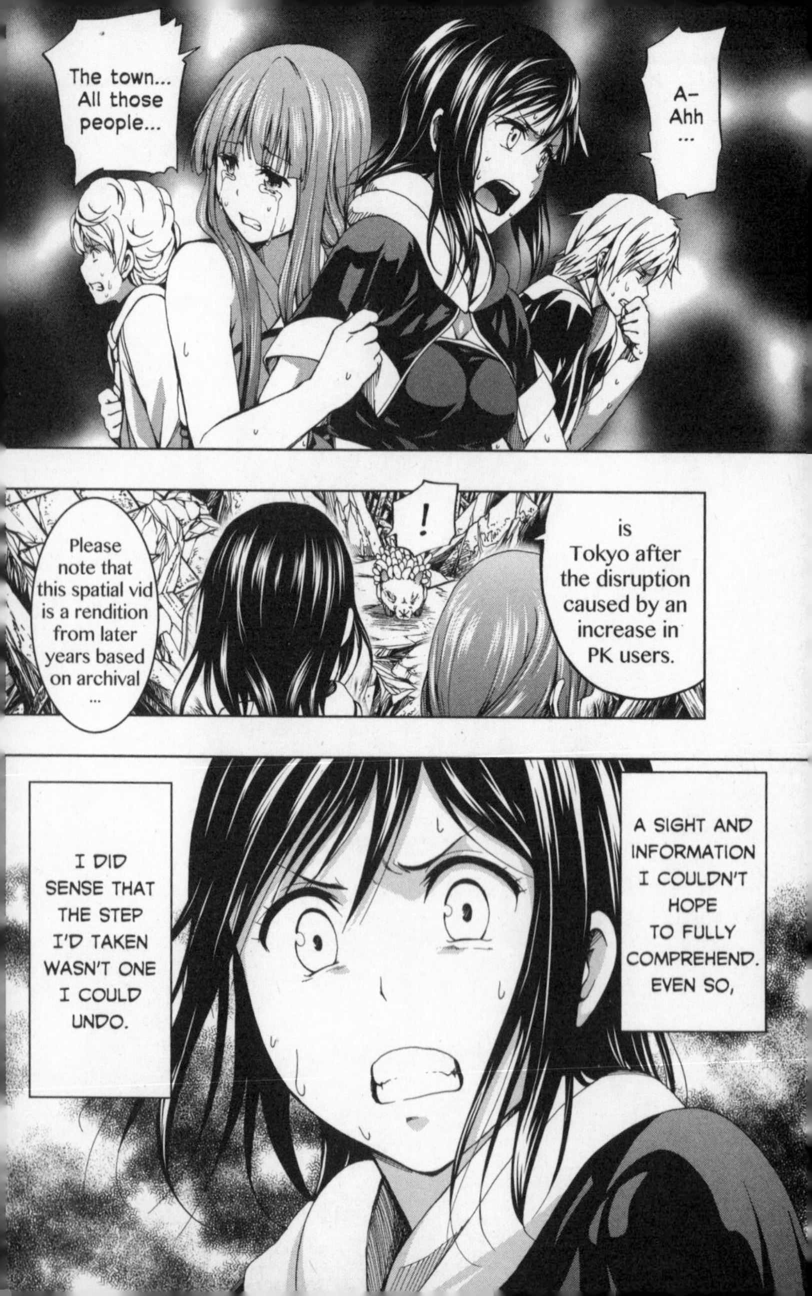
A– Ahh ...
The town... All those people...
is Tokyo after the disruption caused by an increase in PK users.
!
Please note that this spatial vid is a rendition from later years based on archival ...
A SIGHT AND INFORMATION I COULDN'T HOPE TO FULLY COMPREHEND. EVEN SO,
I DID SENSE THAT THE STEP I'D TAKEN WASN'T ONE I COULD UNDO.

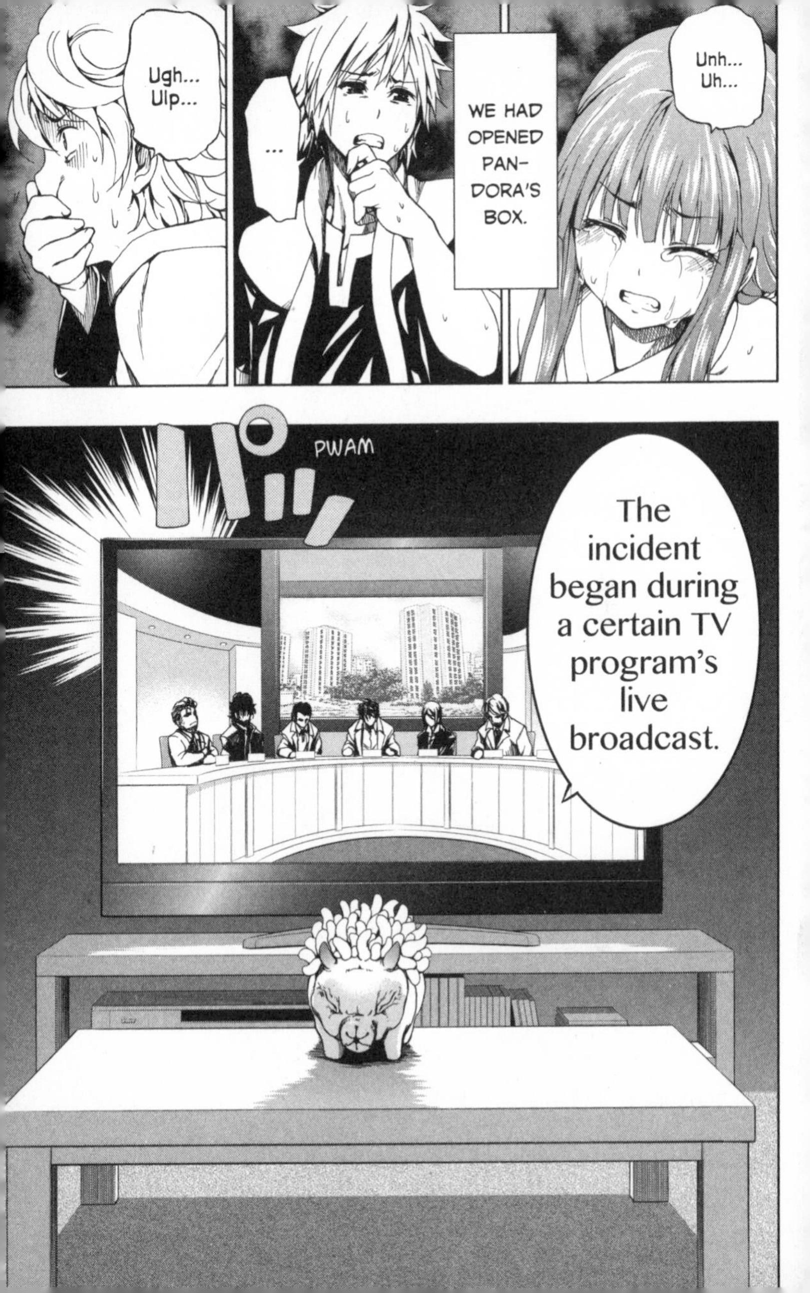
Unh... Uh...
WE HAD OPENED PAN-DORA'S BOX.
...
Ugh... Ulp...
PWAM
The incident began during a certain TV program's live broadcast.

FROM
THE
new
WORLD

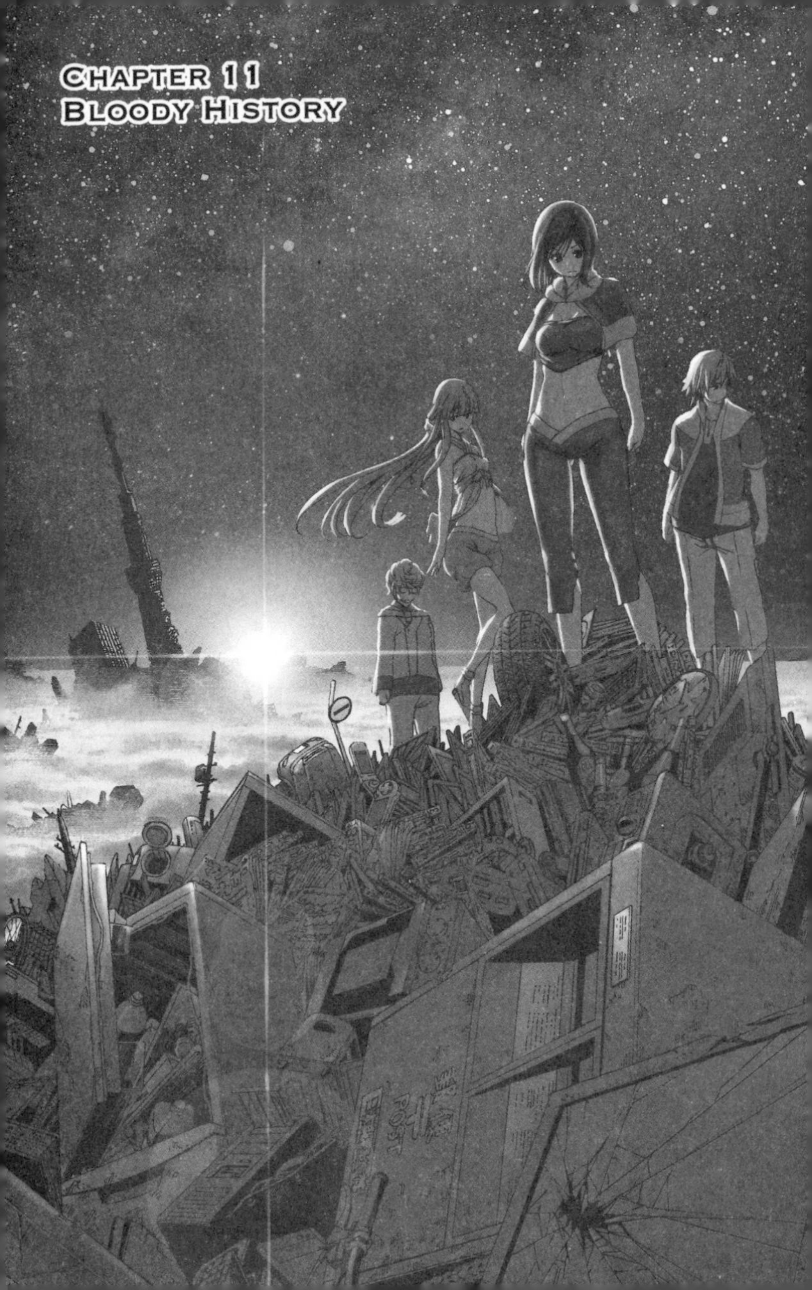
CHAPTER 11
BLOODY HISTORY

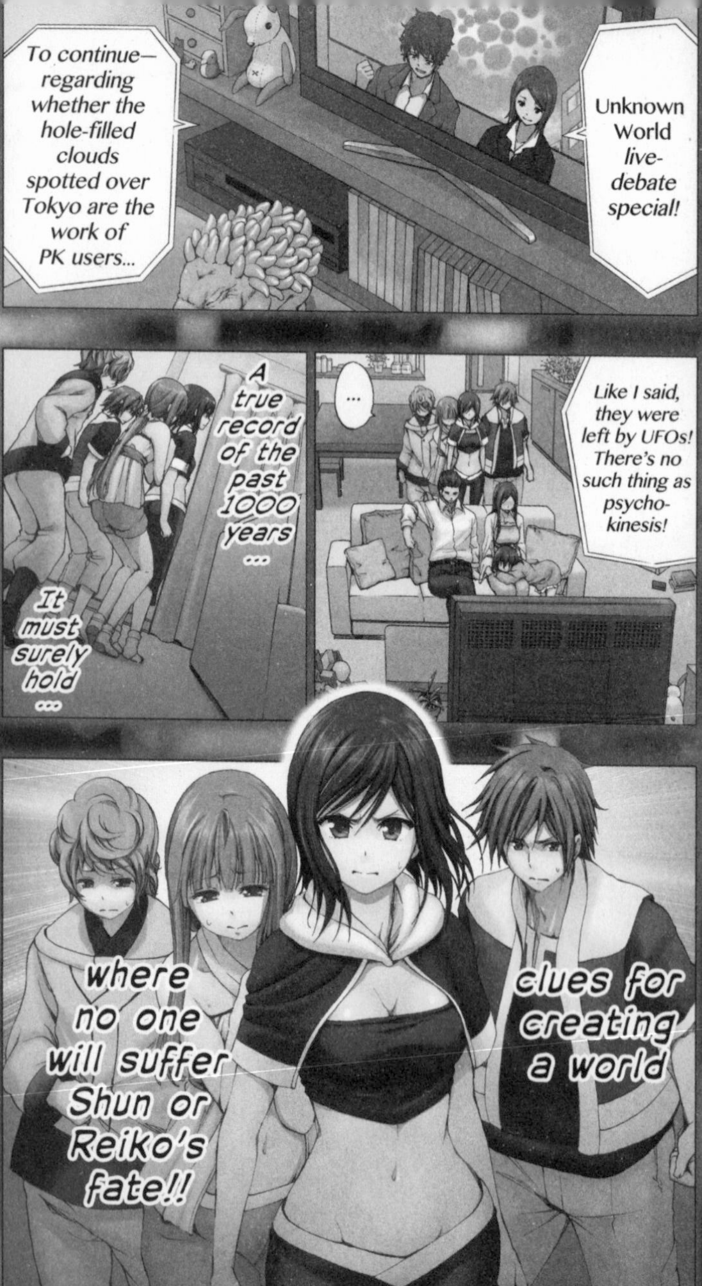
Unknown World live-debate special!
To continue—regarding whether the hole-filled clouds spotted over Tokyo are the work of PK users...
Like I said, they were left by UFOs! There's no such thing as psycho-kinesis!
...
A true record of the past 1000 years...
It must surely hold...
clues for creating a world
where no one will suffer Shun or Reiko's fate!!

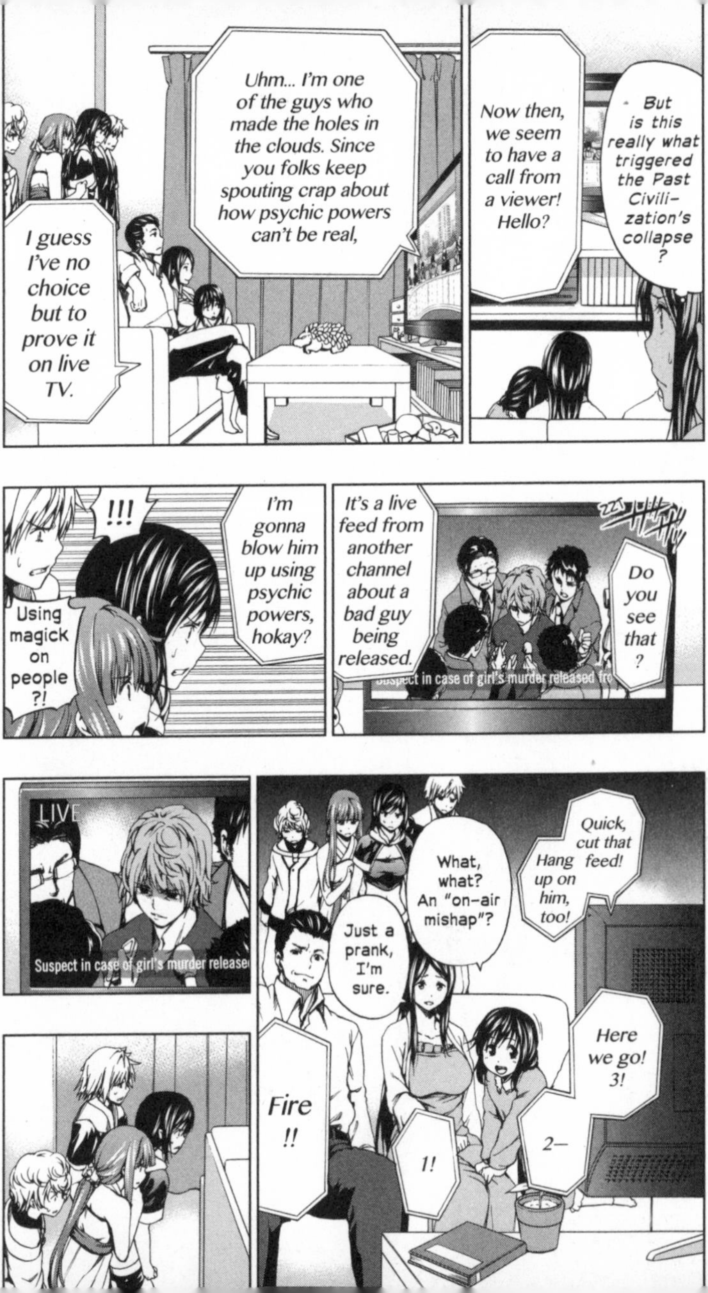
But is this really what triggered the Past Civili-zation's collapse?
Now then, we seem to have a call from a viewer! Hello?
Uhm... I'm one of the guys who made the holes in the clouds. Since you folks keep spouting crap about how psychic powers can't be real,
I guess I've no choice but to prove it on live TV.
Do you see that?
It's a live feed from another channel about a bad guy being released.
Suspect in case of girl's murder released fr
I'm gonna blow him up using psychic powers, hokay?
!!!
Using magick on people?!
Quick, cut that feed!
Hang up on him, too!
What, what? An "on-air mishap"?
Just a prank, I'm sure.
Here we go! 3!
2—
1!
Fire!!
LIVE
Suspect in case of girl's murder releasec

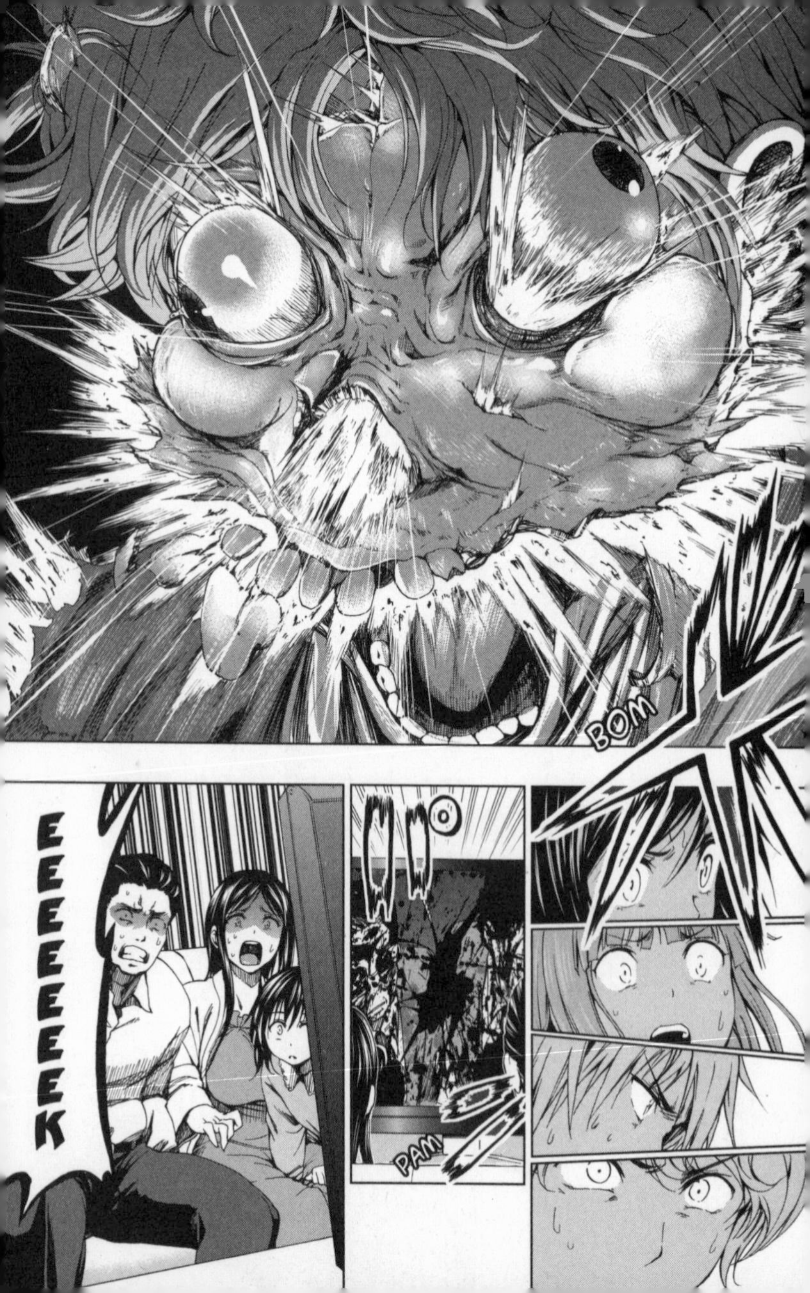
BOM
PAM
EEEEEEEK

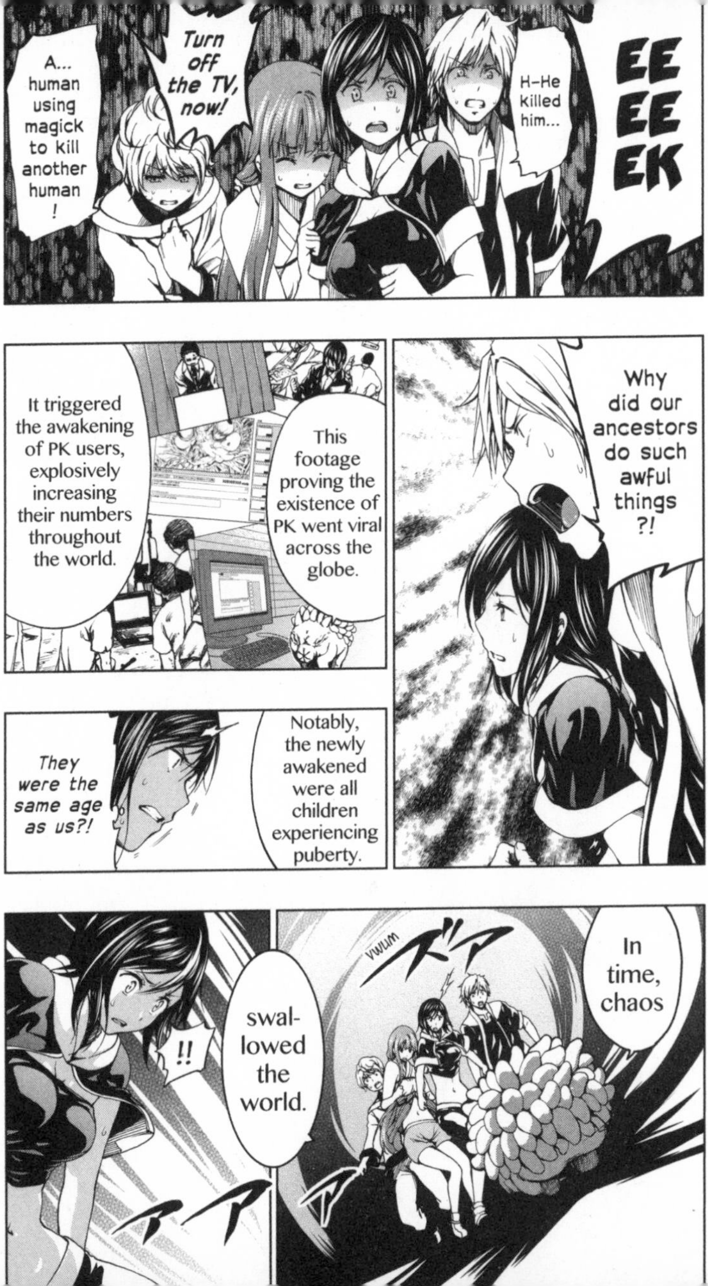
EEEEEK
H-He killed him...
Turn off the TV, now!
A... human using magick to kill another human!
Why did our ancestors do such awful things?!
This footage proving the existence of PK went viral across the globe.
It triggered the awakening of PK users, explosively increasing their numbers throughout the world.
Notably, the newly awakened were all children experiencing puberty.
They were the same age as us?!
In time, chaos
VWUM
swal-lowed the world.
!!

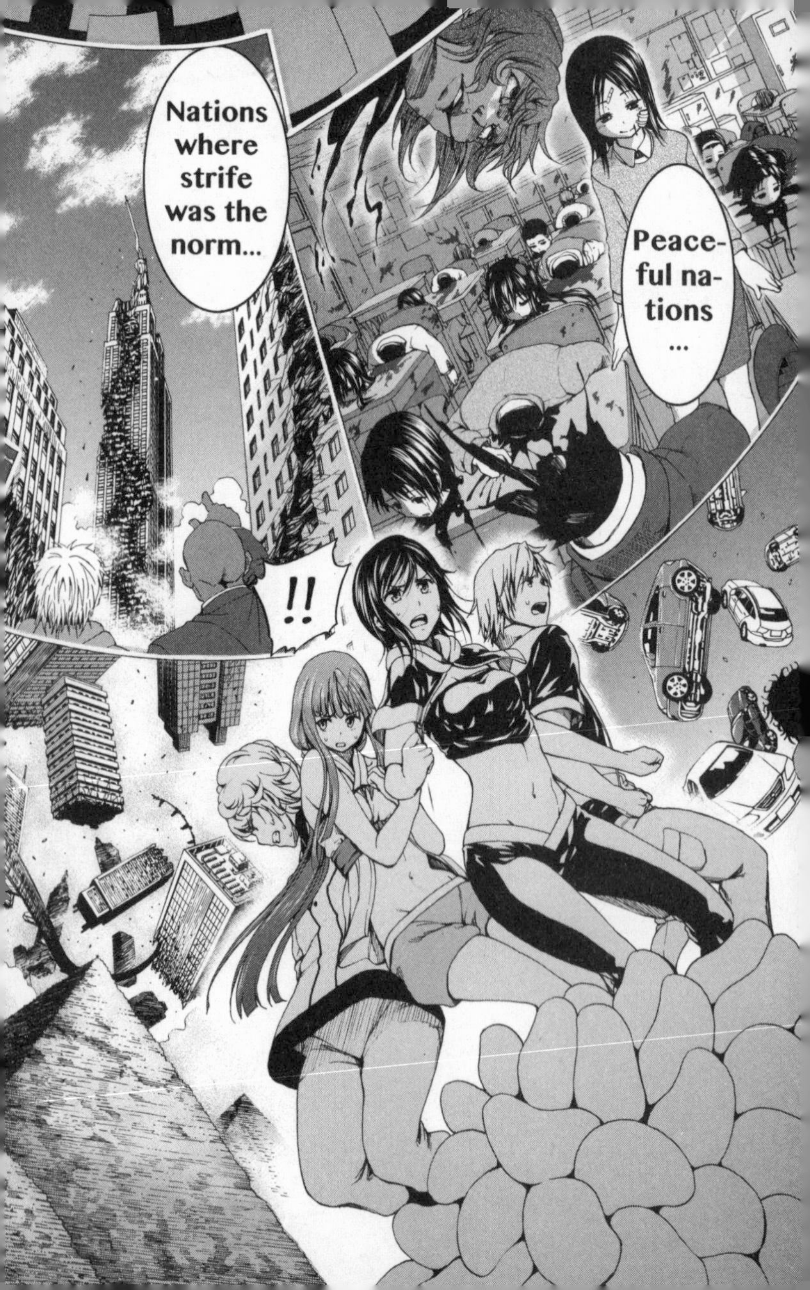
Peace-ful na-tions ...
Nations where strife was the norm...
!!

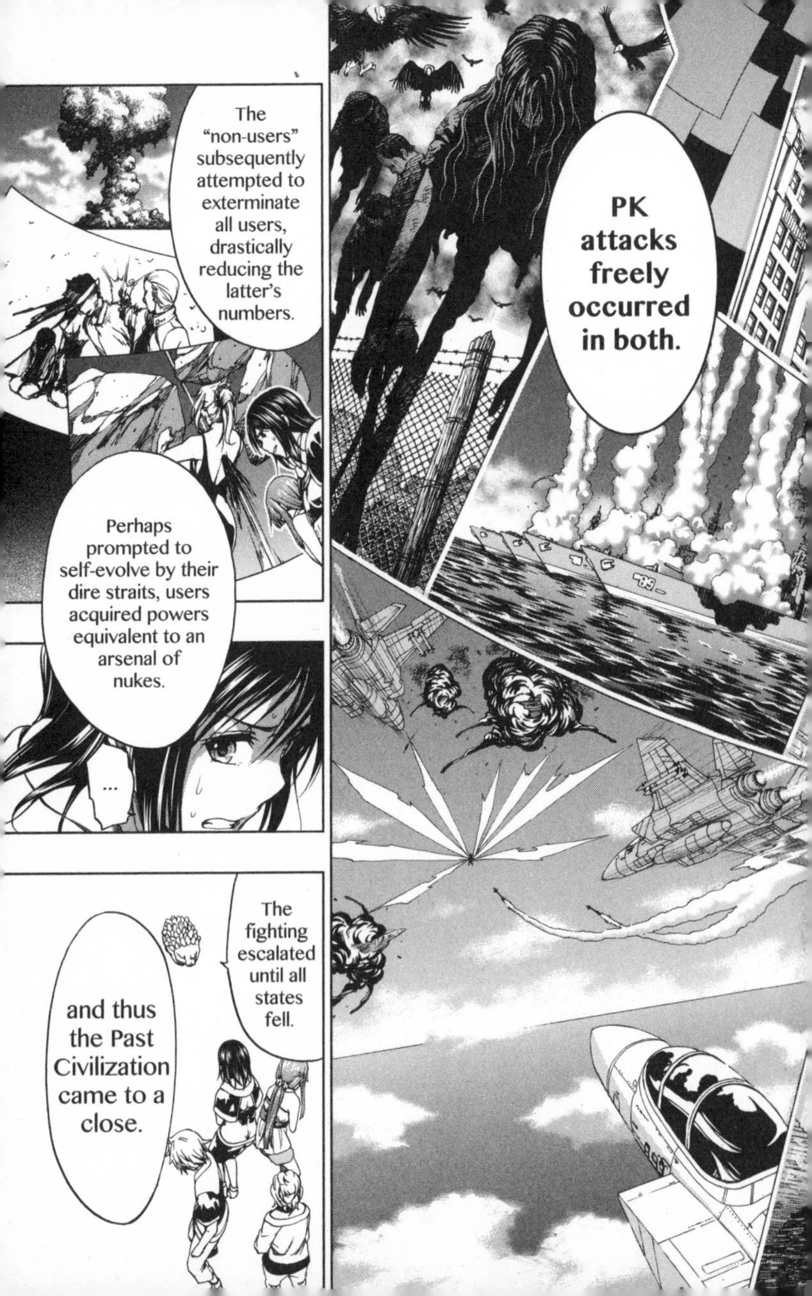
PK attacks freely occurred in both.
The "non-users" subsequently attempted to exterminate all users, drastically reducing the latter's numbers.
Perhaps prompted to self-evolve by their dire straits, users acquired powers equivalent to an arsenal of nukes.
...
The fighting escalated until all states fell.
and thus the Past Civilization came to a close.

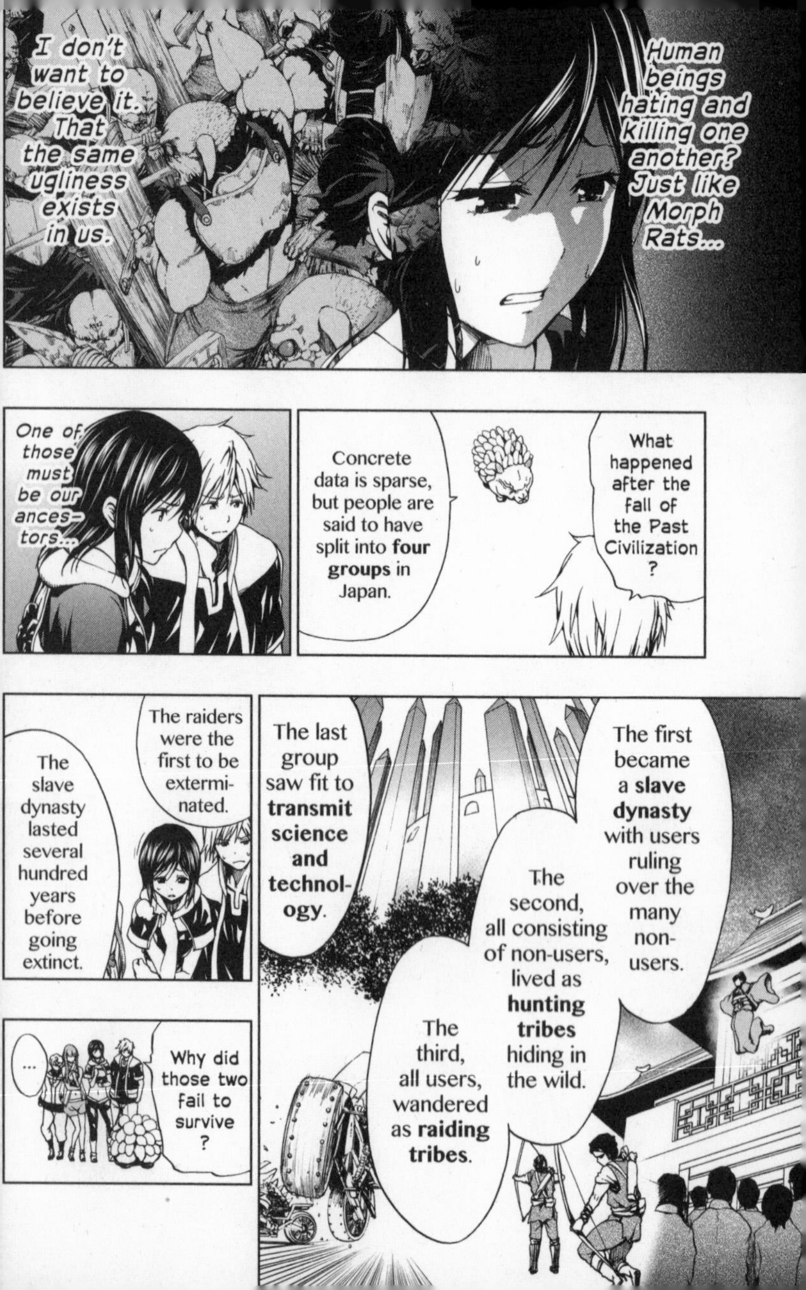
Human beings hating and killing one another? Just like Morph Rats...
I don't want to believe it. That the same ugliness exists in us.
What happened after the fall of the Past Civilization?
Concrete data is sparse, but people are said to have split into four groups in Japan.
One of those must be our ancestors...
The first became a slave dynasty with users ruling over the many non-users.
The second, all consisting of non-users, lived as hunting tribes hiding in the wild.
The third, all users, wandered as raiding tribes.
The last group saw fit to transmit science and technology.
The raiders were the first to be exterminated.
The slave dynasty lasted several hundred years before going extinct.
Why did those two fail to survive?
...

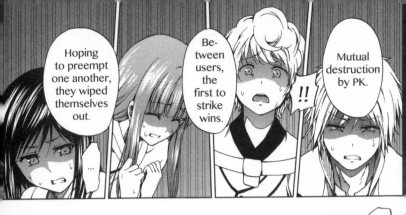

Mutual destruction by PK.
!!
Be-tween users, the first to strike wins.
Hoping to preempt one another, they wiped themselves out.
...
Why ...
Why didn't our ancestors try to find another solution ?!
They went on killing each other even after the fall of civilization ?!
No detailed data has survived,
but studies seem to have been conducted.
In the latter days of the Past Civilization, the secondmost researched topic after
"How to kill PK users"

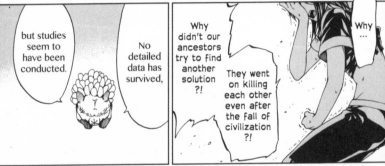

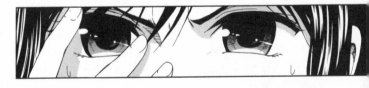

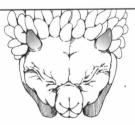

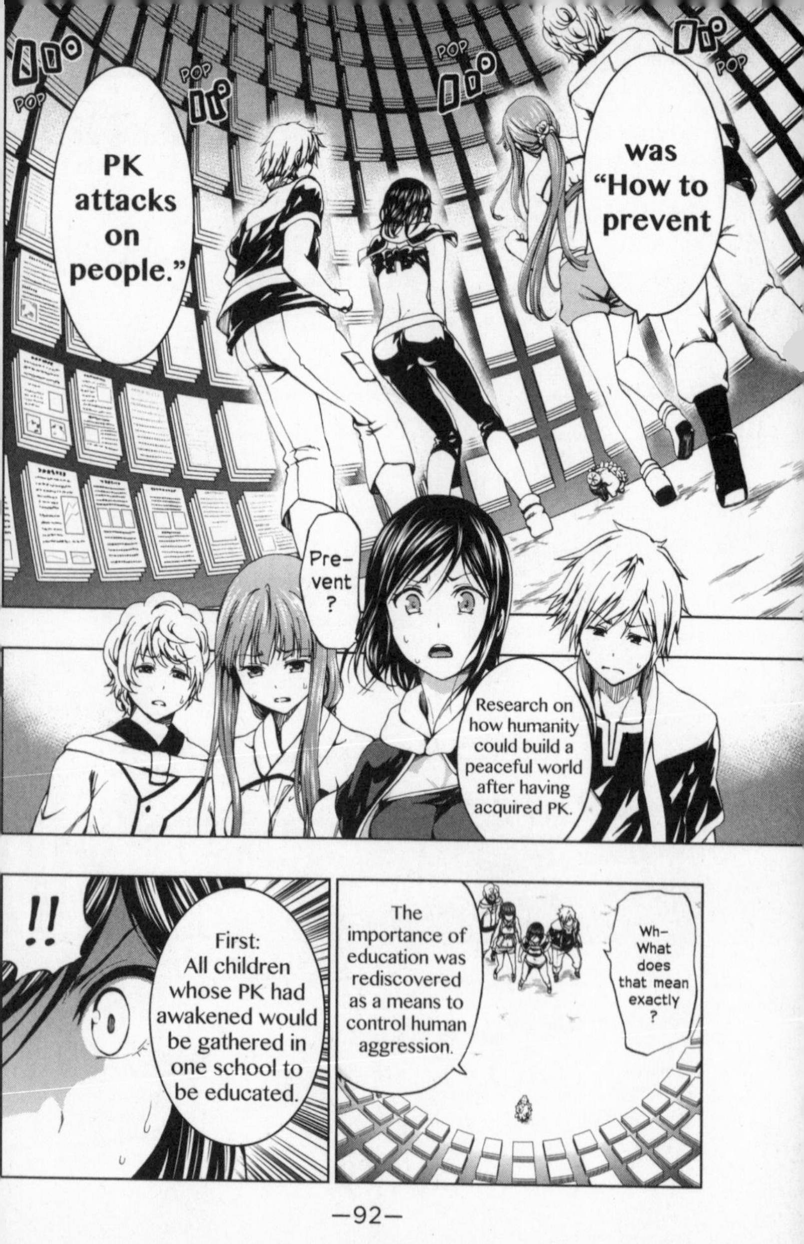
POP
POP
was "How to prevent
PK attacks on people."
POP
POP
Pre-vent?
Research on how humanity could build a peaceful world after having acquired PK.
Wh- What does that mean exactly?
The importance of education was rediscovered as a means to control human aggression.
!!
First: All children whose PK had awakened would be gathered in one school to be educated.

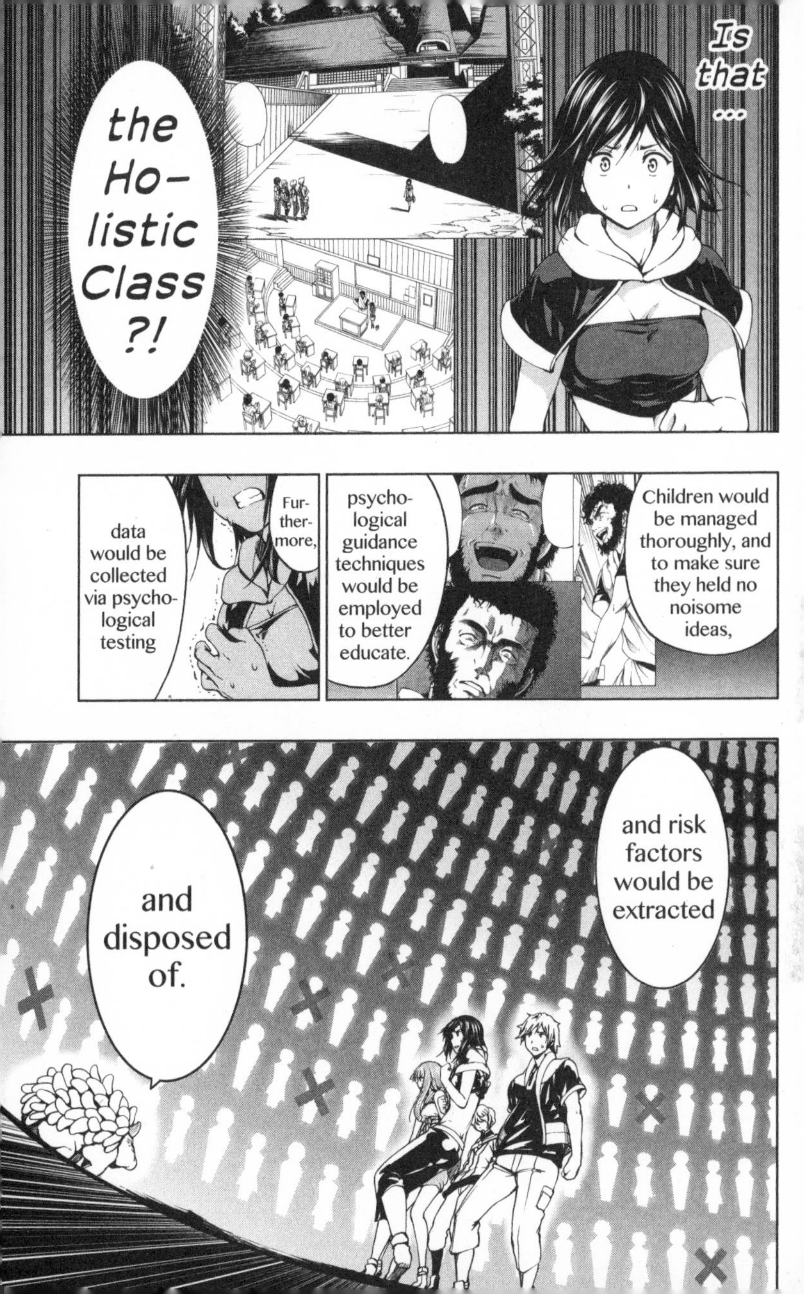
Is that ...
the Ho-listic Class?!
Children would be managed thoroughly, and to make sure they held no noisome ideas,
psycho-logical guidance techniques would be employed to better educate.
Fur-ther-more,
data would be collected via psycho-logical testing
and risk factors would be extracted
and disposed of.

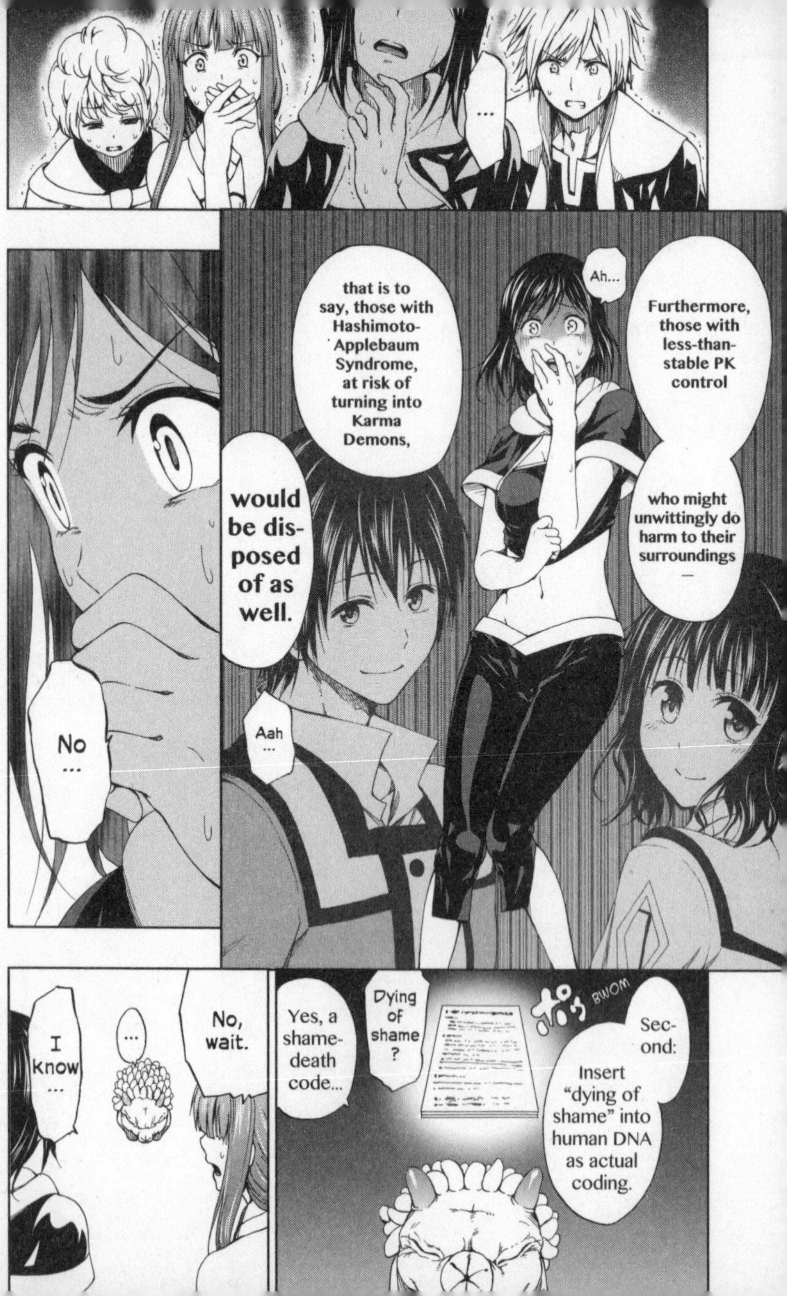
...
Furthermore, those with less-than-stable PK control
who might unwittingly do harm to their surroundings —
Ah...
that is to say, those with Hashimoto-Applebaum Syndrome, at risk of turning into Karma Demons,
would be disposed of as well.
Aah ...
No ...
Second:
Insert "dying of shame" into human DNA as actual coding.
BWOM
Dying of shame?
Yes, a shame-death code...
No, wait.
...
I know ...

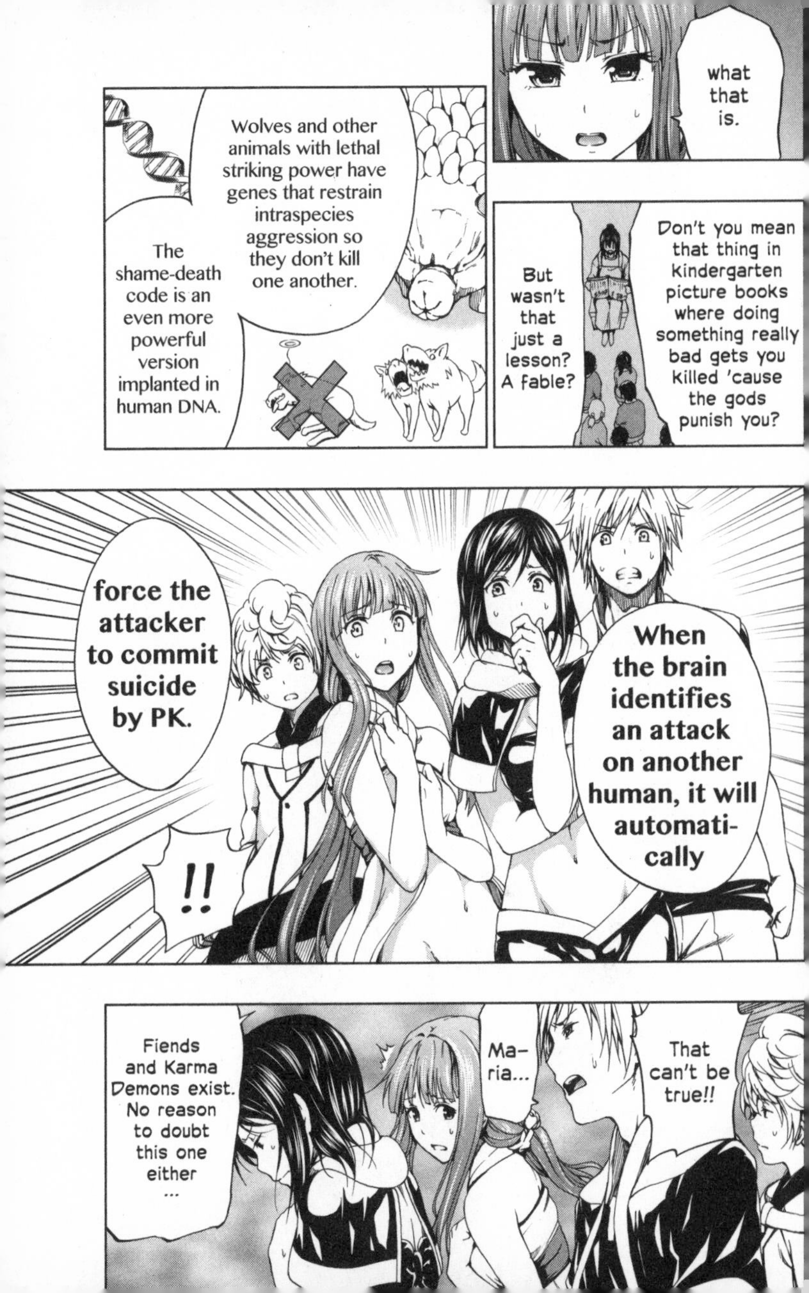
what that is.
Don't you mean that thing in kindergarten picture books where doing something really bad gets you killed 'cause the gods punish you?
But wasn't that just a lesson? A fable?
Wolves and other animals with lethal striking power have genes that restrain intraspecies aggression so they don't kill one another.
The shame-death code is an even more powerful version implanted in human DNA.
When the brain identifies an attack on another human, it will automatically
force the attacker to commit suicide by PK.
!!
That can't be true!!
Ma-ria...
Fiends and Karma Demons exist. No reason to doubt this one either ...

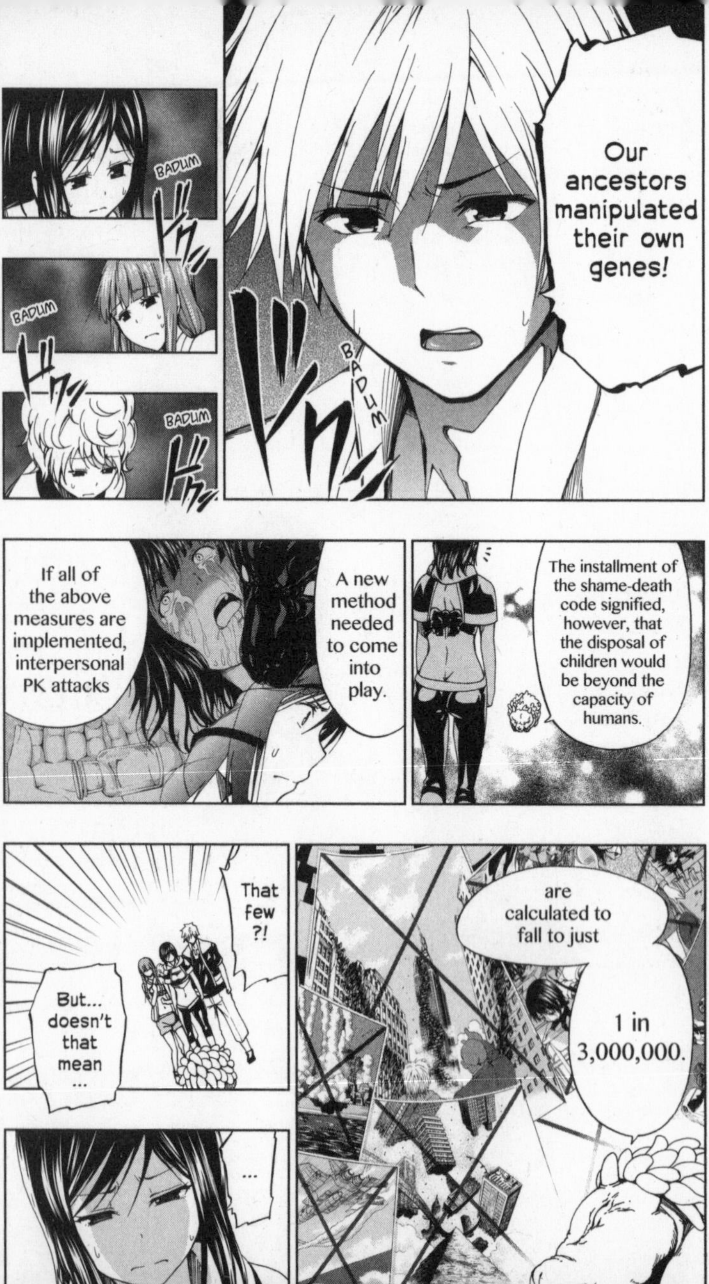

Our ancestors manipulated their own genes!
BADUM
BADUM
BADUM
BADUM
The installment of the shame-death code signified, however, that the disposal of children would be beyond the capacity of humans.
A new method needed to come into play.
If all of the above measures are implemented, interpersonal PK attacks
are calculated to fall to just
1 in 3,000,000.
That few ?!
But... doesn't that mean ...
...

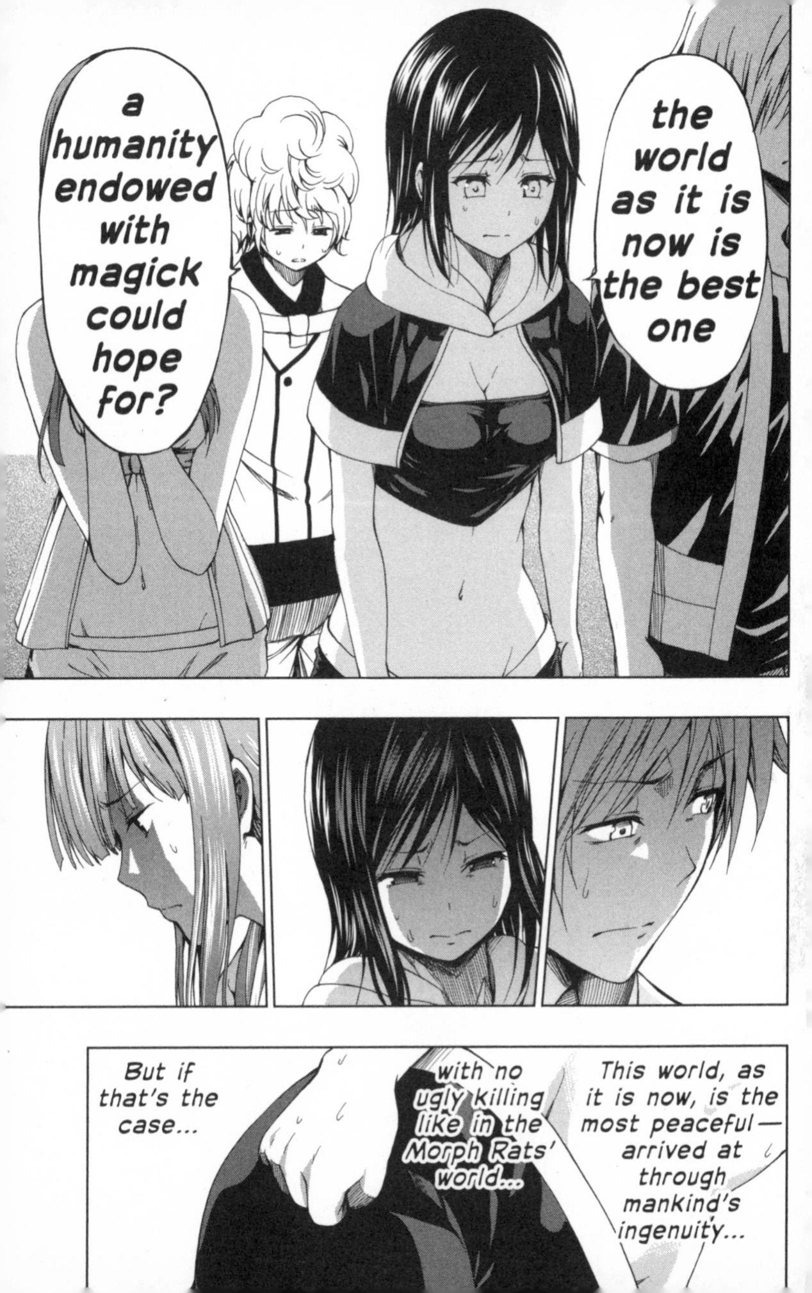
the world as it is now is the best one
a humanity endowed with magick could hope for?
This world, as it is now, is the most peaceful— arrived at through mankind's ingenuity...
with no ugly killing like in the Morph Rats' world...
But if that's the case...

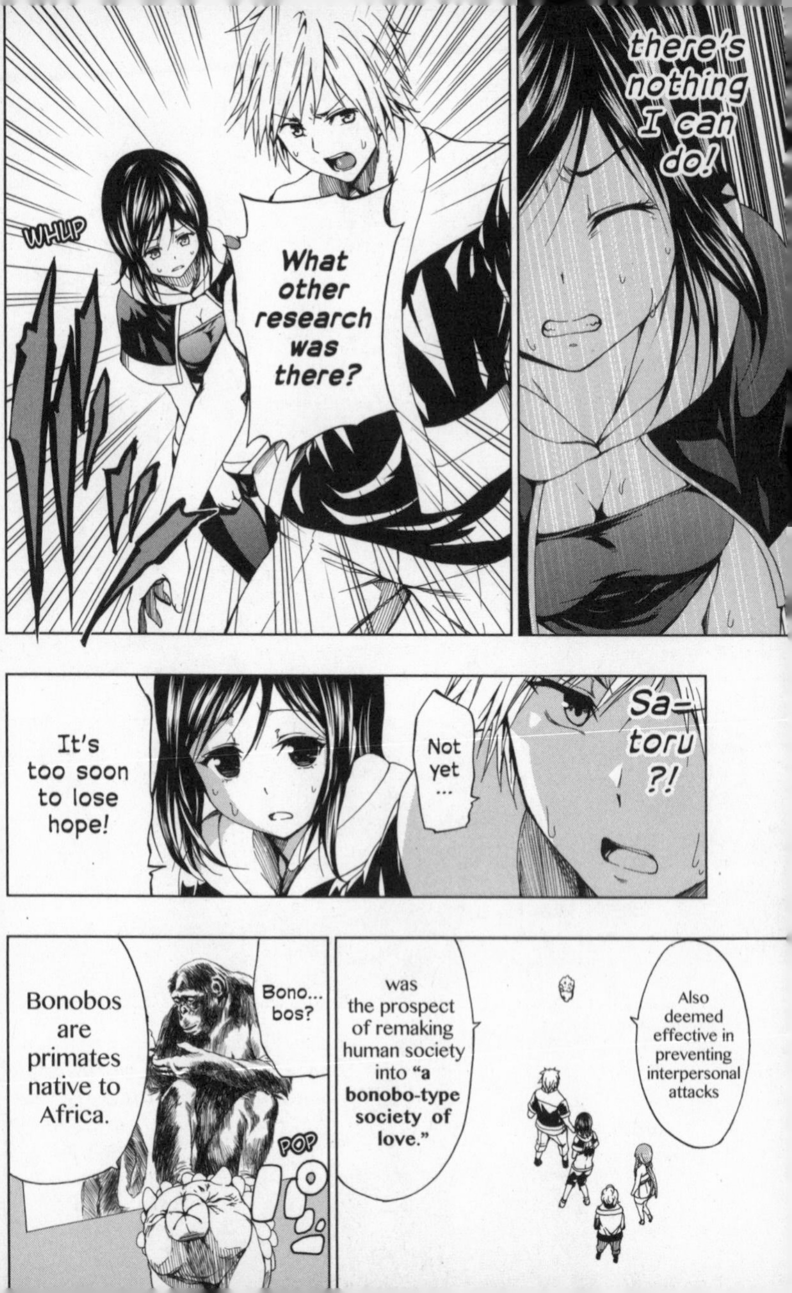
there's nothing I can do!
What other research was there?
WHUP
Sa-toru?!
Not yet...
It's too soon to lose hope!
Also deemed effective in preventing interpersonal attacks
was the prospect of remaking human society into "a bonobo-type society of love."
Bono... bos?
Bonobos are primates native to Africa.
POP

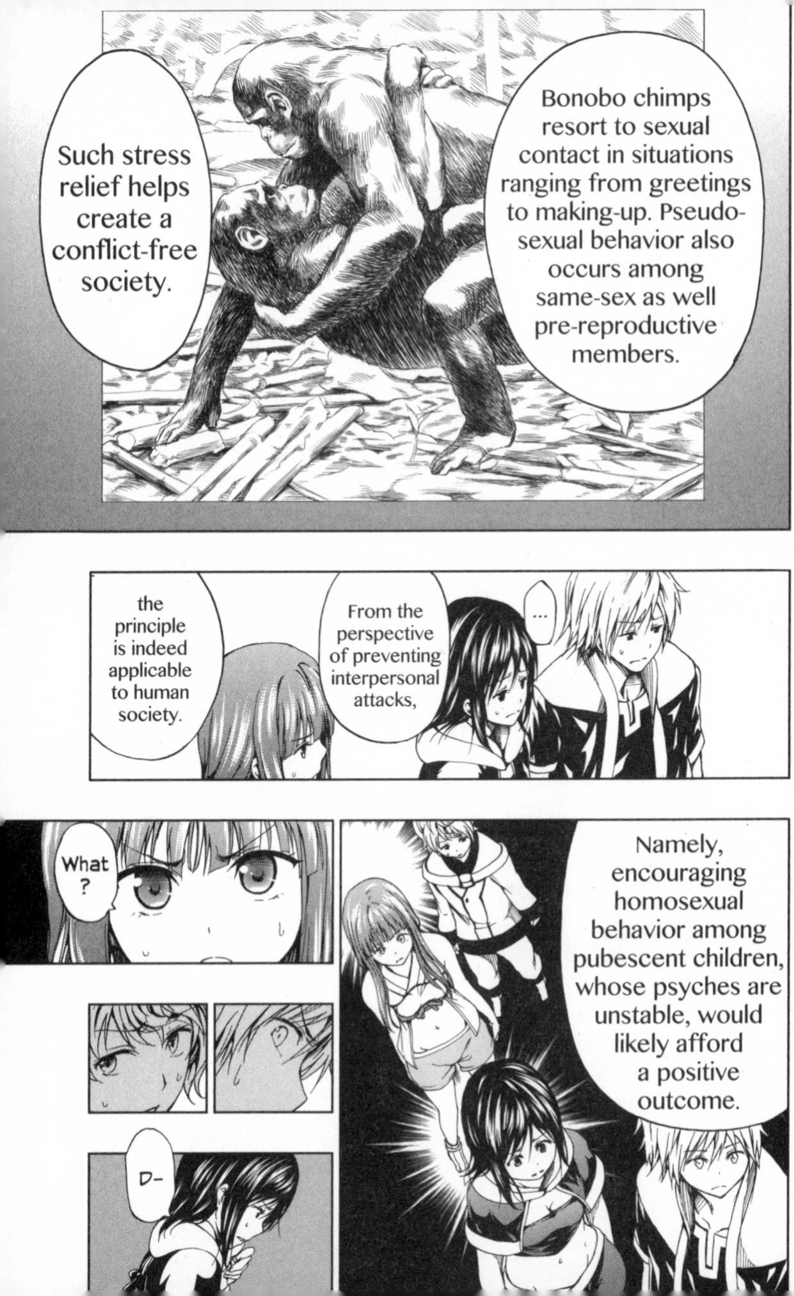

Bonobo chimps resort to sexual contact in situations ranging from greetings to making-up. Pseudo-sexual behavior also occurs among same-sex as well pre-reproductive members.
Such stress relief helps create a conflict-free society.
...
From the perspective of preventing interpersonal attacks,
the principle is indeed applicable to human society.
Namely, encouraging homosexual behavior among pubescent children, whose psyches are unstable, would likely afford a positive outcome.
What?
D-

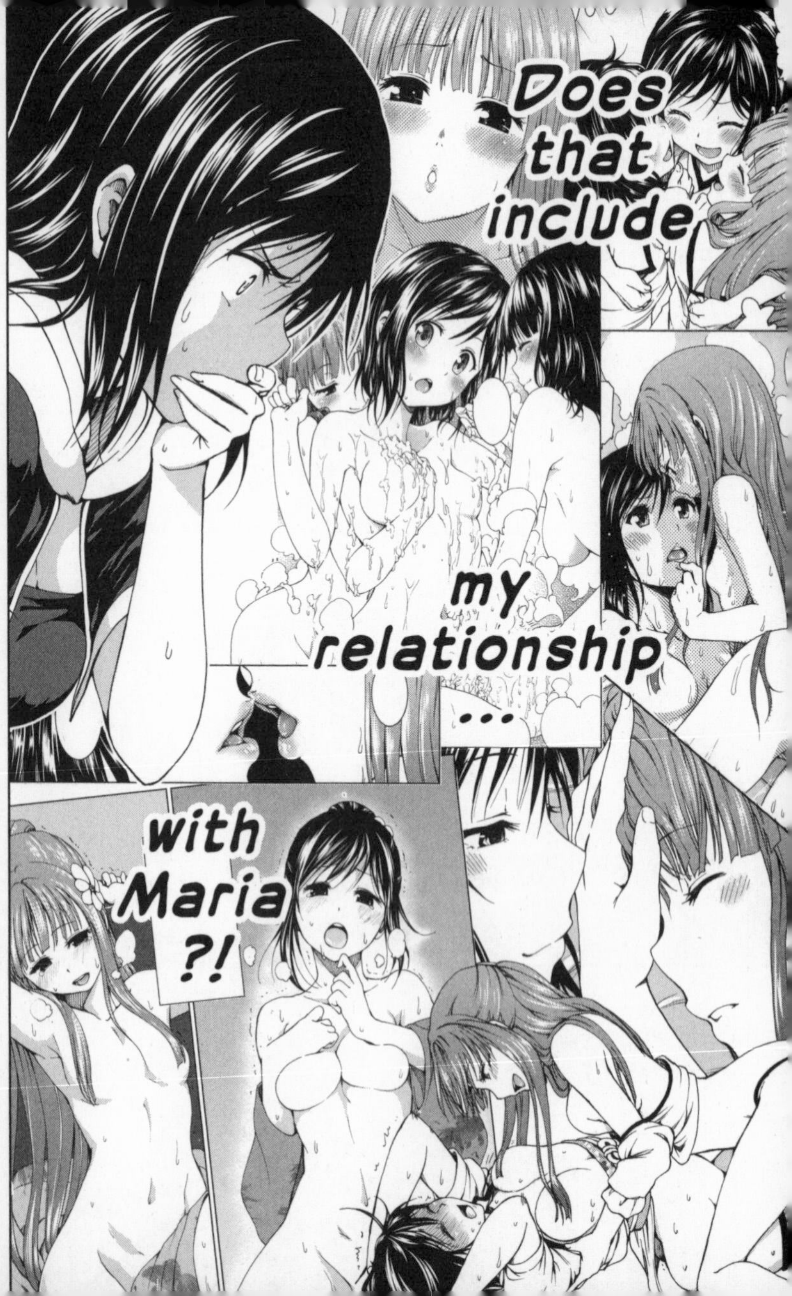
Does that include
my relationship...
with Maria?!

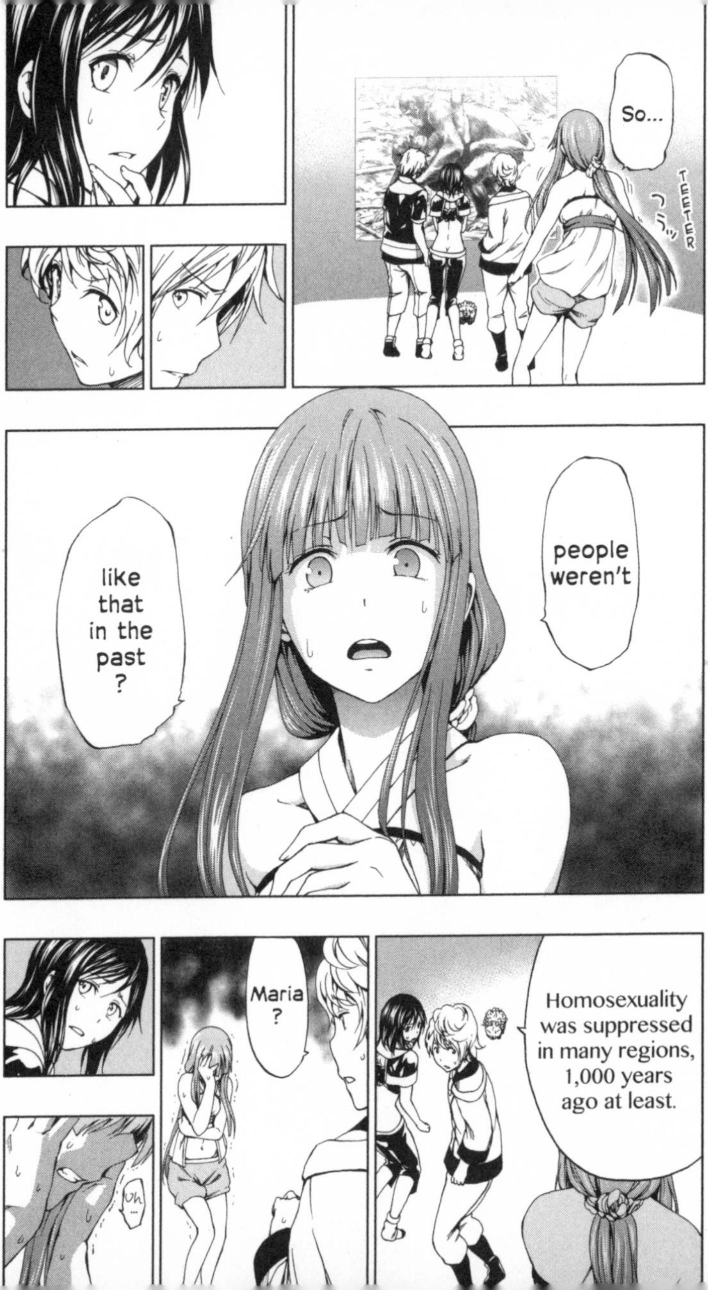
So...
TEETER
people weren't
like that in the past ?
Homosexuality was suppressed in many regions, 1,000 years ago at least.
Maria ?
Uh...

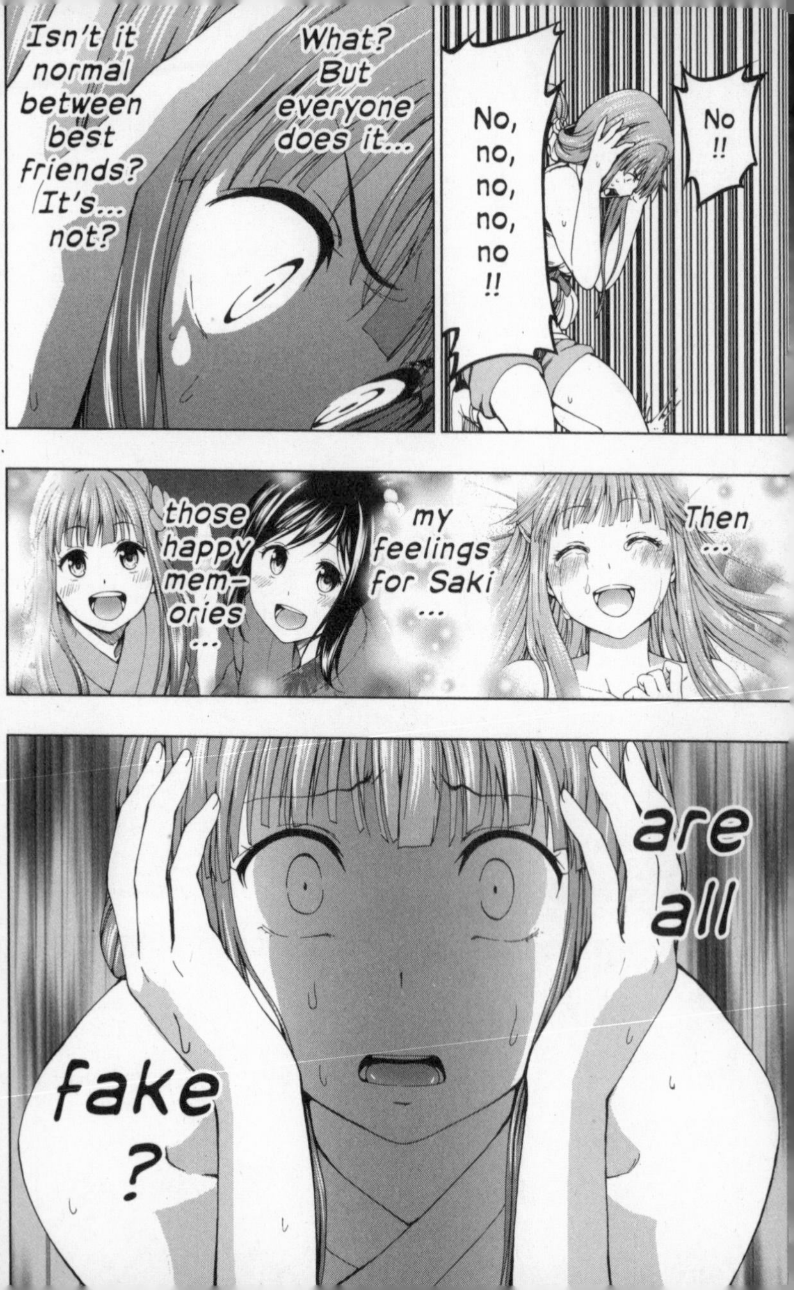
No !!
No, no, no, no, no !!
What? But everyone does it...
Isn't it normal between best friends? It's... not?
Then ...
my feelings for Saki ...
those happy mem-ories ...
are all
fake ?

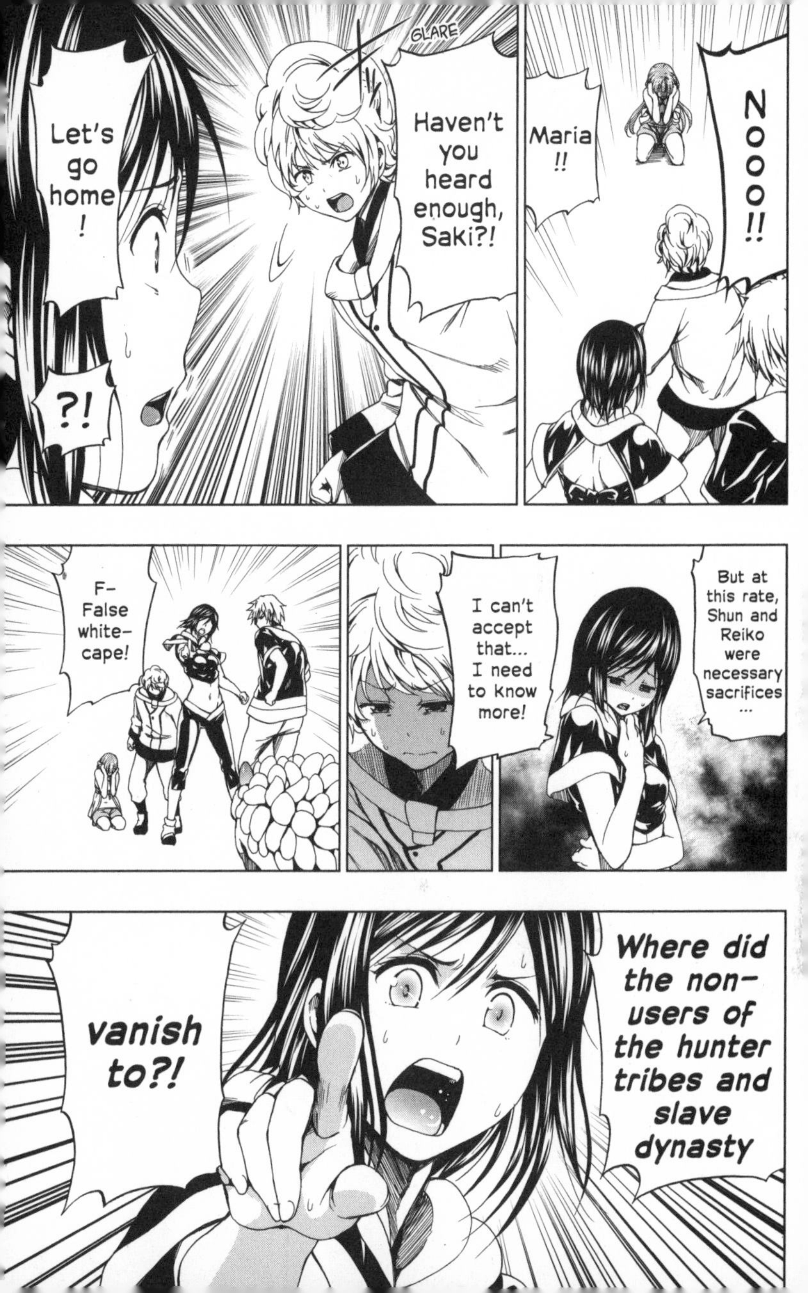
NOOOO!!
Maria !!
GLARE
Haven't you heard enough, Saki?!
Let's go home!
?!
But at this rate, Shun and Reiko were necessary sacrifices ...
I can't accept that... I need to know more!
F- False white-cape!
Where did the non-users of the hunter tribes and slave dynasty
vanish to?!

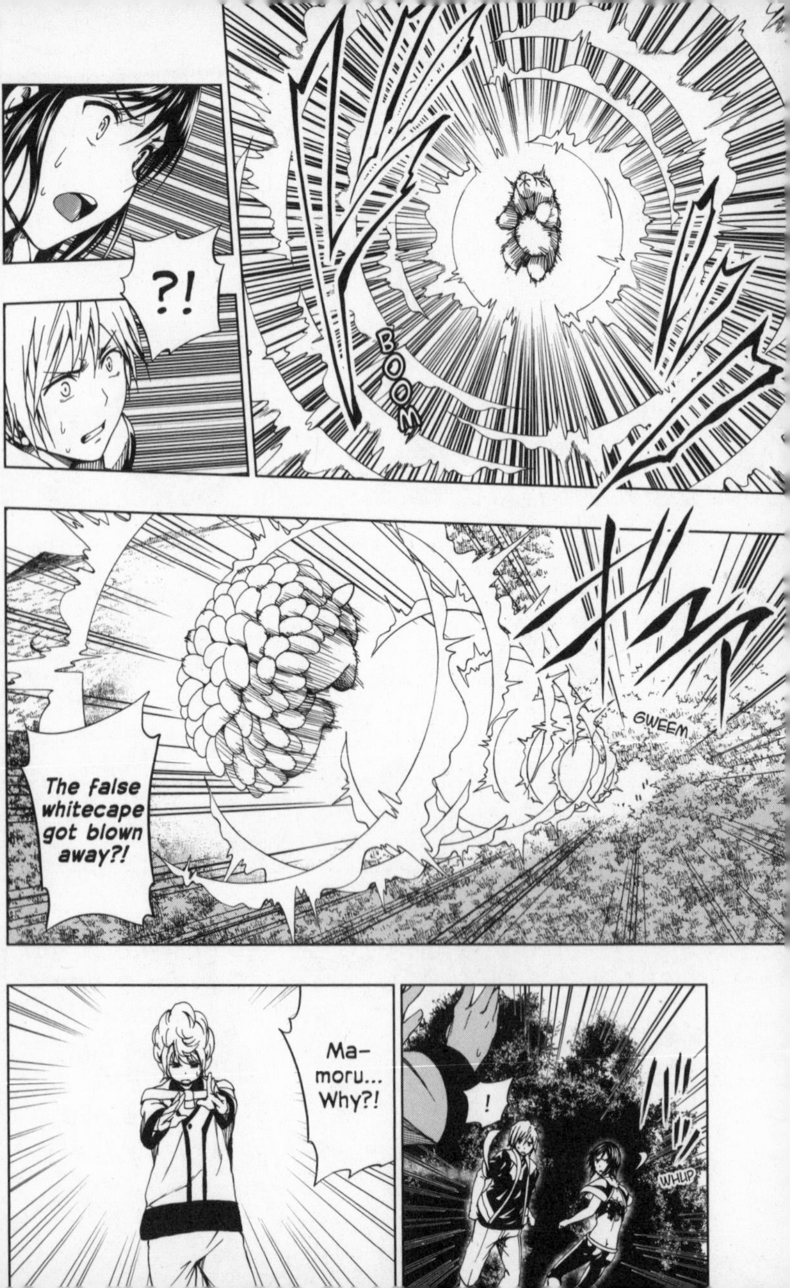
BOOM
?!
GWEEM
The false whitecape got blown away?!
!
WHLUP
Ma-moru... Why?!

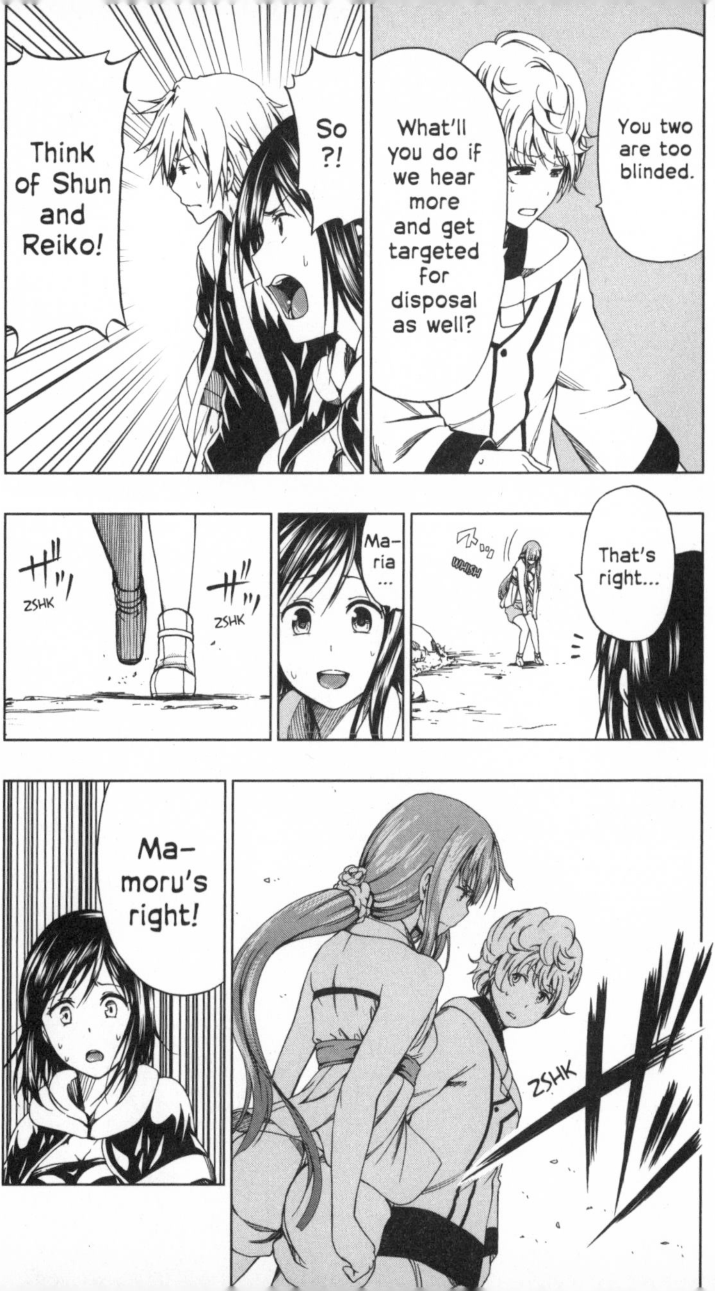
You two are too blinded.
What'll you do if we hear more and get targeted for disposal as well?
So ?!
Think of Shun and Reiko!
That's right...
WHISH
Ma-ria ...
ZSHK
ZSHK
ZSHK
Ma-moru's right!

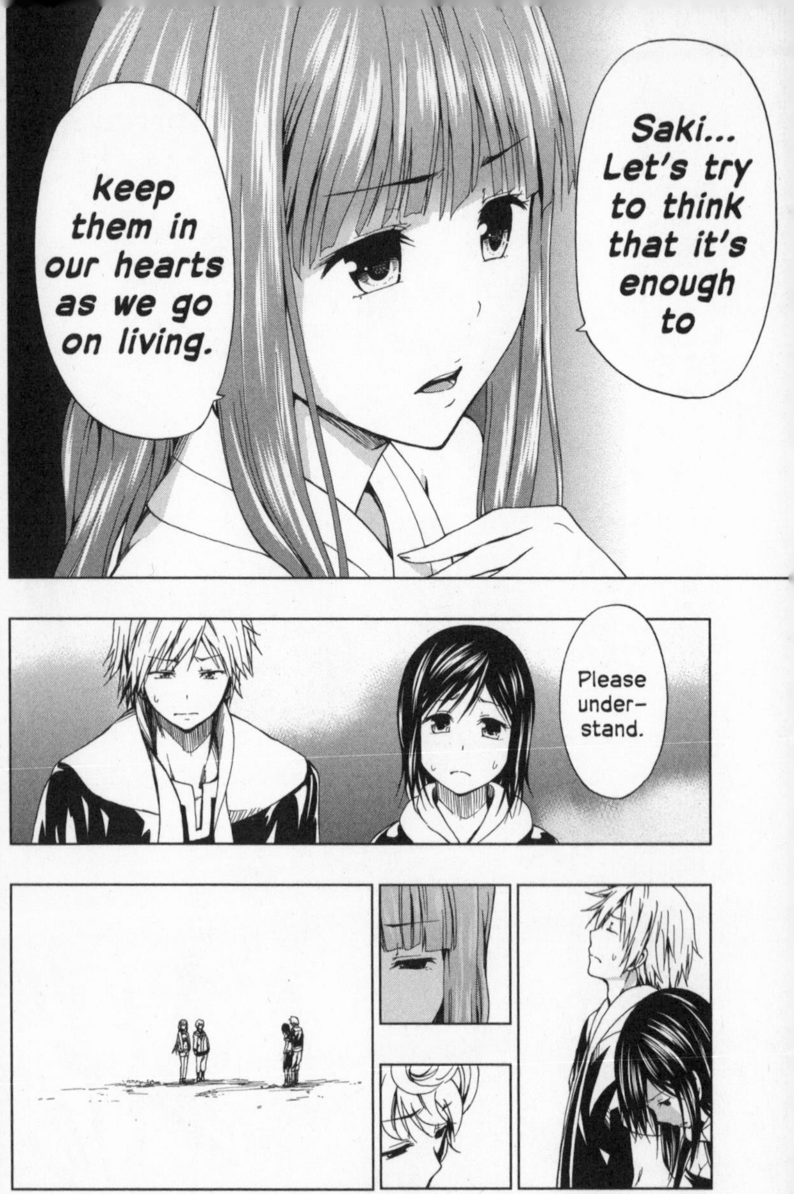
Saki... Let's try to think that it's enough to
keep them in our hearts as we go on living.
Please under-stand.

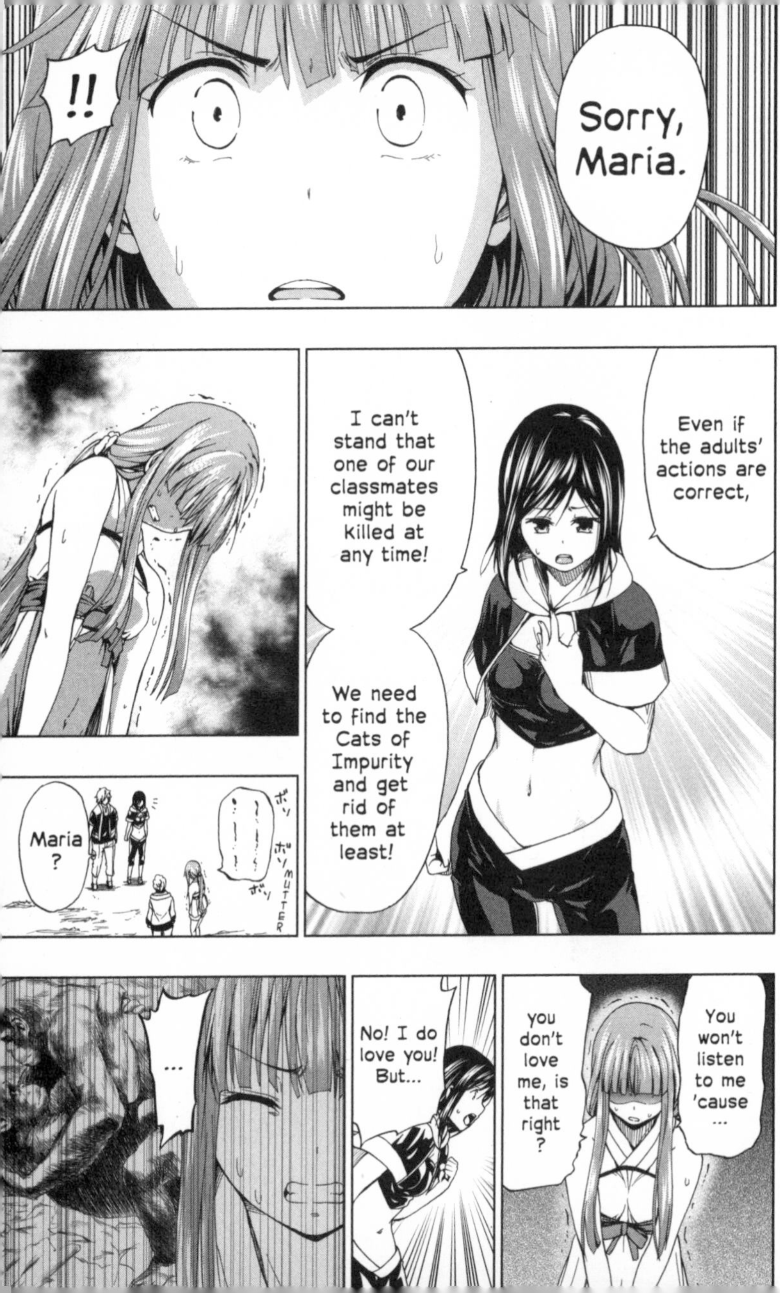
Sorry, Maria.
!!
Even if the adults' actions are correct,
I can't stand that one of our classmates might be killed at any time!
We need to find the Cats of Impurity and get rid of them at least!
ボソ ボソ ボソ
MUTTER
Maria?
You won't listen to me 'cause ...
you don't love me, is that right?
No! I do love you! But...
...

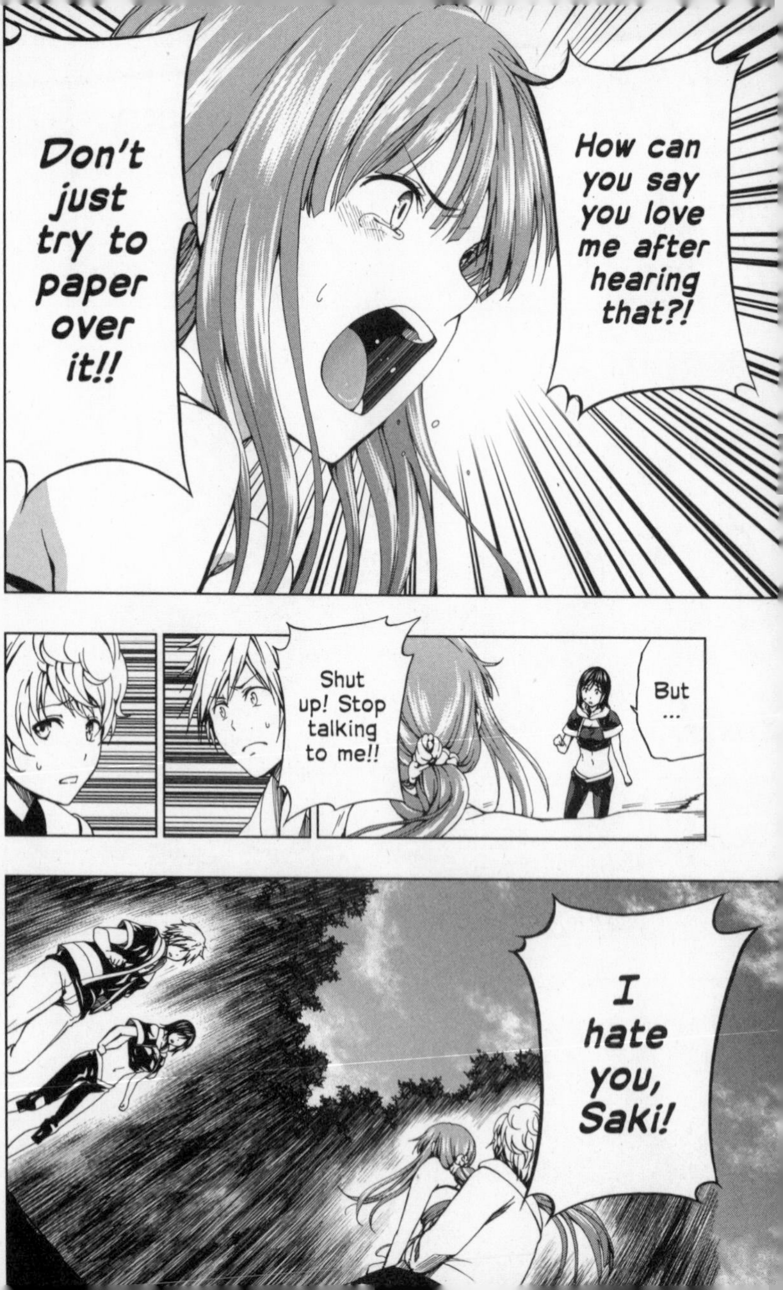
How can you say you love me after hearing that?!
Don't just try to paper over it!!
But ...
Shut up! Stop talking to me!!
I hate you, Saki!

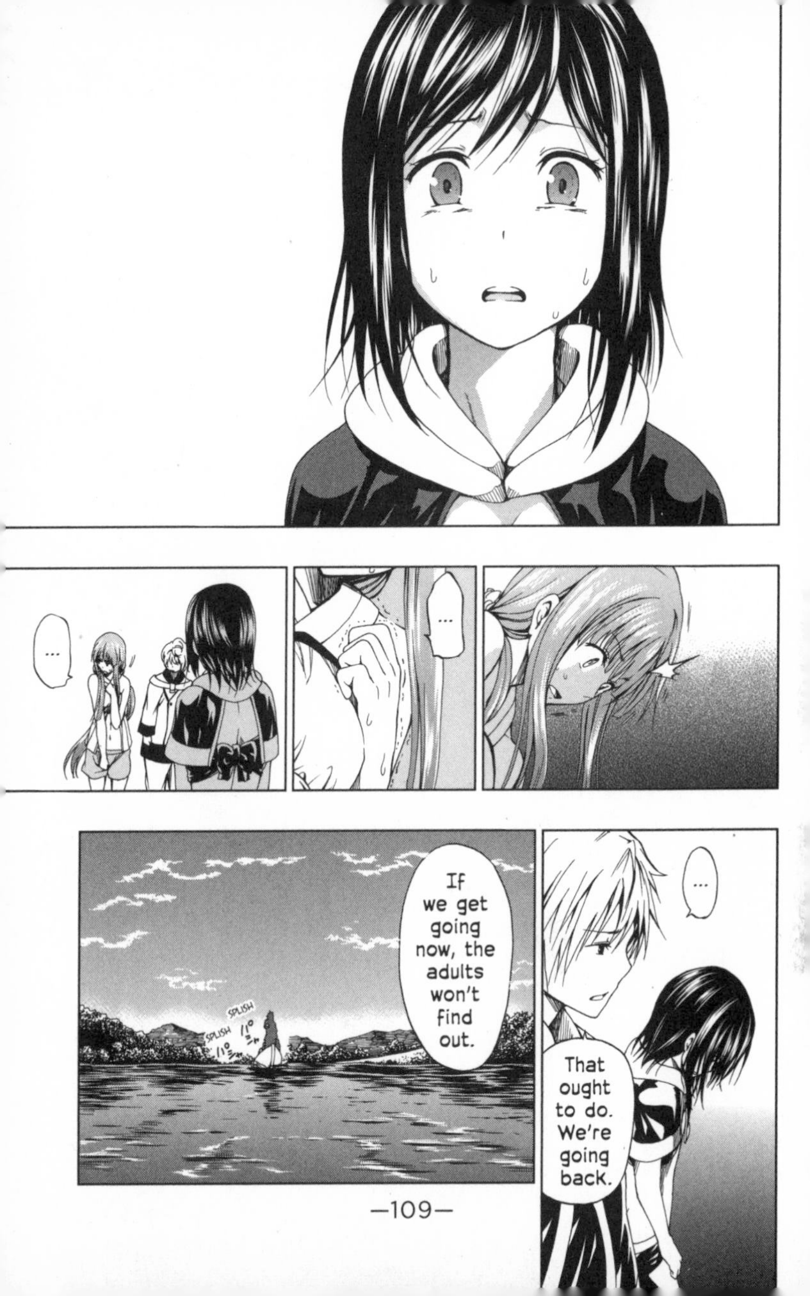
...
...
...
That ought to do. We're going back.
If we get going now, the adults won't find out.
SPLISH
SPLISH

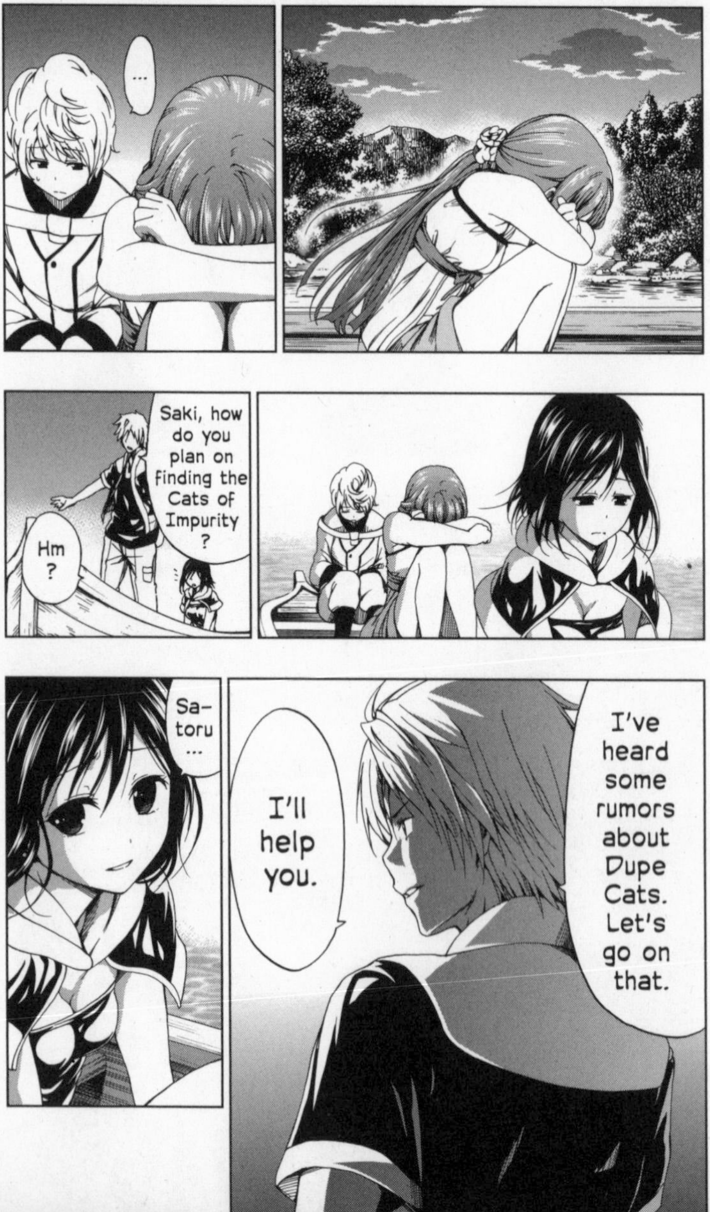
...
Saki, how do you plan on finding the Cats of Impurity?
Hm?
I've heard some rumors about Dupe Cats. Let's go on that.
I'll help you.
Sa-toru...

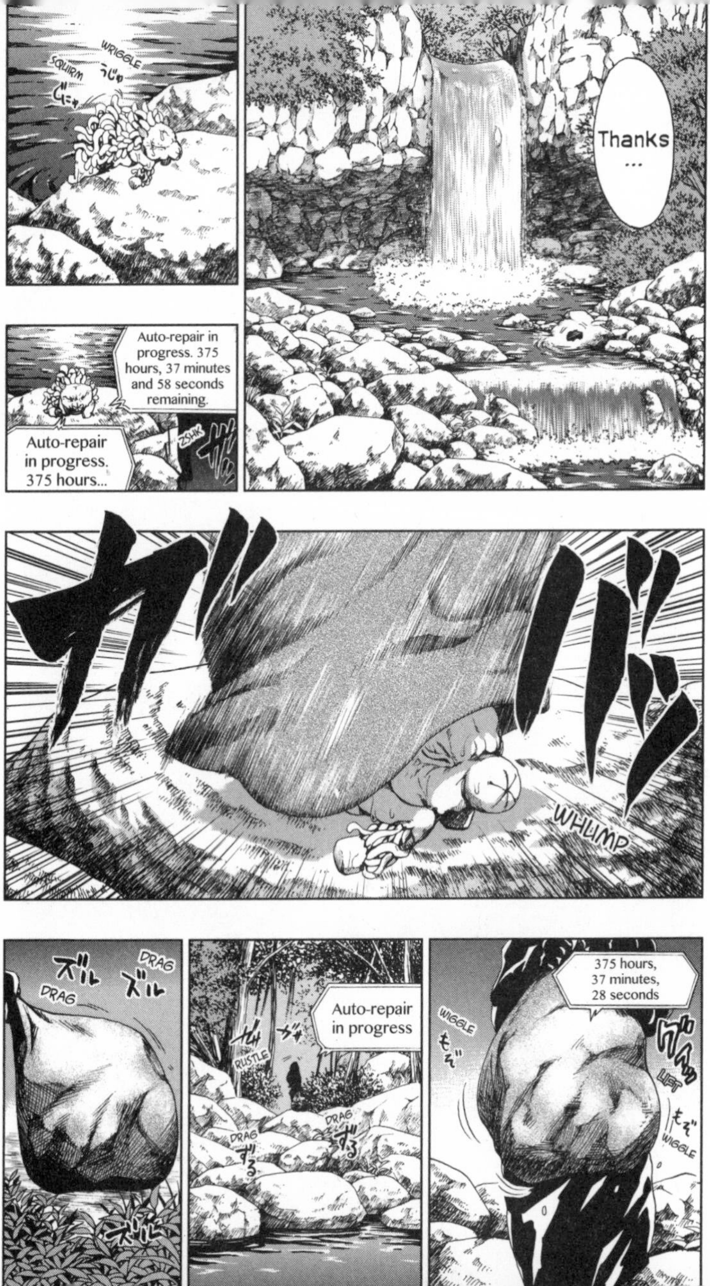

Thanks ...
WRIGGLE
うじゃ
SQUIRM
ぐにゃ
Auto-repair in progress. 375 hours, 37 minutes and 58 seconds remaining.
Auto-repair in progress. 375 hours...
ZSHK
WHLIMP
375 hours, 37 minutes, 28 seconds
WIGGLE
もぞ
LIFT
もぞ
WIGGLE
Auto-repair in progress
RUSTLE
DRAG
ずる
DRAG
ずる
DRAG
DRAG

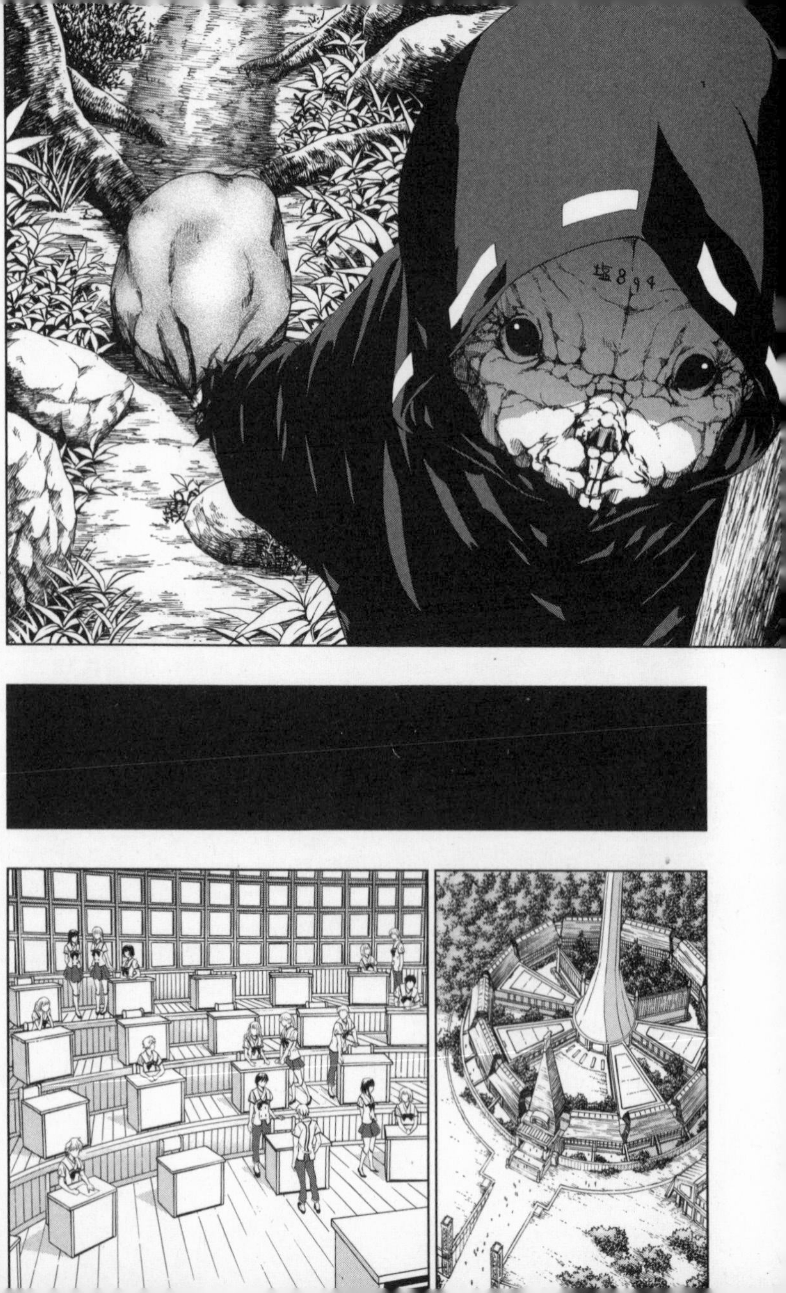
塩894

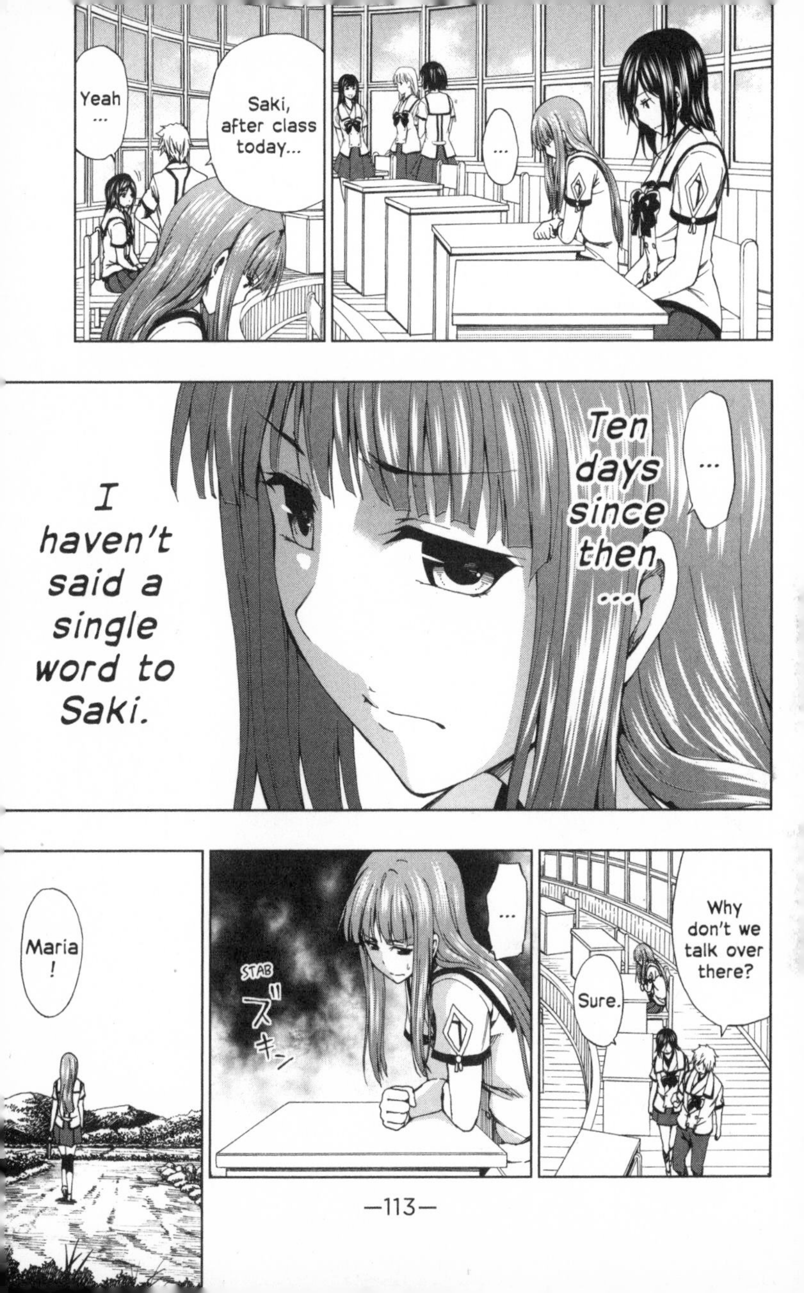
...
Saki, after class today...
Yeah ...
...
Ten days since then ...
I haven't said a single word to Saki.
Why don't we talk over there?
Sure.
...
STAB
ズキン
Maria!

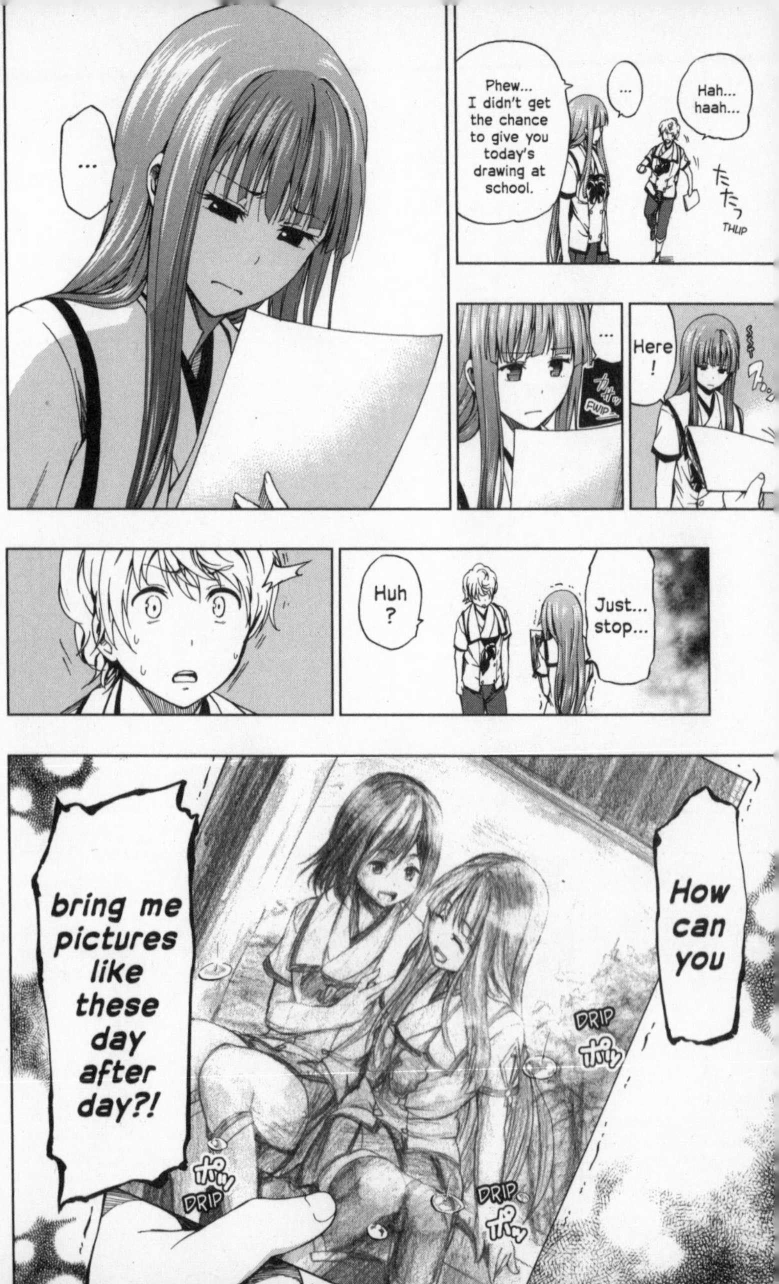
Hah... haah...
THUP
...
Phew... I didn't get the chance to give you today's drawing at school.
Here!
...
FWIP
...
Just... stop...
Huh?
How can you
DRIP
DRIP
DRIP
bring me pictures like these day after day?!

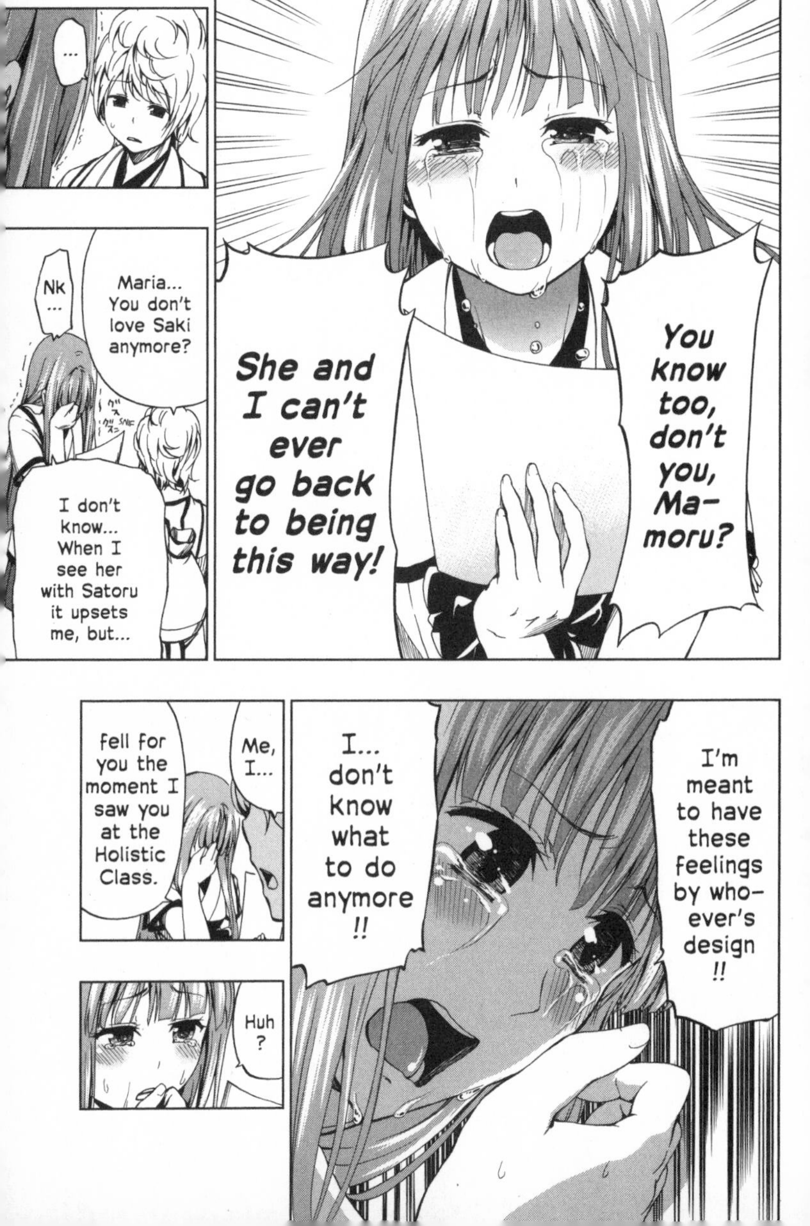
You know too, don't you, Mamoru?
She and I can't ever go back to being this way!
...
Maria... You don't love Saki anymore?
Nk ...
SNIF
I don't know... When I see her with Satoru it upsets me, but...
I'm meant to have these feelings by who-ever's design !!
I... don't know what to do anymore !!
Me, I...
fell for you the moment I saw you at the Holistic Class.
Huh ?

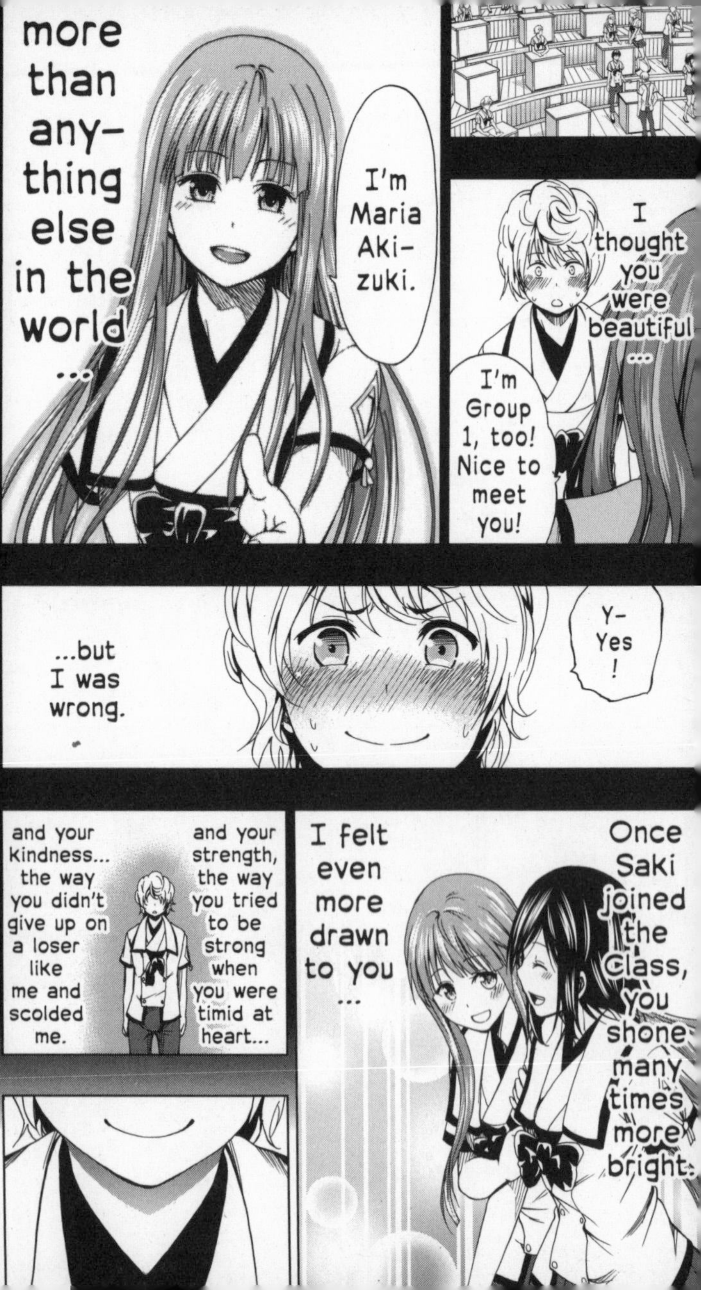
I thought you were beautiful...
I'm Group 1, too! Nice to meet you!
I'm Maria Aki-zuki.
more than any-thing else in the world...
Y-Yes!
...but I was wrong.
Once Saki joined the Class, you shone many times more bright.
I felt even more drawn to you...
and your strength, the way you tried to be strong when you were timid at heart...
and your kindness... the way you didn't give up on a loser like me and scolded me.

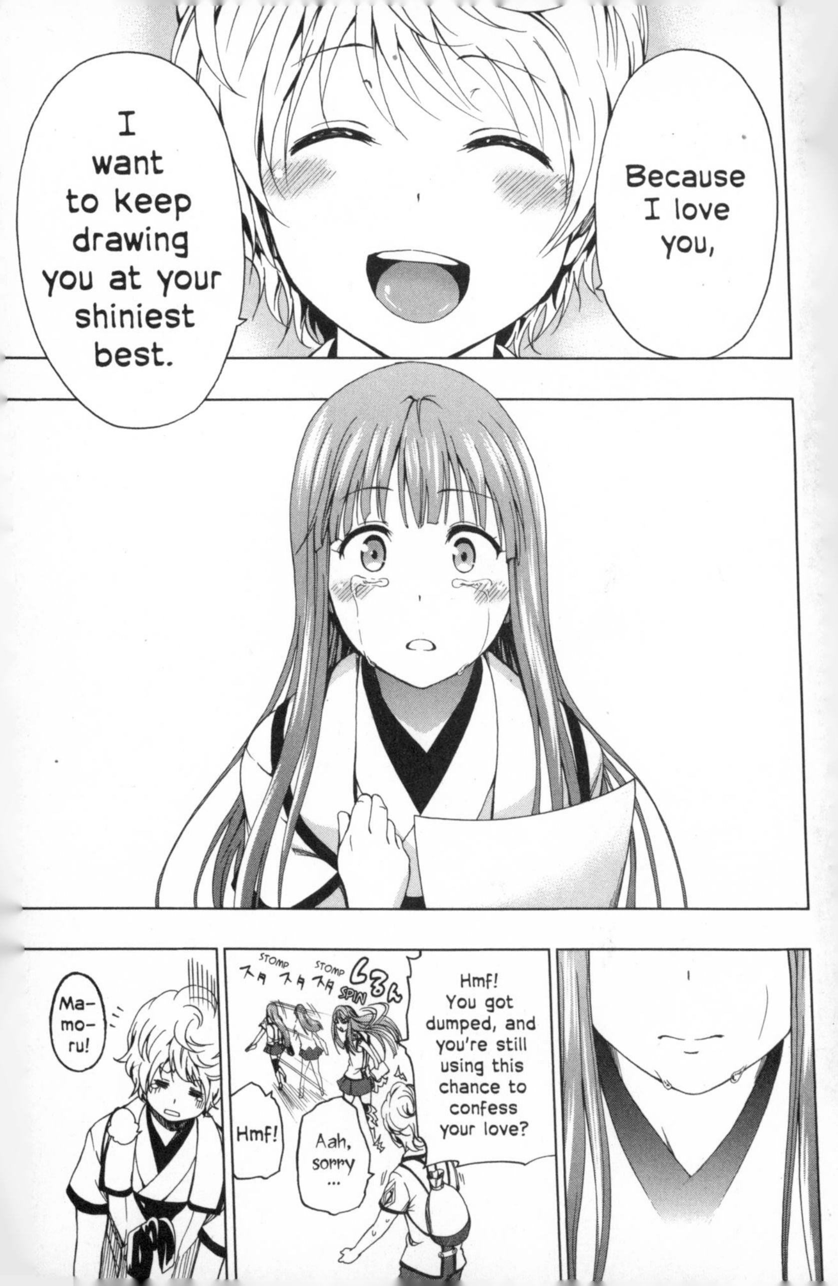
Because I love you,
I want to keep drawing you at your shiniest best.
Hmf! You got dumped, and you're still using this chance to confess your love?
STOMP STOMP
SPIN
Hmf!
Aah, sorry ...
Ma-mo-ru!

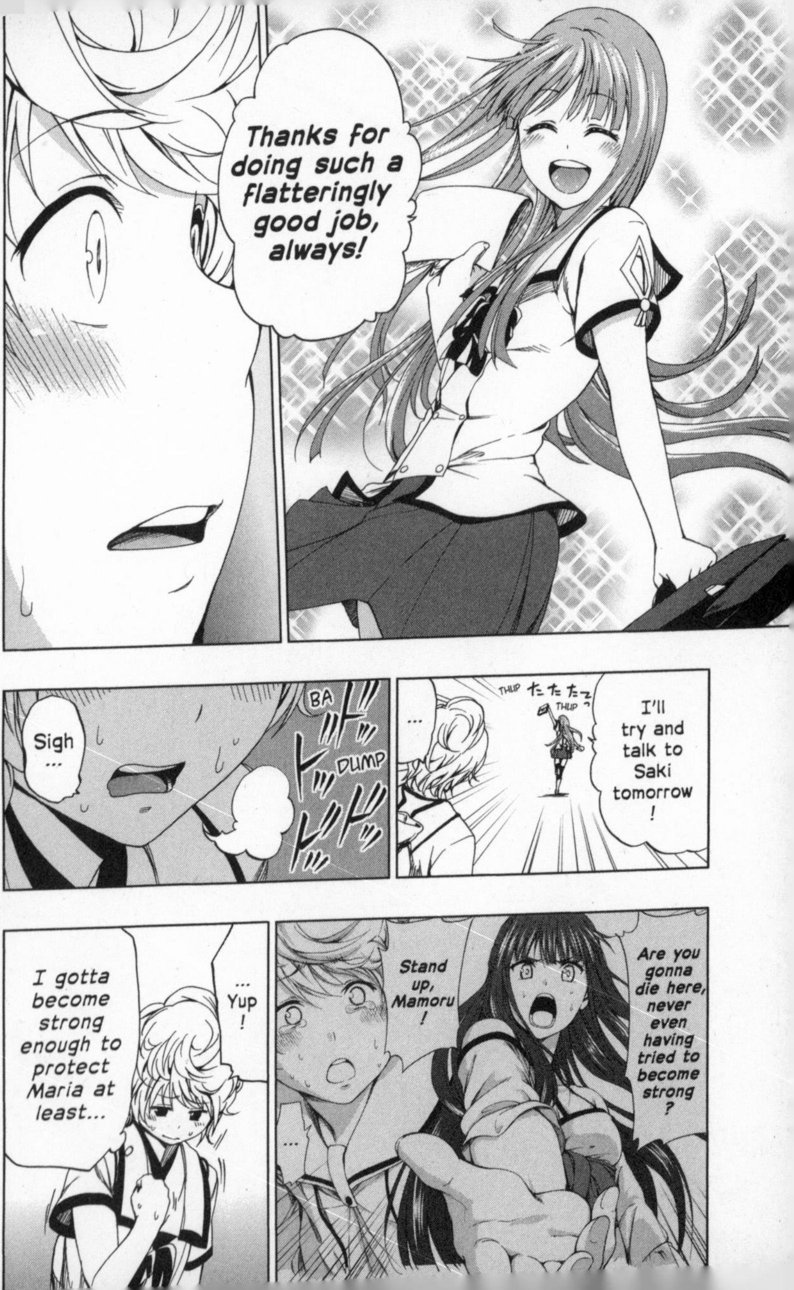
Thanks for doing such a flatteringly good job, always!
I'll try and talk to Saki tomorrow!
THUP たたたっ THUP
...
BA
DUMP
Sigh ...
Are you gonna die here, never even having tried to become strong?
Stand up, Mamoru!
...
... Yup!
I gotta become strong enough to protect Maria at least...

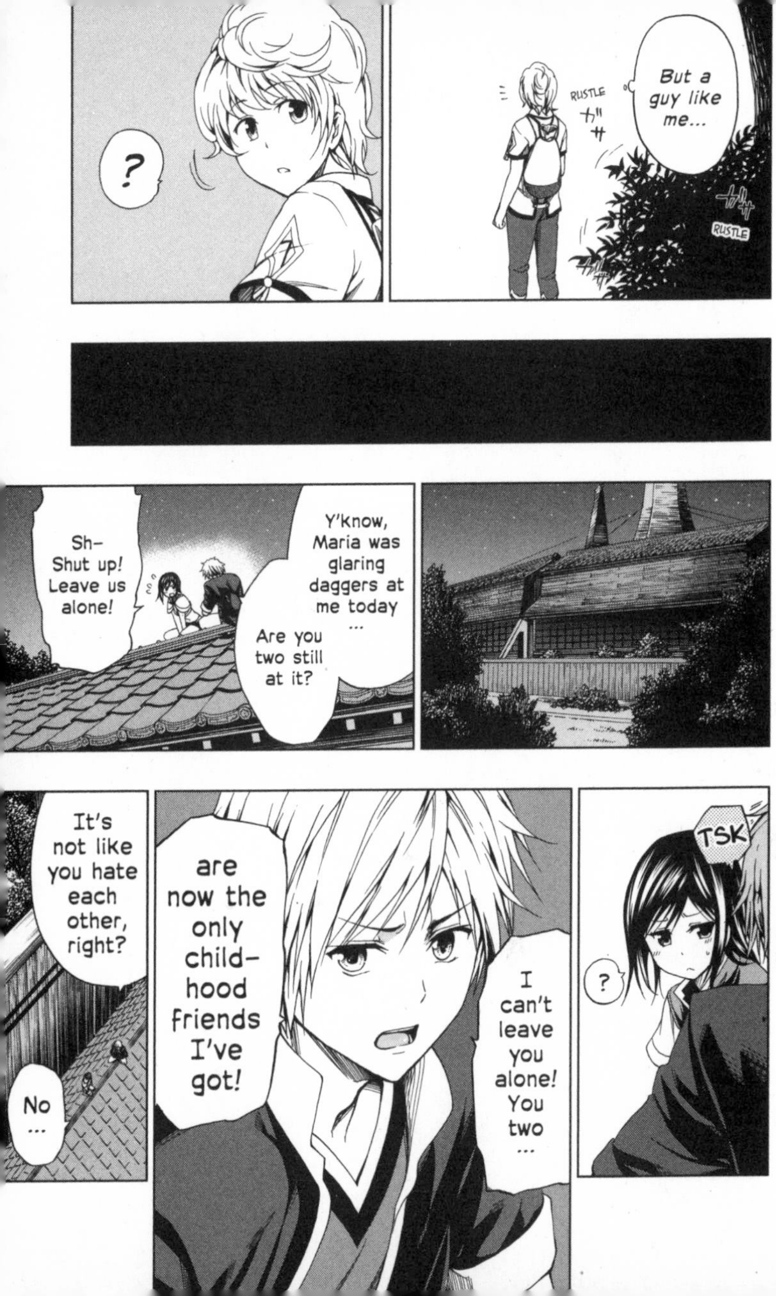
But a guy like me...
RUSTLE
RUSTLE
?
Y'know, Maria was glaring daggers at me today ...
Are you two still at it?
Sh- Shut up! Leave us alone!
TSK
?
I can't leave you alone! You two ...
are now the only child- hood friends I've got!
It's not like you hate each other, right?
No ...

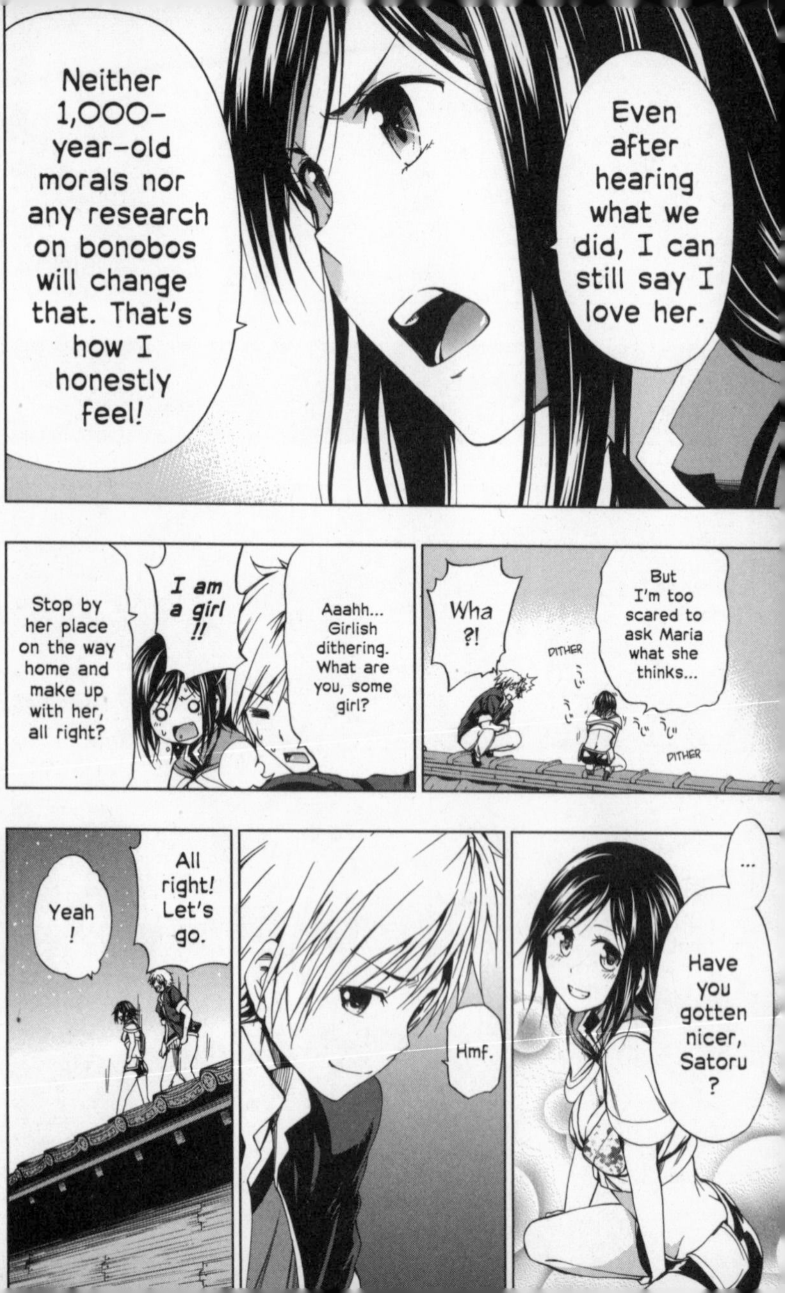
Even after hearing what we did, I can still say I love her.
Neither 1,000-year-old morals nor any research on bonobos will change that. That's how I honestly feel!
But I'm too scared to ask Maria what she thinks...
Wha ?!
DITHER
DITHER
Aaahh... Girlish dithering. What are you, some girl?
I am a girl !!
Stop by her place on the way home and make up with her, all right?
...
Have you gotten nicer, Satoru ?
Hmf.
All right! Let's go.
Yeah !

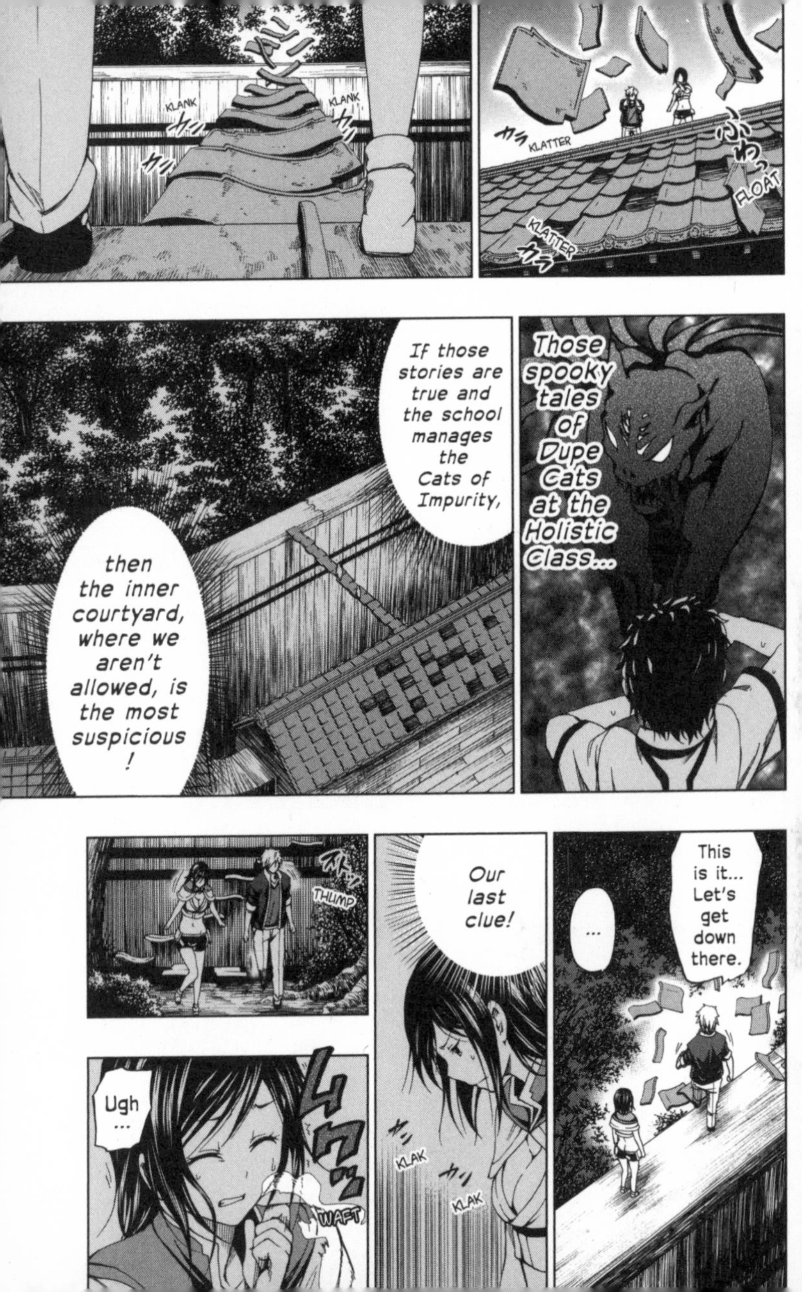
KLATTER
FLOAT
KLATTER
KLANK
KLANK
Those spooky tales of Dupe Cats at the Holistic Class...
If those stories are true and the school manages the Cats of Impurity,
then the inner courtyard, where we aren't allowed, is the most suspicious!
This is it... Let's get down there.
...
Our last clue!
KLAK
KLAK
THUMP
Ugh...
WAFT

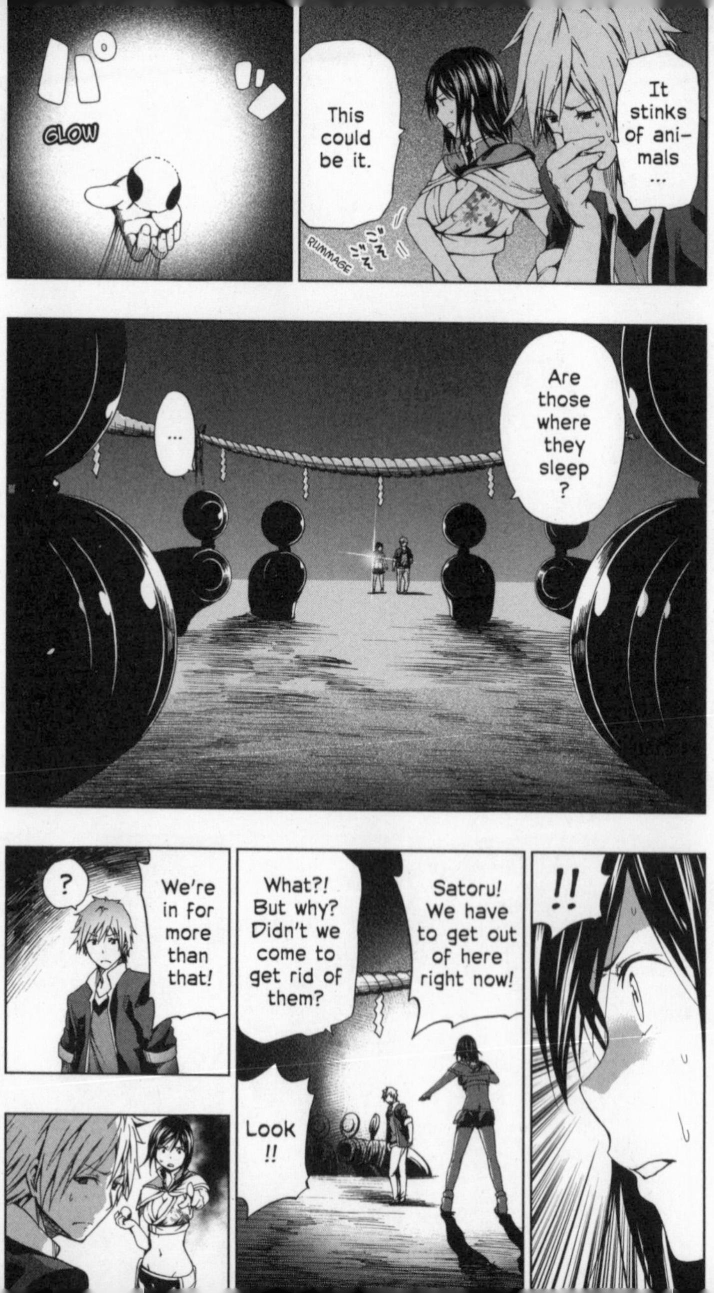

It stinks of animals ...
This could be it.
RUMMAGE
GLOW
Are those where they sleep?
...
!!
Satoru! We have to get out of here right now!
What?! But why? Didn't we come to get rid of them?
Look !!
?
We're in for more than that!

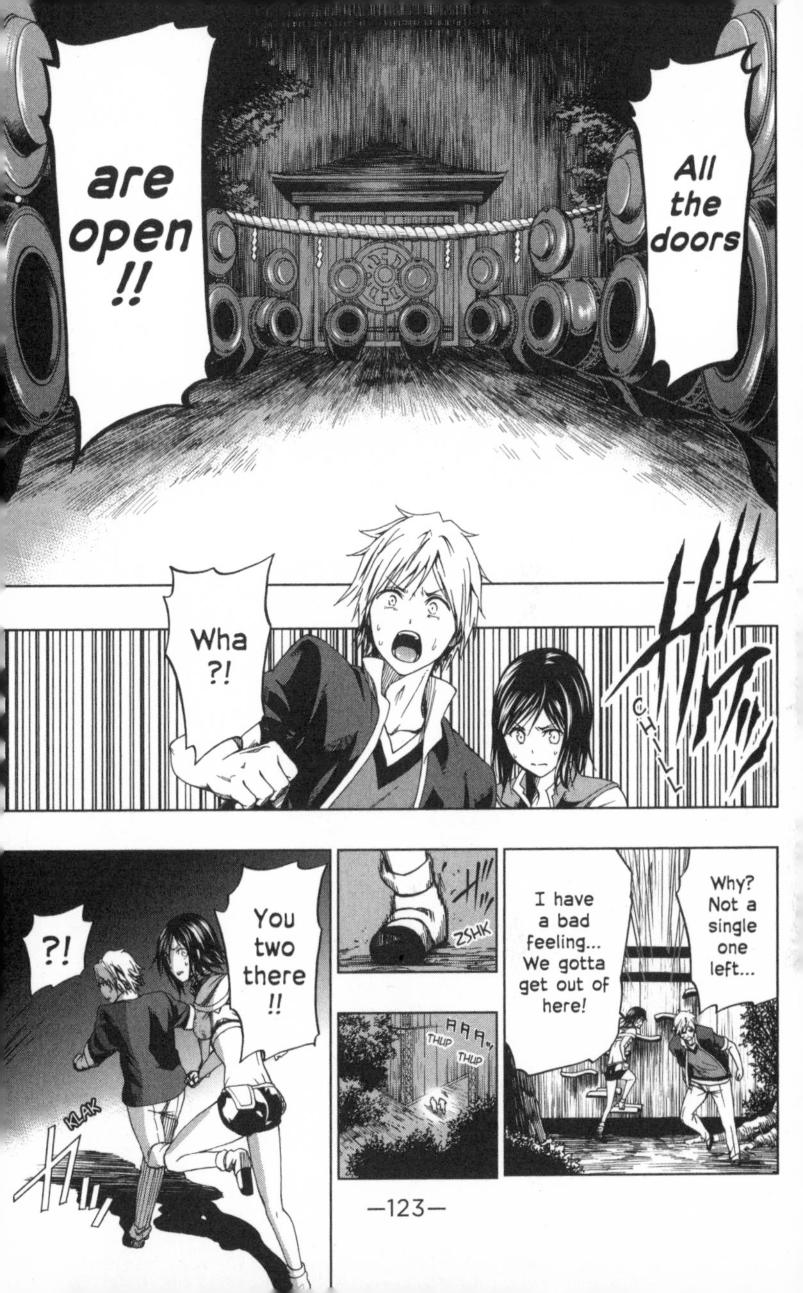
All the doors
are open !!
Wha ?!
CHILL
Why? Not a single one left...
I have a bad feeling... We gotta get out of here!
ZSHK
THUP THUP
You two there !!
?!
KLAK

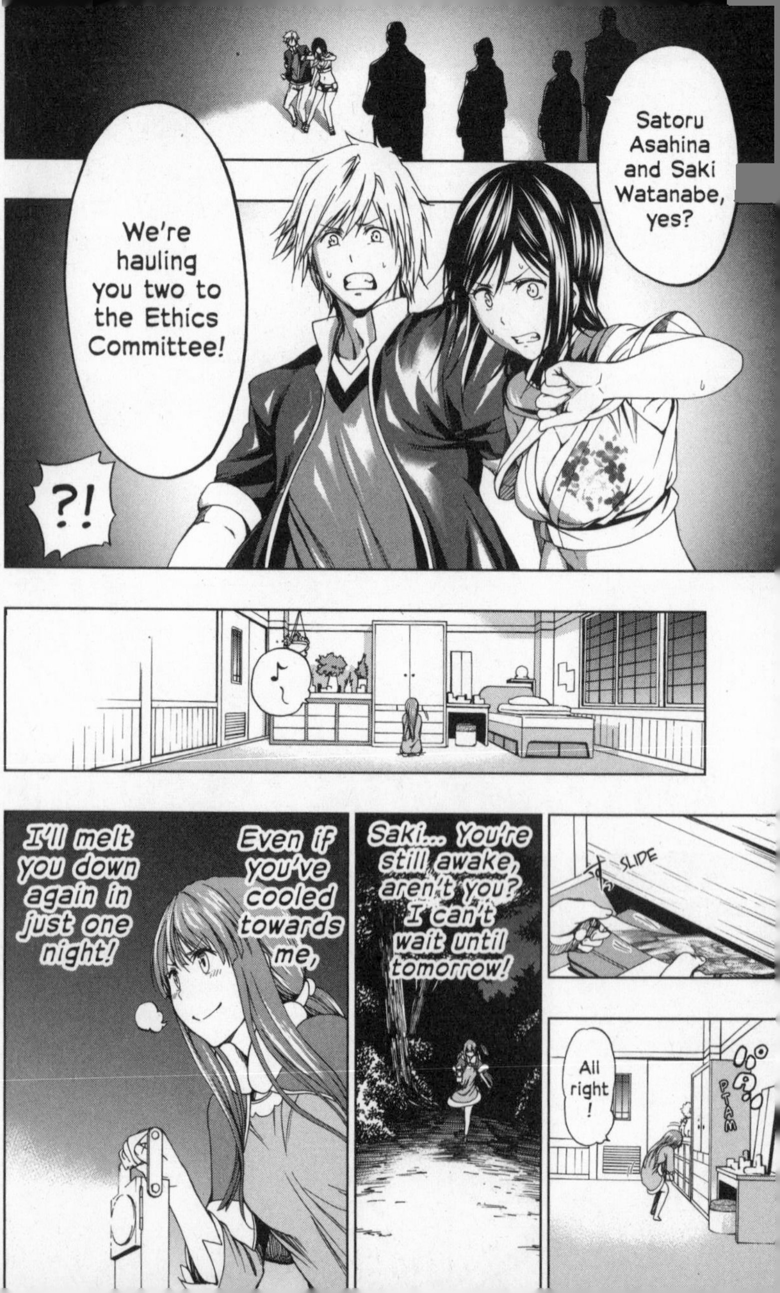
Satoru Asahina and Saki Watanabe, yes?
We're hauling you two to the Ethics Committee!
?!
♪
SLIDE
All right!
PTAM
Saki... You're still awake, aren't you? I can't wait until tomorrow!
Even if you've cooled towards me,
I'll melt you down again in just one night!

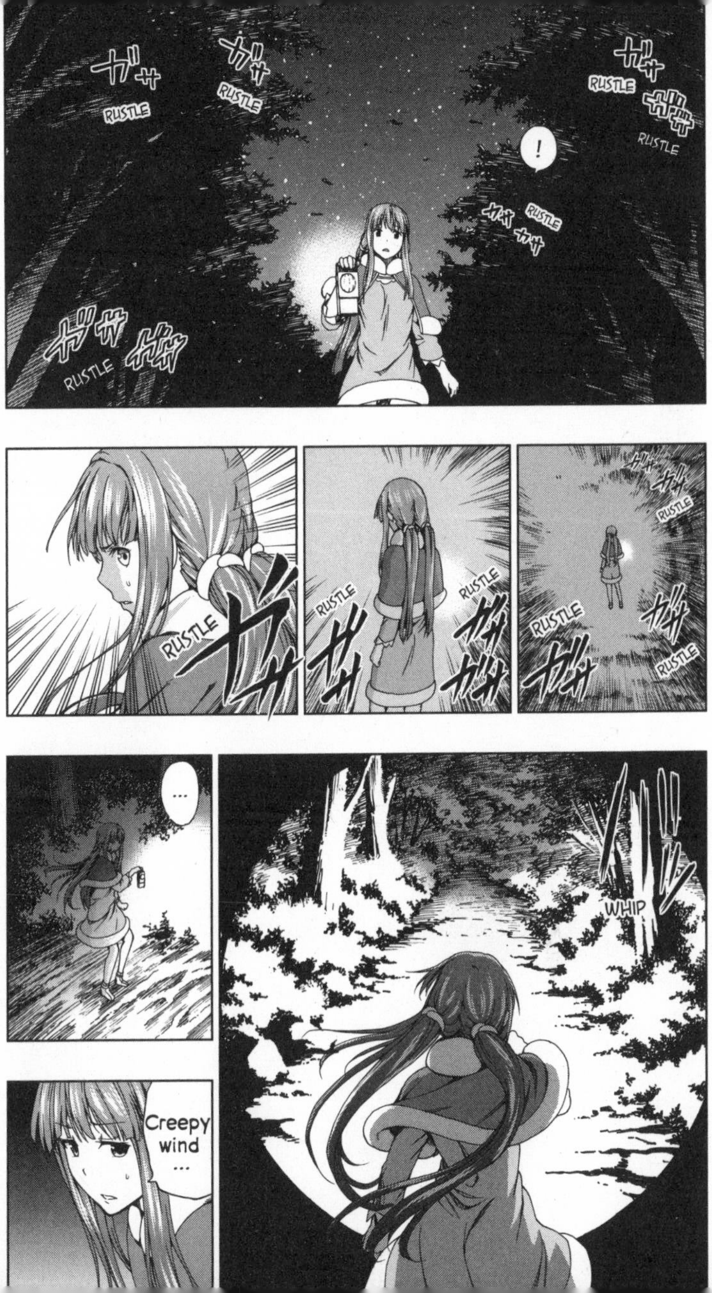
RUSTLE
RUSTLE
!
RUSTLE
RUSTLE
RUSTLE
RUSTLE
RUSTLE
RUSTLE
RUSTLE
RUSTLE
RUSTLE
RUSTLE
WHIP
...
Creepy wind ...

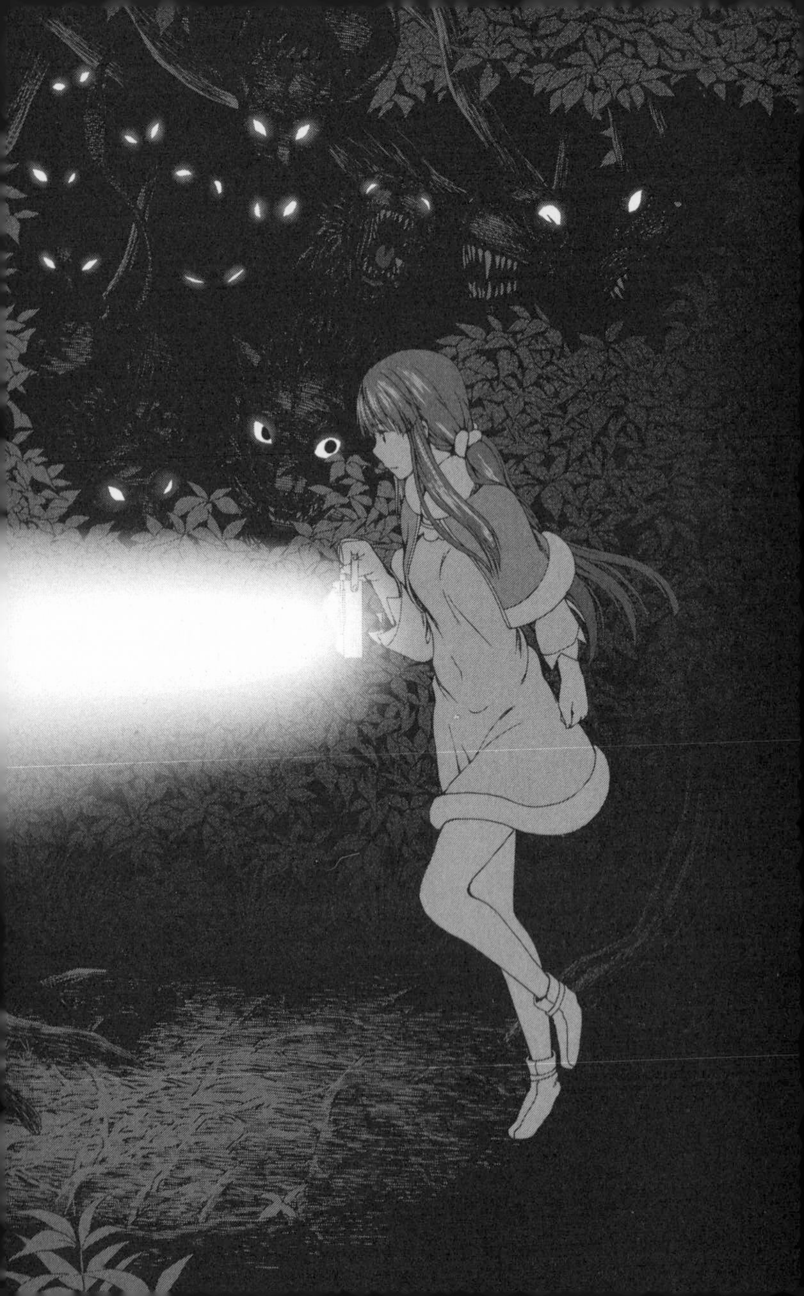

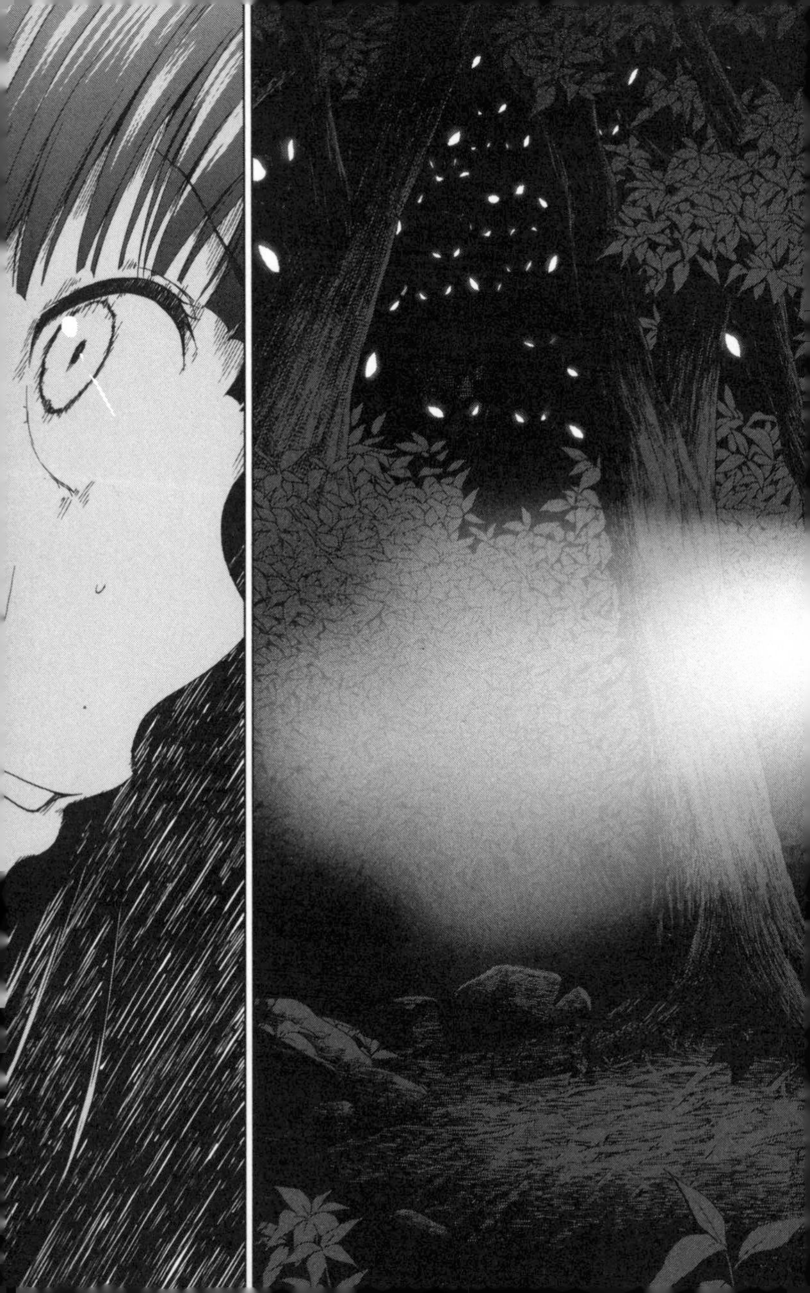

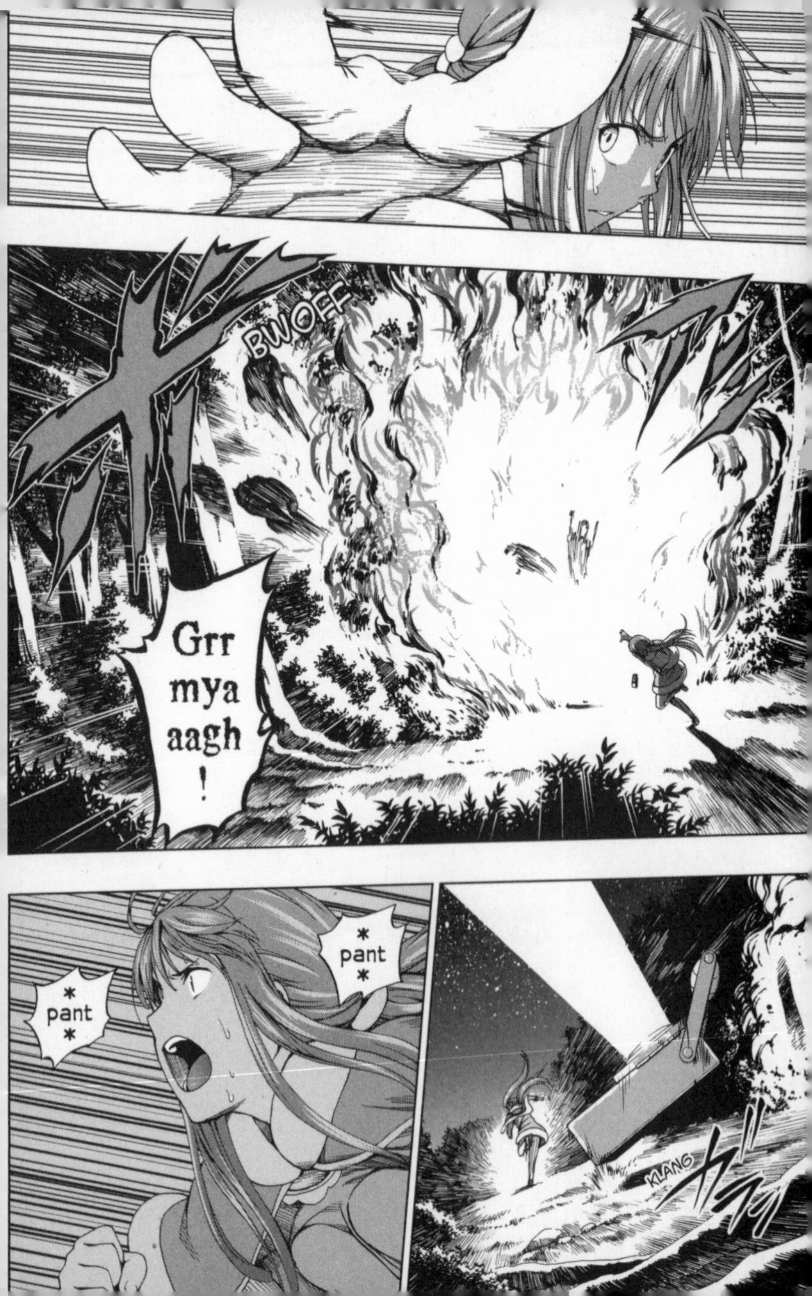
BWOFF
Grr mya aagh!
* pant *
* pant *
KLANG

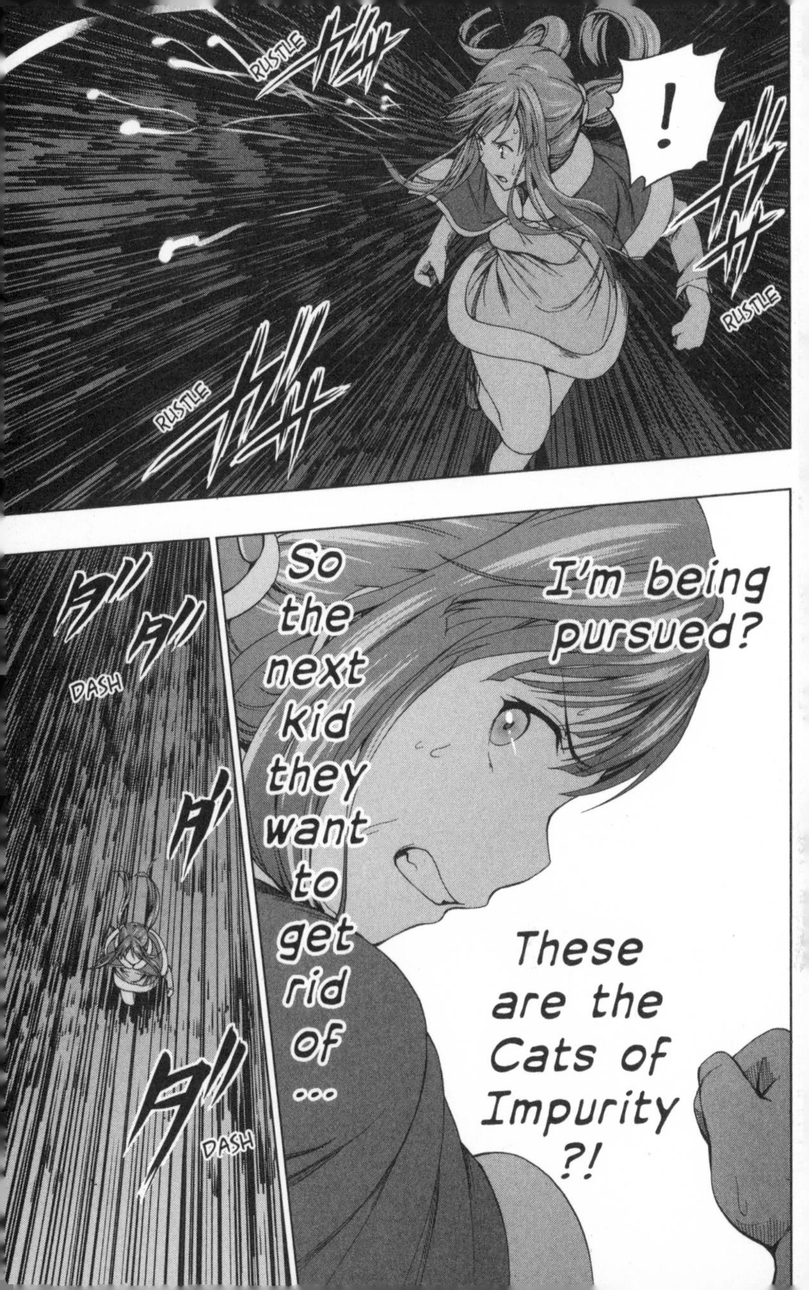
!
RUSTLE
RUSTLE
RUSTLE
I'm being pursued?
So the next kid they want to get rid of...
These are the Cats of Impurity?!
DASH
DASH

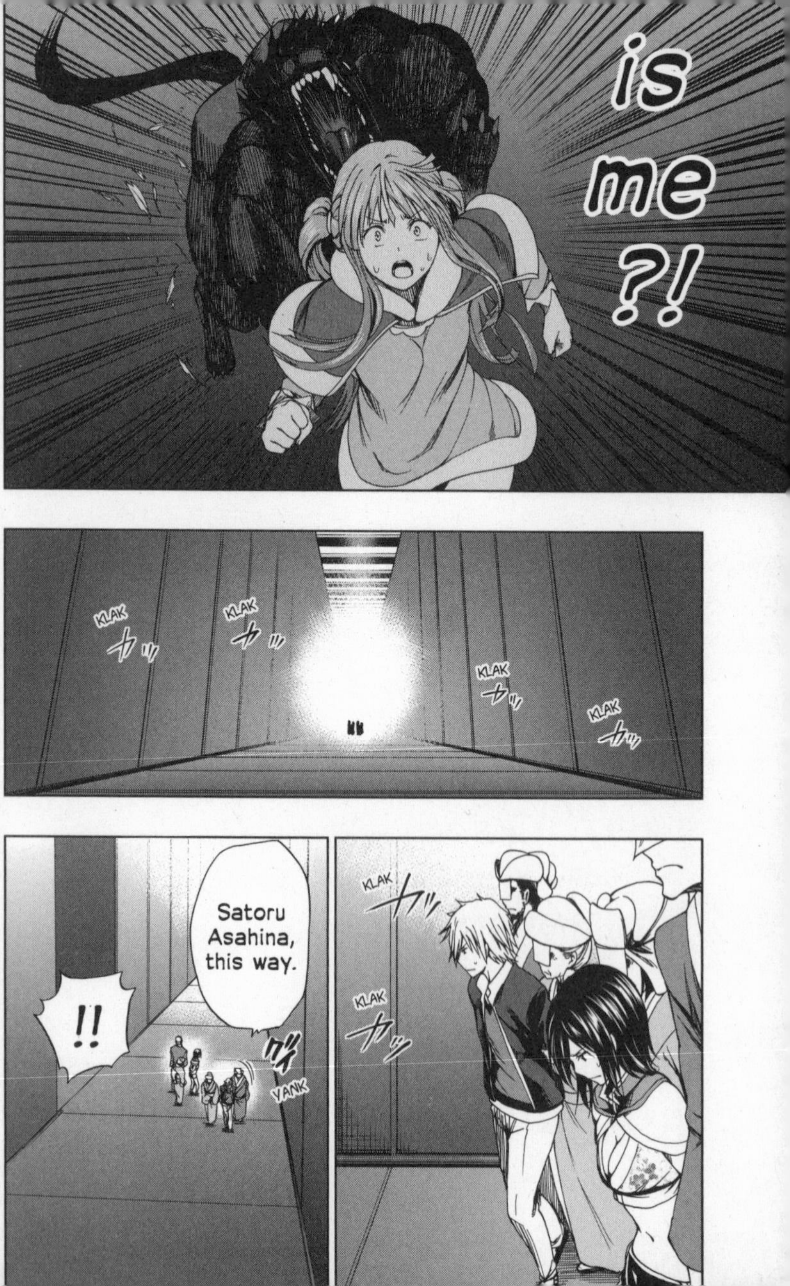

is me ?!
KLAK
KLAK
KLAK
KLAK
KLAK
KLAK
Satoru Asahina, this way.
!!
YANK

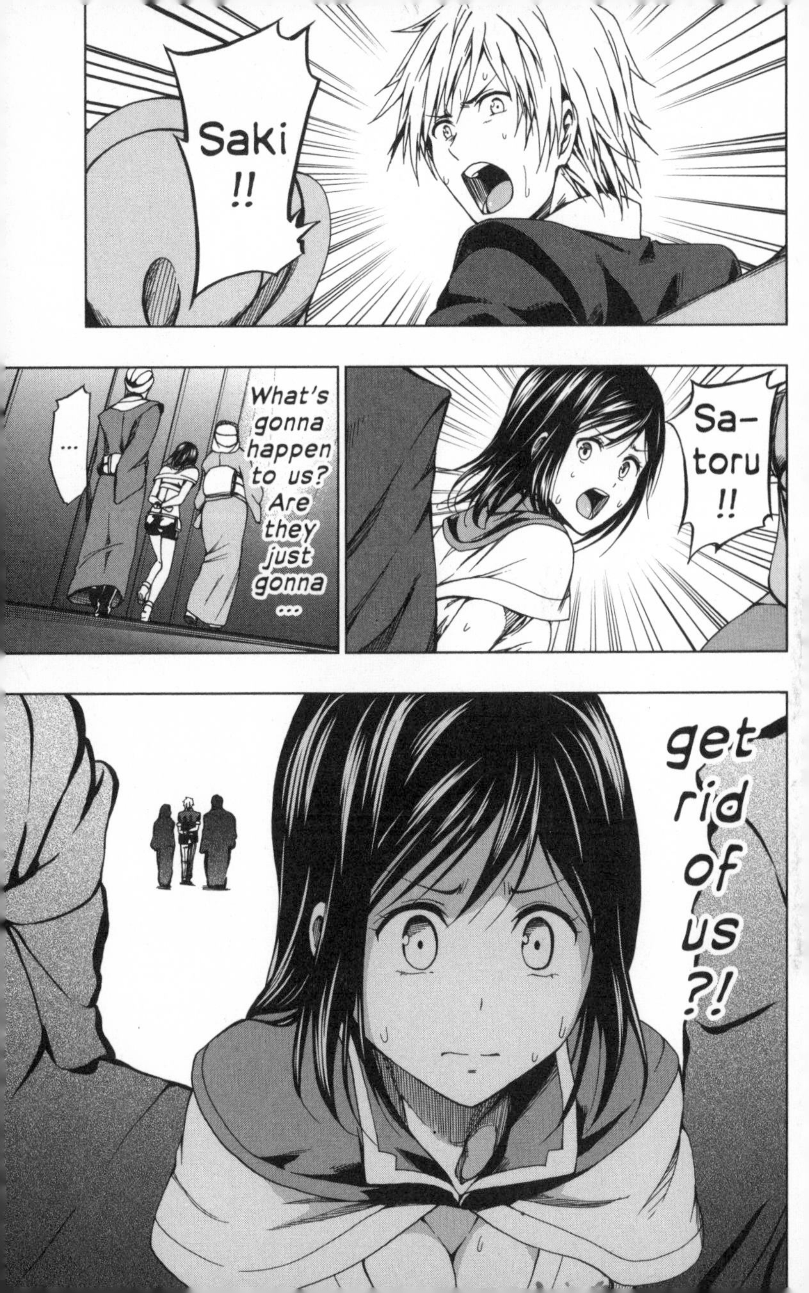
Saki !!
Sa-toru !!
...
What's gonna happen to us? Are they just gonna ...
get rid of us ?!

FROM THE NEW WORLD

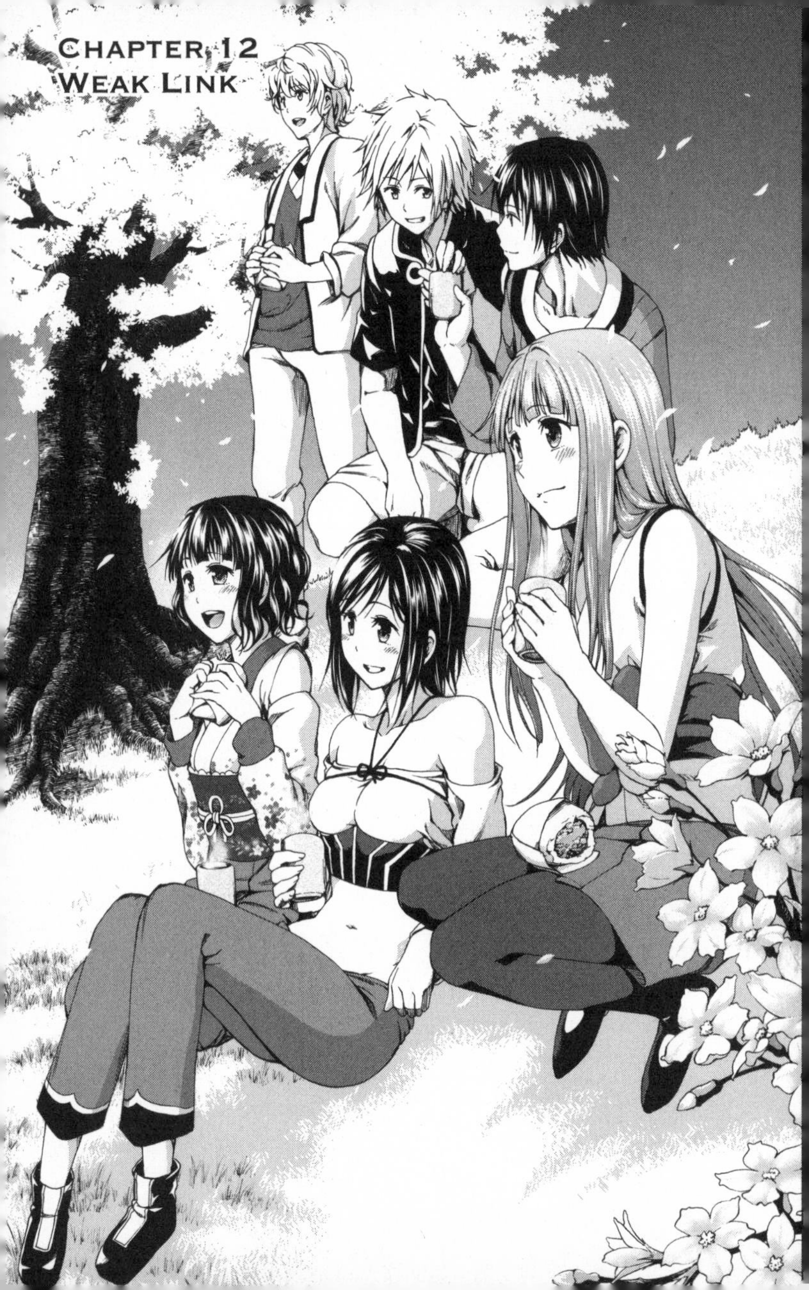
CHAPTER 12
WEAK LINK

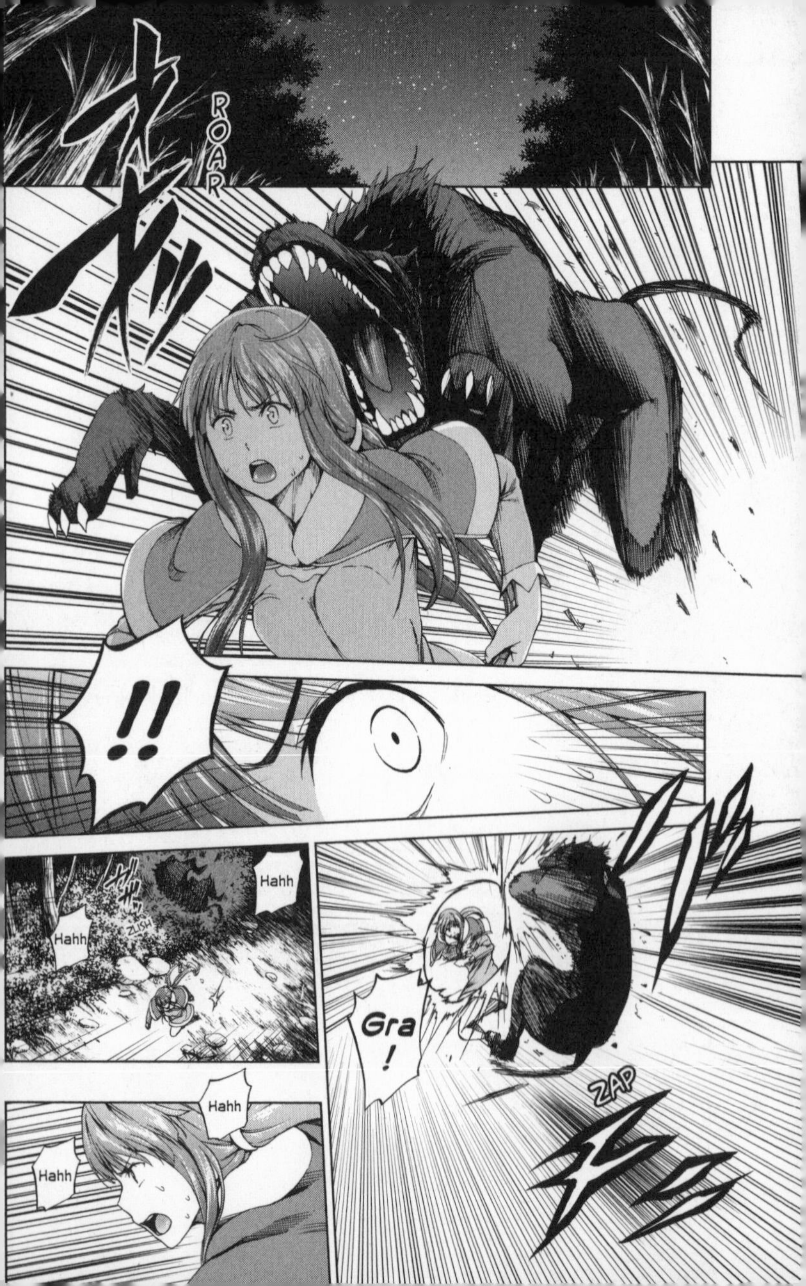
ROAR
!!
Gra!
ZAP
Hahh
Hahh
ZLISH
Hahh
Hahh

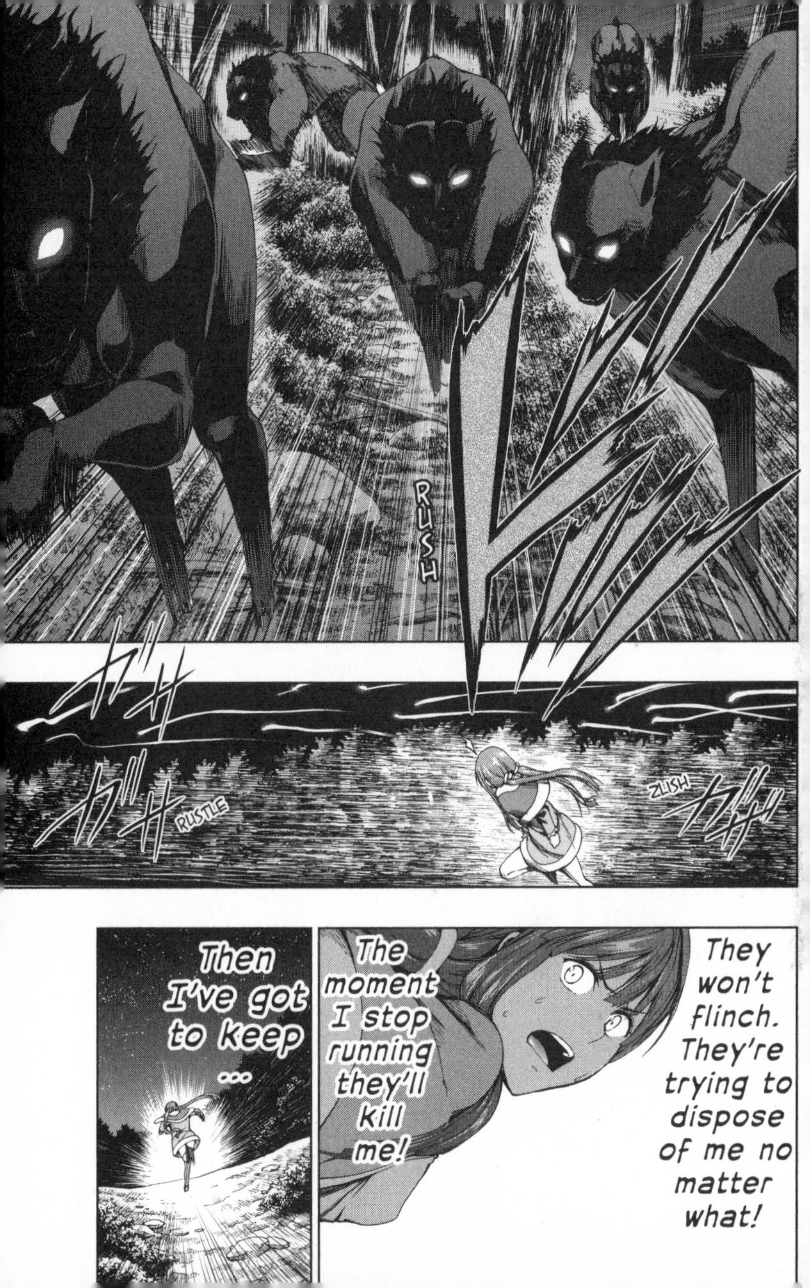
RUSH
ガサ
ZLISH
ガサ
ガサ
RUSTLE
They won't flinch. They're trying to dispose of me no matter what!
The moment I stop running they'll kill me!
Then I've got to keep ...

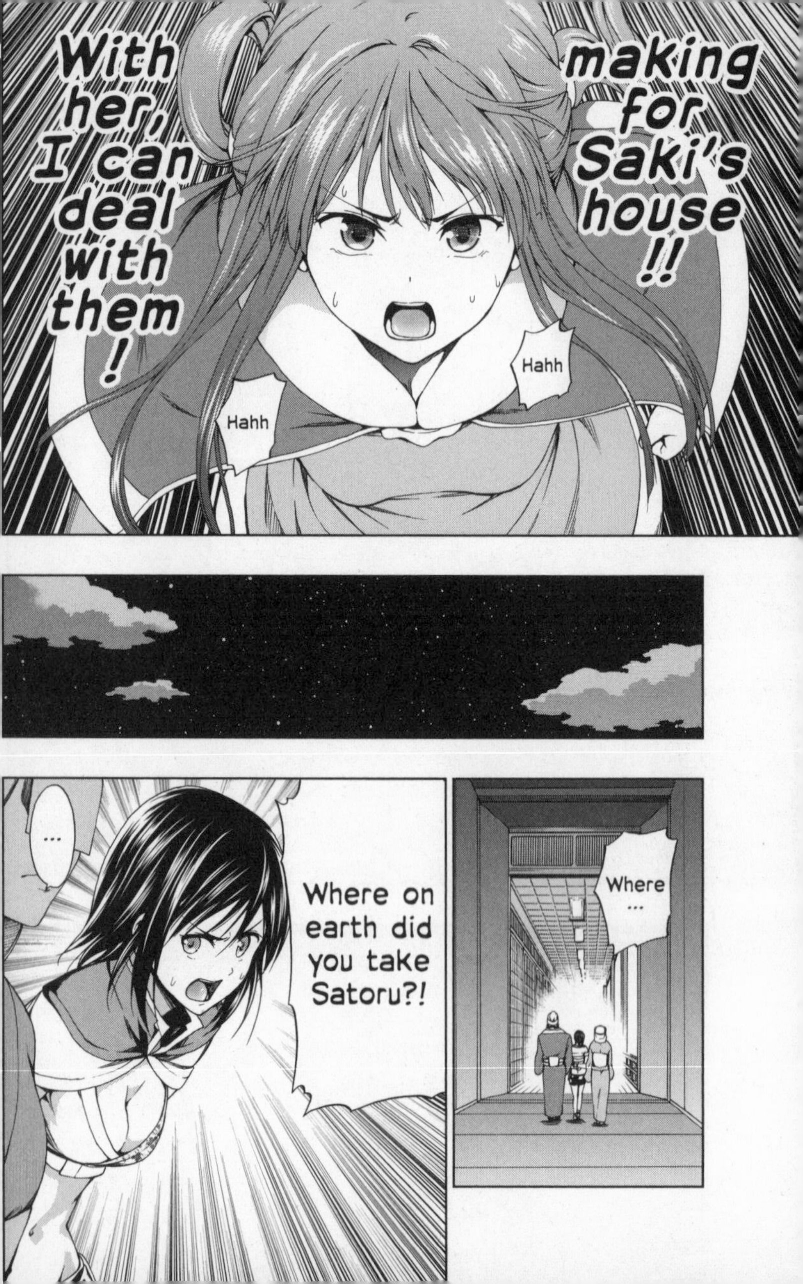
making for Saki's house!!
With her, I can deal with them!
Hahh
Hahh
Where ...
Where on earth did you take Satoru?!
...

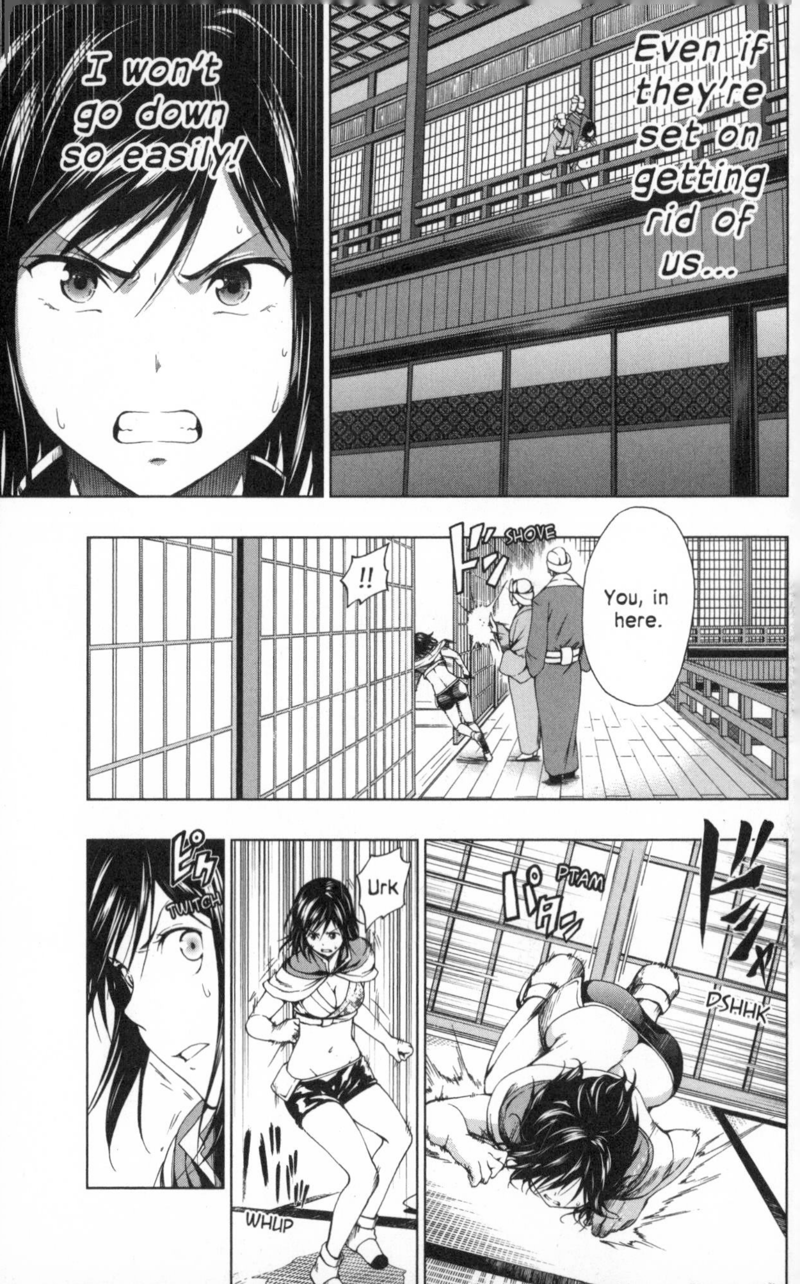
Even if they're set on getting rid of us...
I won't go down so easily!
You, in here.
SHOVE
!!
DSHHK
PTAM
Urk
WHUP
TWITCH

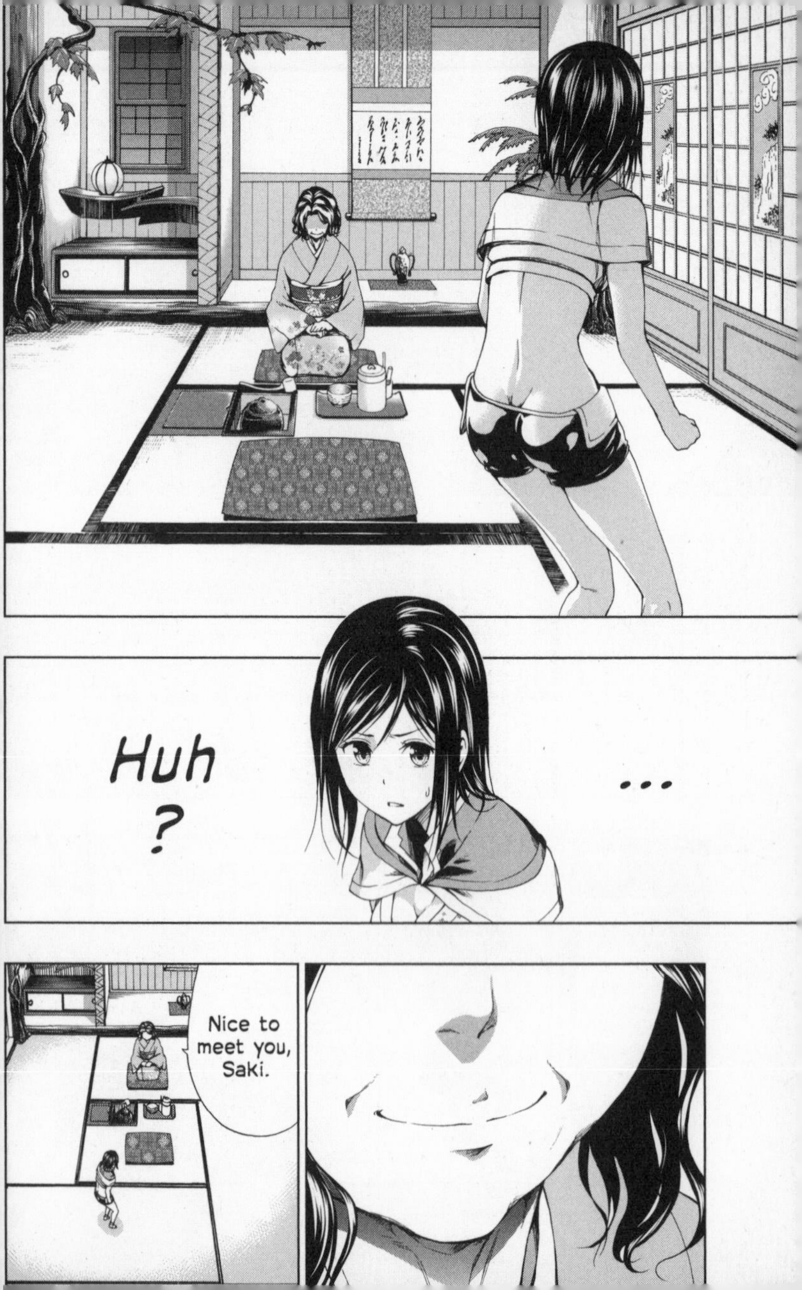
...
Huh
?
Nice to meet you, Saki.

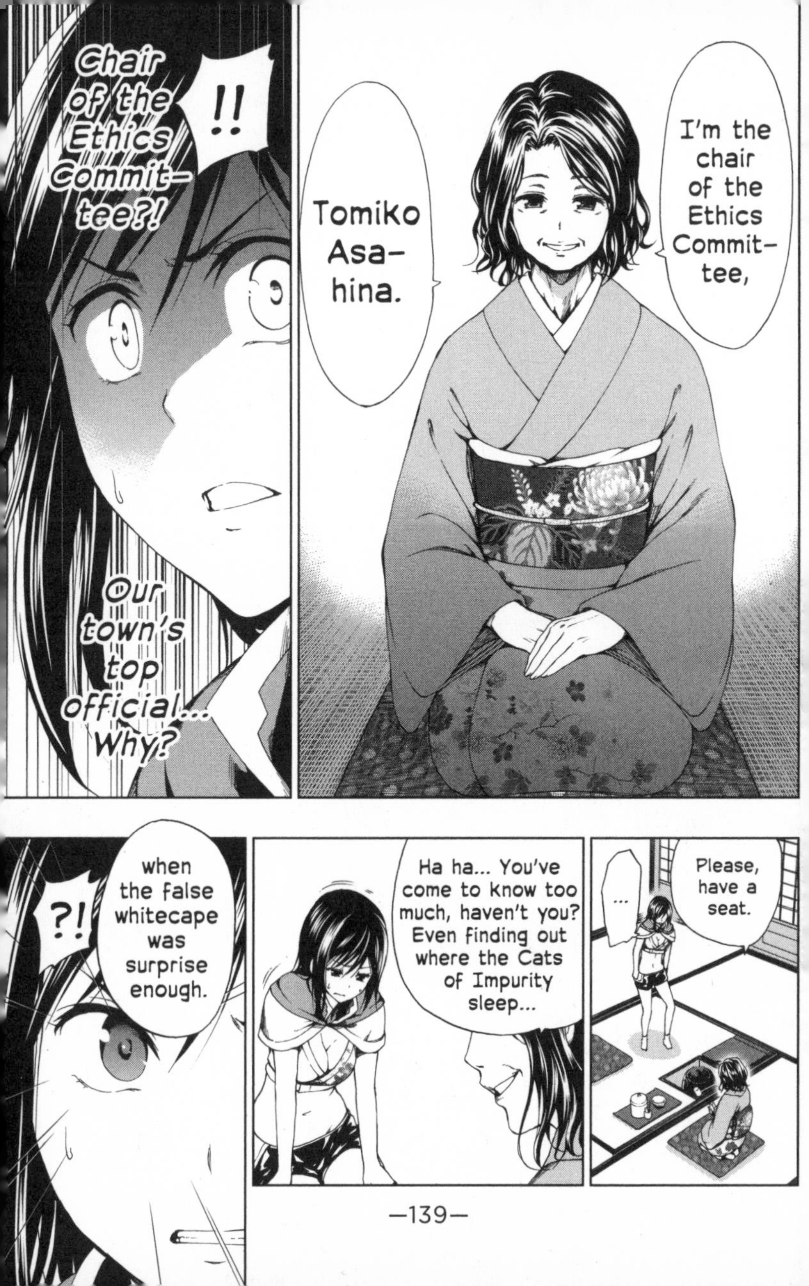
I'm the chair of the Ethics Commit-tee,
Tomiko Asa-hina.
!!
Chair of the Ethics Commit-tee?!
Our town's top official... Why?
Please, have a seat.
...
Ha ha... You've come to know too much, haven't you? Even finding out where the Cats of Impurity sleep...
when the false whitecape was surprise enough.
?!

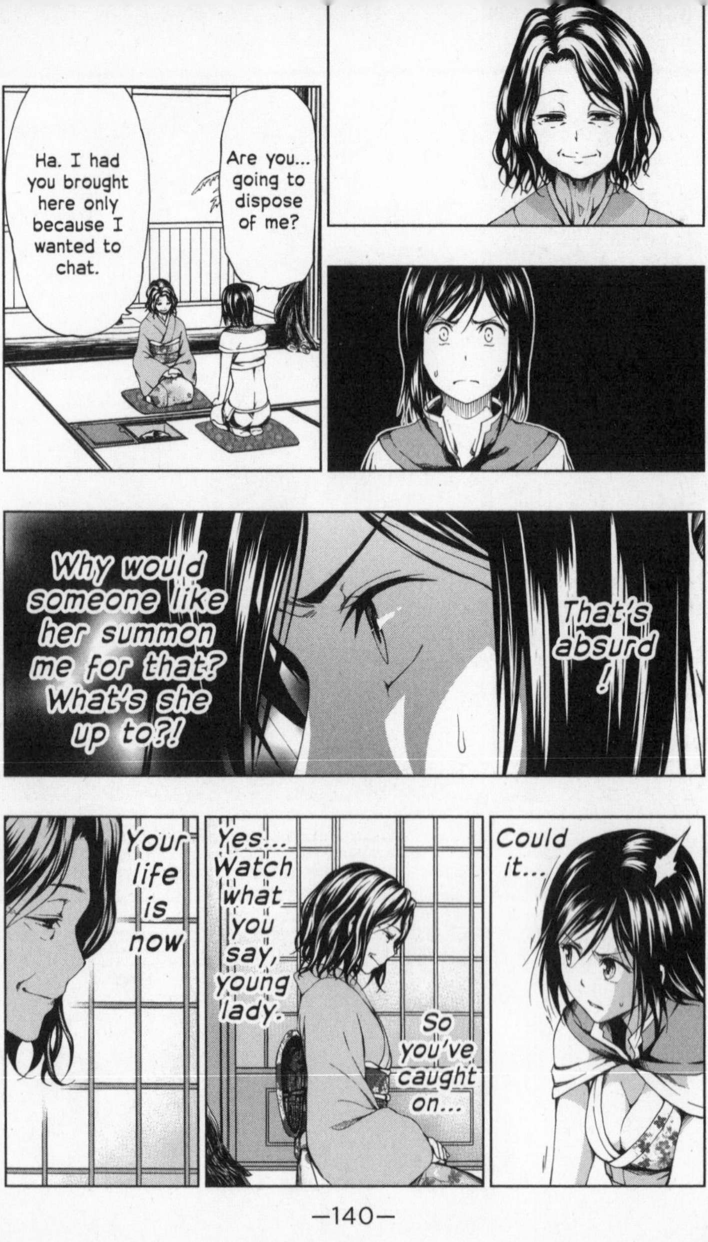

Are you... going to dispose of me?
Ha. I had you brought here only because I wanted to chat.
That's absurd!
Why would someone like her summon me for that? What's she up to?!
Could it...
So you've caught on...
Yes... Watch what you say, young lady.
Your life is now

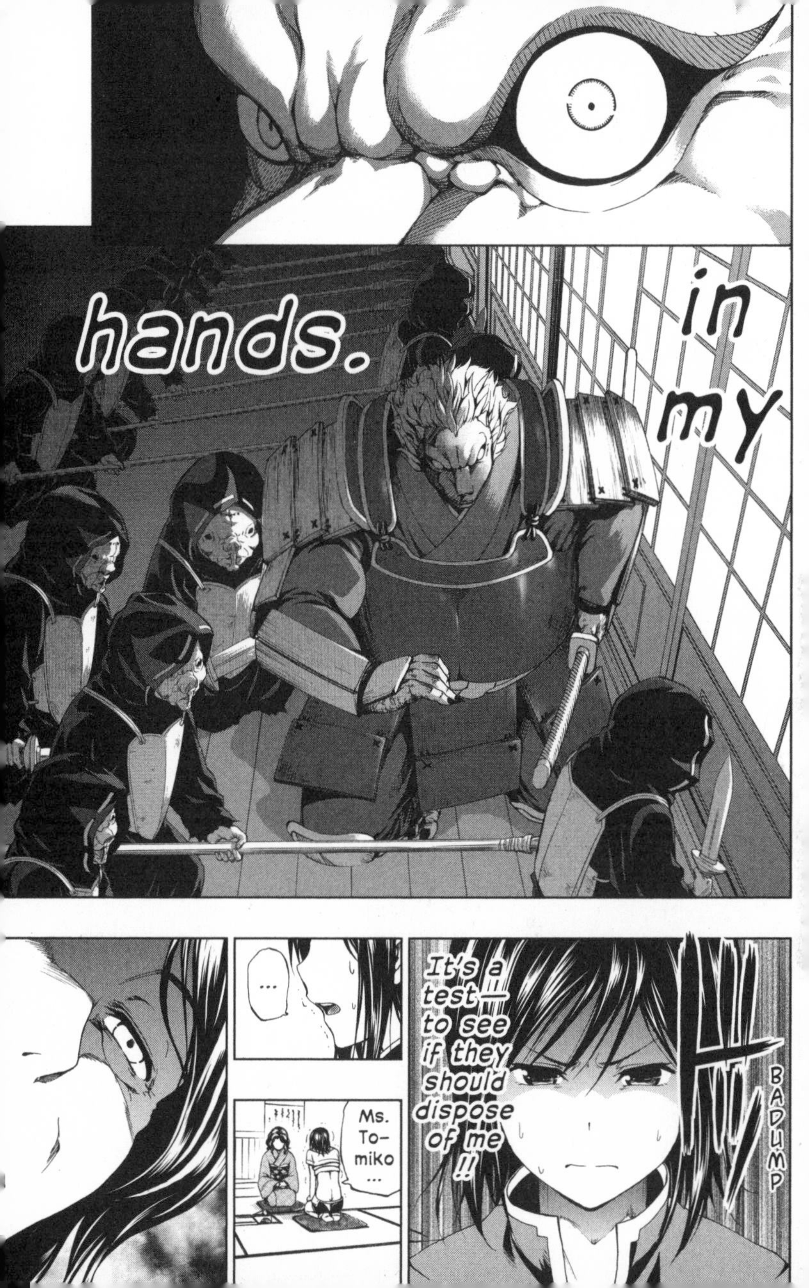
in my
hands.
It's a test—to see if they should dispose of me!!
BADUMP
...
Ms. To-miko ...

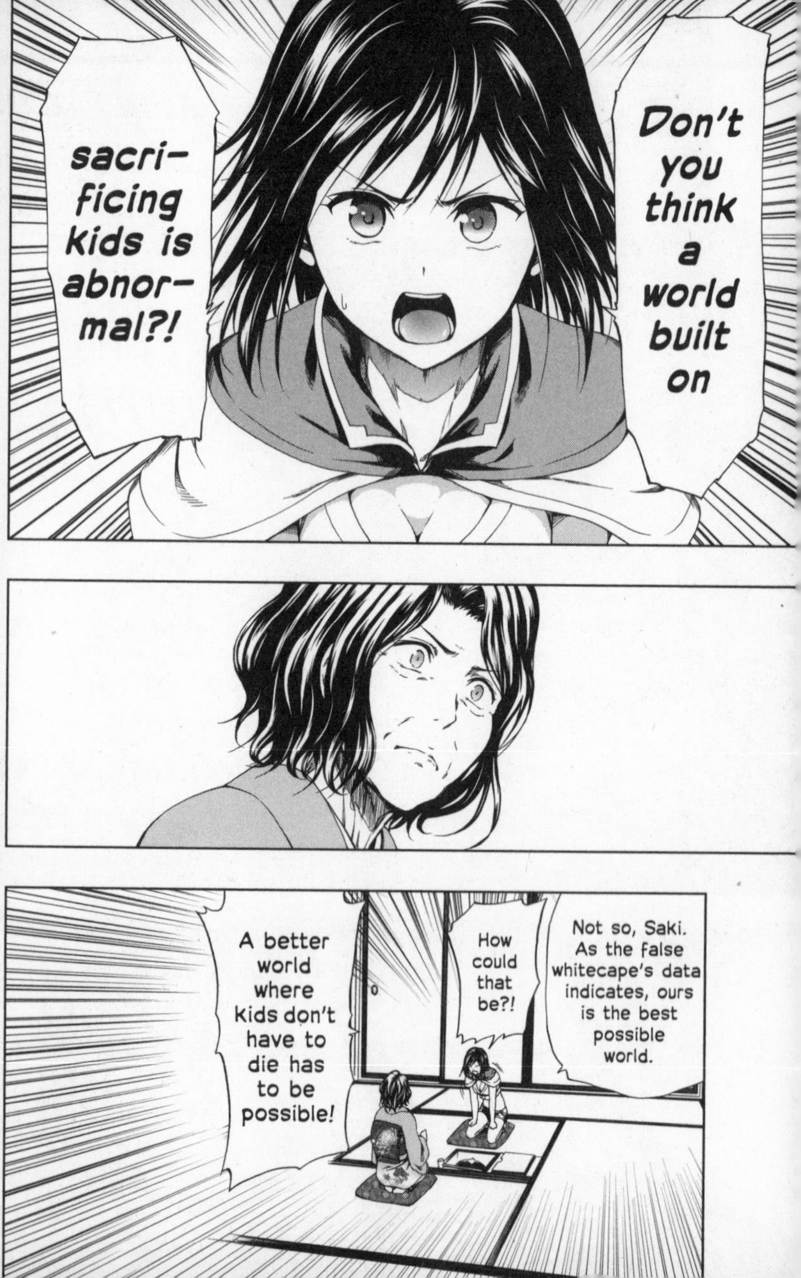
Don't you think a world built on
sacri-ficing kids is abnor-mal?!
Not so, Saki. As the false whitecape's data indicates, ours is the best possible world.
How could that be?!
A better world where kids don't have to die has to be possible!

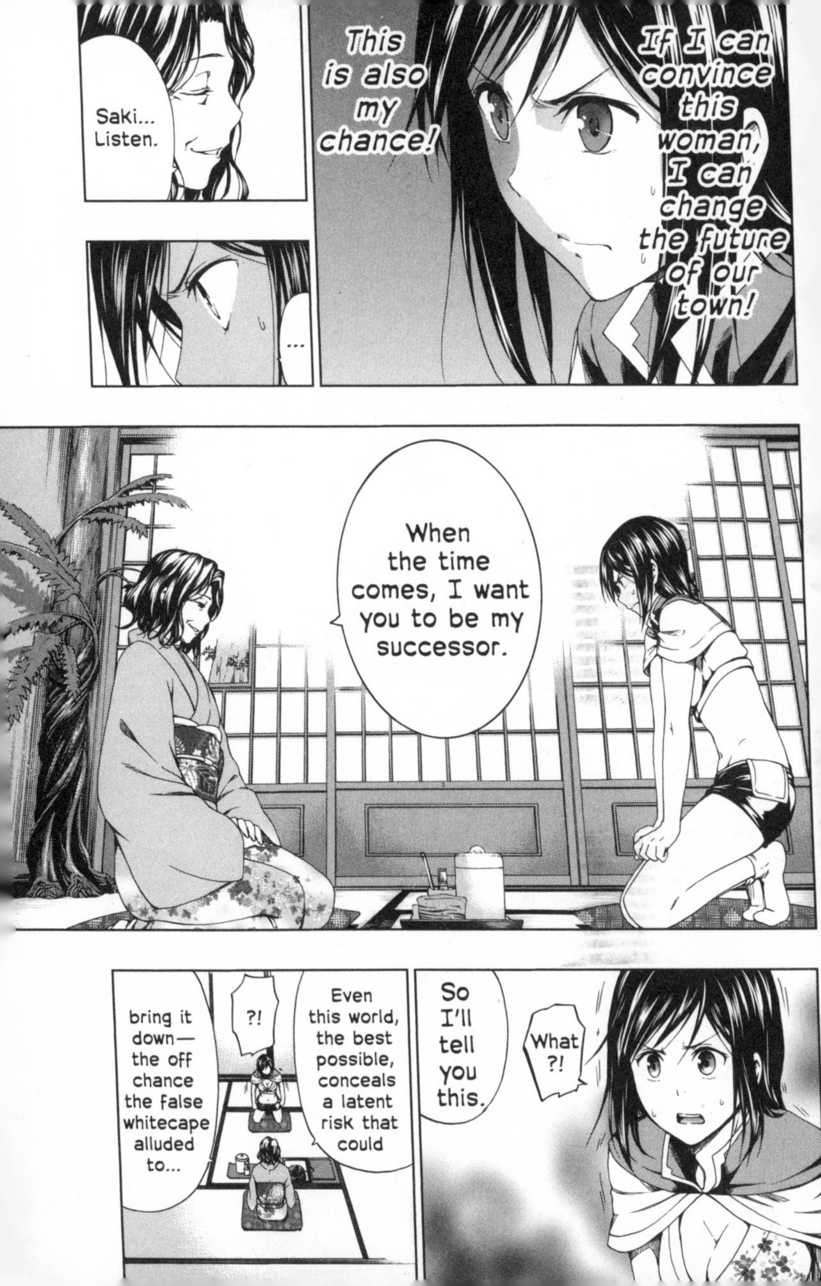
If I can convince this woman, I can change the future of our town!
This is also my chance!
Saki... Listen.
...
When the time comes, I want you to be my successor.
What?!
So I'll tell you this.
Even this world, the best possible, conceals a latent risk that could
?!
bring it down— the off chance the false whitecape alluded to...

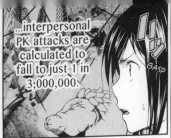

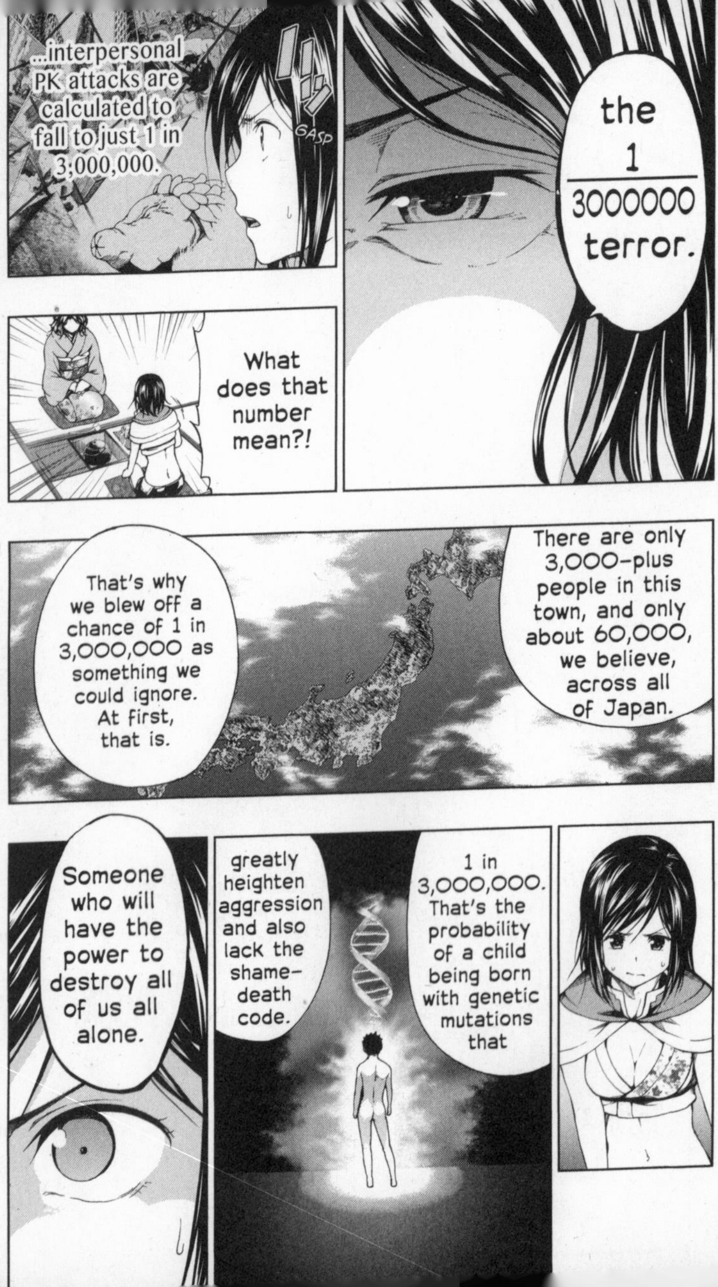

the 1/3000000 terror.
...interpersonal PK attacks are calculated to fall to just 1 in 3,000,000.
GASP
What does that number mean?!
There are only 3,000-plus people in this town, and only about 60,000, we believe, across all of Japan.
That's why we blew off a chance of 1 in 3,000,000 as something we could ignore. At first, that is.
1 in 3,000,000. That's the probability of a child being born with genetic mutations that
greatly heighten aggression and also lack the shame-death code.
Someone who will have the power to destroy all of us all alone.

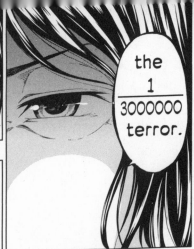

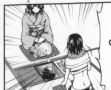

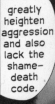

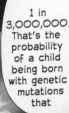

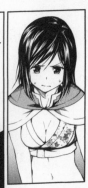

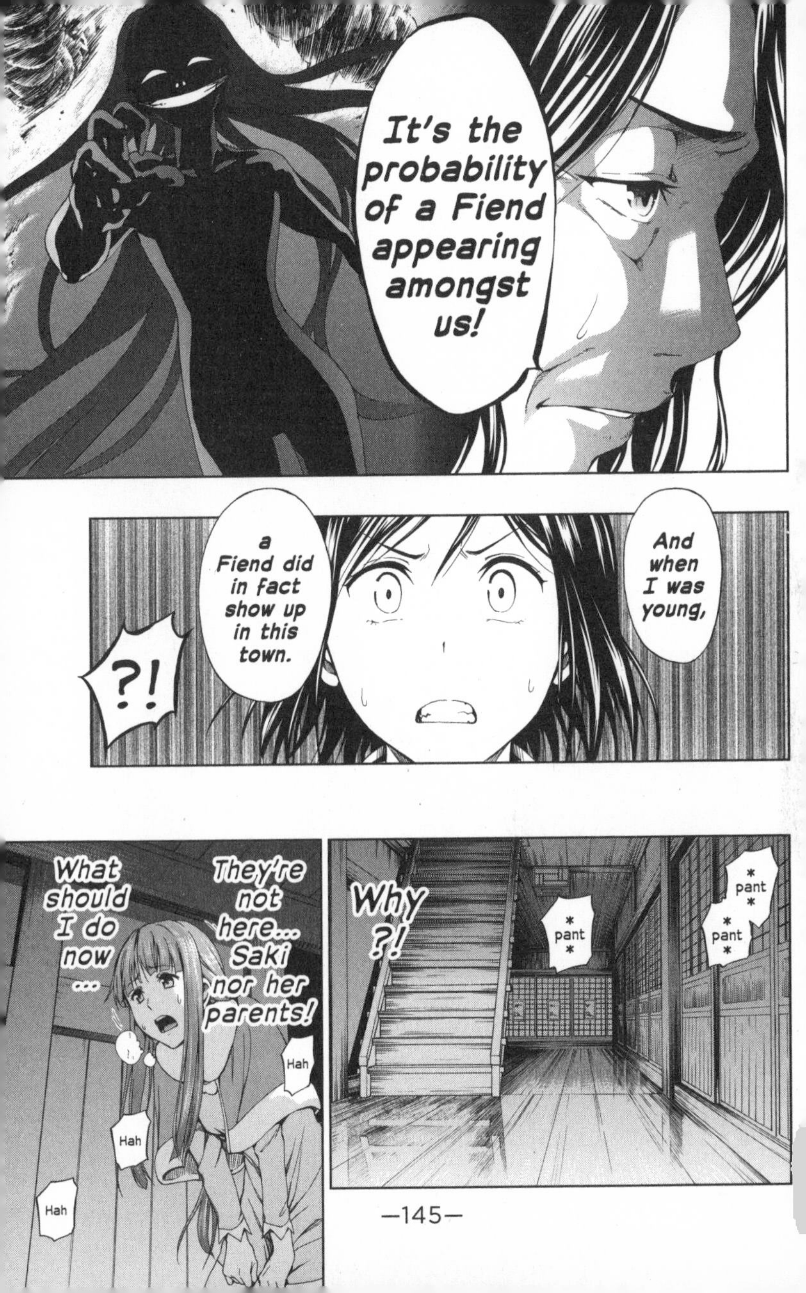
It's the probability of a Fiend appearing amongst us!
And when I was young,
a Fiend did in fact show up in this town.
?!
* pant *
* pant *
* pant *
Why ?!
They're not here... Saki nor her parents!
What should I do now ...
Hah
Hah
Hah

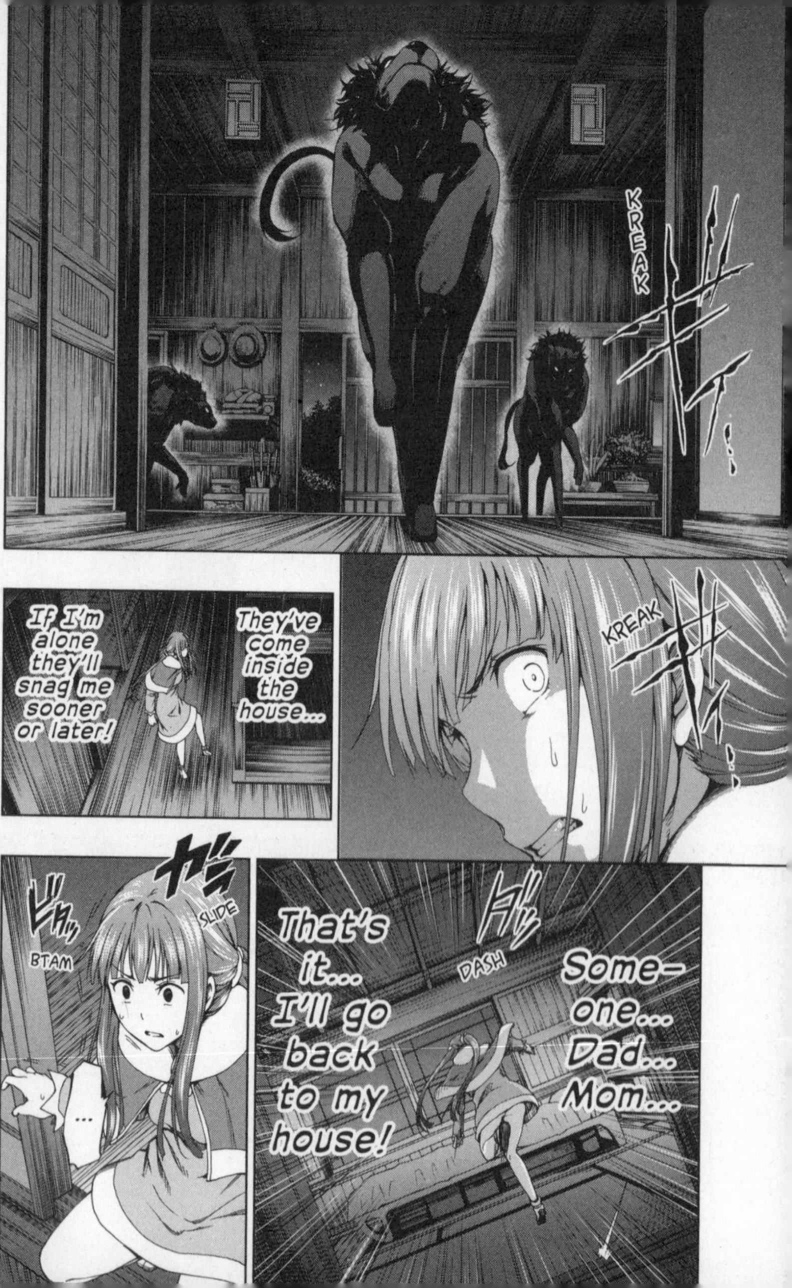
KREAK
KREAK
They've come inside the house...
If I'm alone they'll snag me sooner or later!
DASH
Some-one... Dad... Mom...
That's it... I'll go back to my house!
SLIDE
BTAM
...

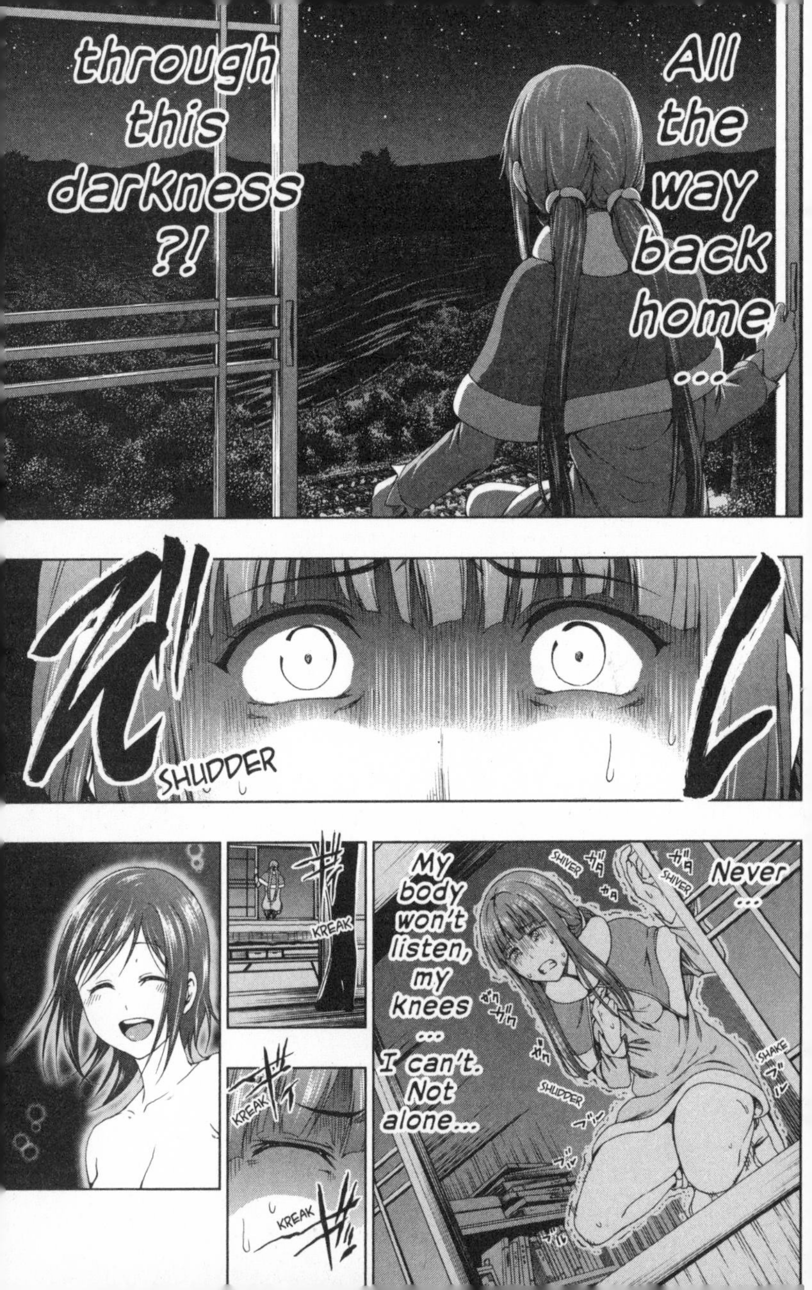
All the way back home...
through this darkness?!
SHUDDER
Never...
SHIVER
SHIVER
My body won't listen, my knees... I can't. Not alone...
SHAKE
SHUDDER
KREAK
KREAK
KREAK

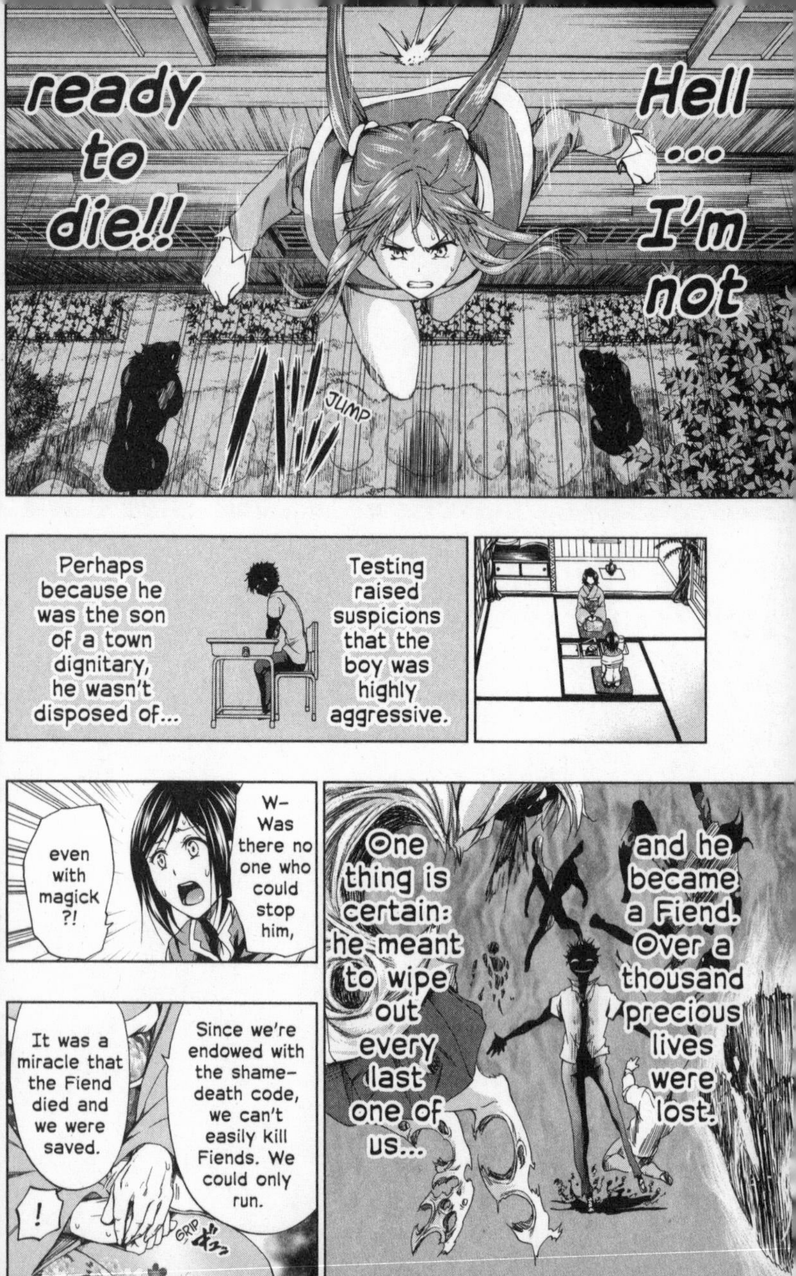

Hell... I'm not
ready to die!!
JUMP
Testing raised suspicions that the boy was highly aggressive.
Perhaps because he was the son of a town dignitary, he wasn't disposed of...
and he became a Fiend. Over a thousand precious lives were lost.
One thing is certain: he meant to wipe out every last one of us...
W- Was there no one who could stop him,
even with magick?!
Since we're endowed with the shame-death code, we can't easily kill Fiends. We could only run.
It was a miracle that the Fiend died and we were saved.
GRIP
!

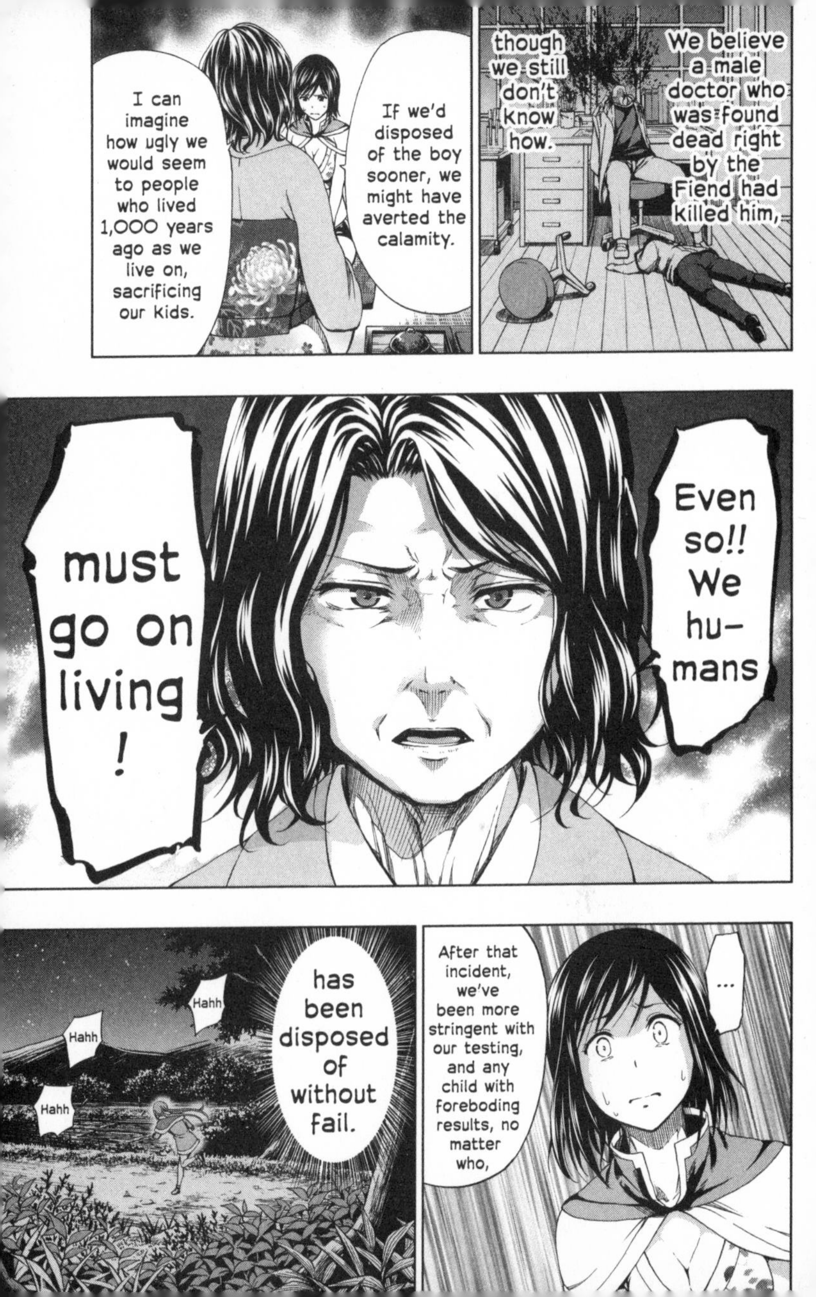
We believe a male doctor who was found dead right by the Fiend had killed him,
though we still don't know how.
If we'd disposed of the boy sooner, we might have averted the calamity.
I can imagine how ugly we would seem to people who lived 1,000 years ago as we live on, sacrificing our kids.
Even so!! We hu-mans
must go on living!
...
After that incident, we've been more stringent with our testing, and any child with foreboding results, no matter who,
has been disposed of without fail.
Hahh
Hahh
Hahh

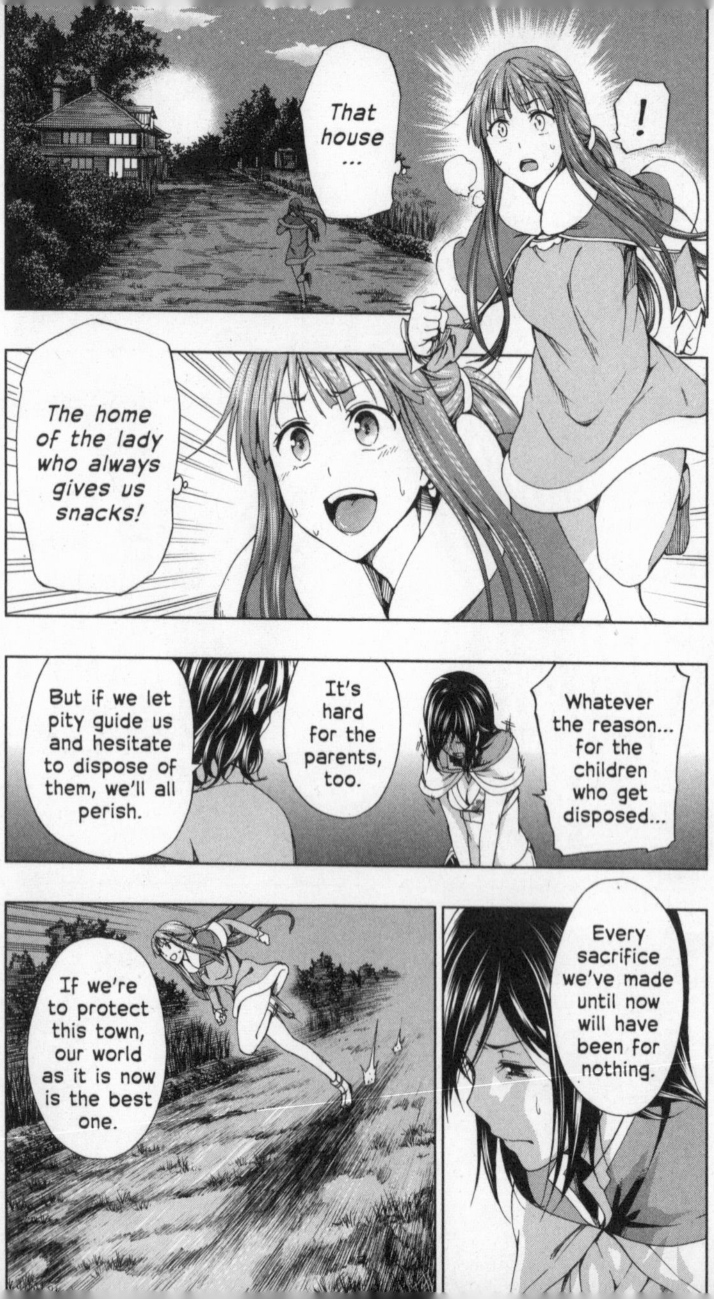
!
That house ...
The home of the lady who always gives us snacks!
Whatever the reason... for the children who get disposed...
It's hard for the parents, too.
But if we let pity guide us and hesitate to dispose of them, we'll all perish.
Every sacrifice we've made until now will have been for nothing.
If we're to protect this town, our world as it is now is the best one.

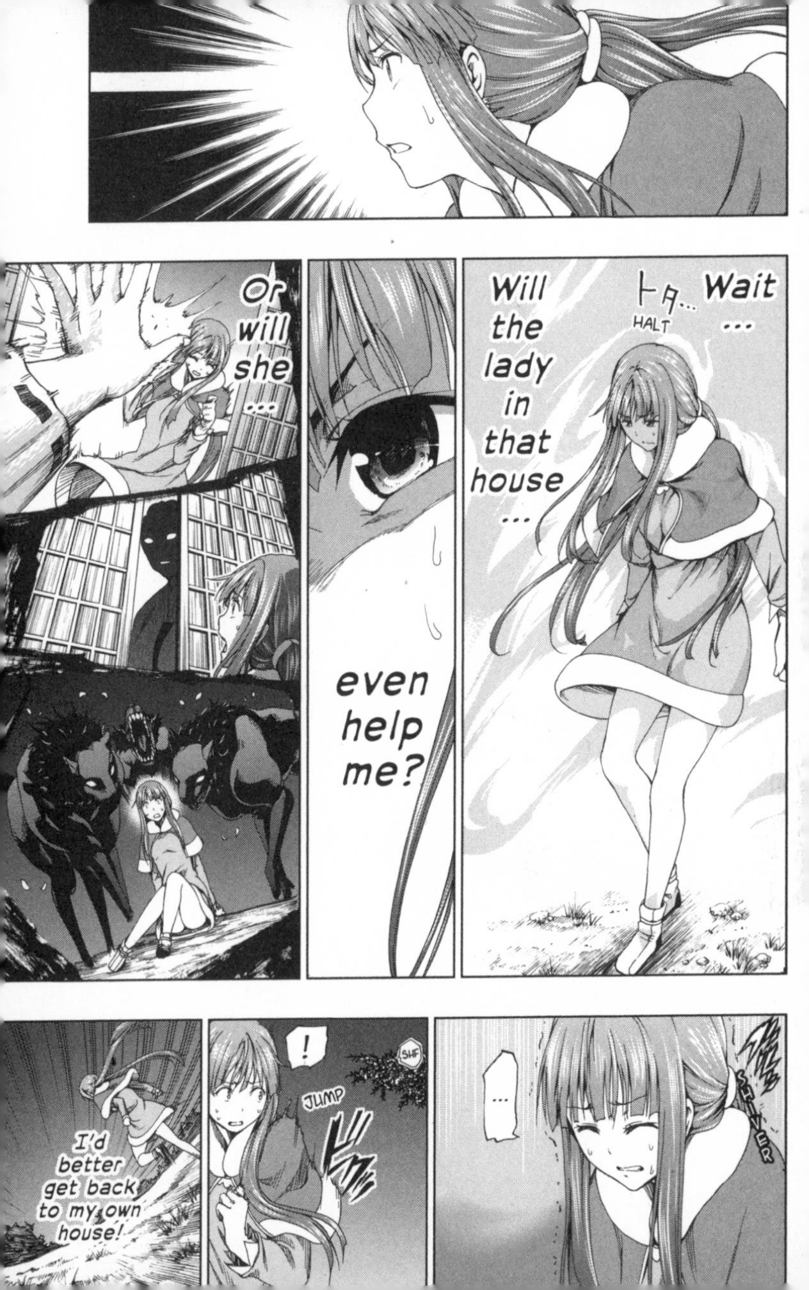
Wait ...
トタ...
HALT
Will the lady in that house ...
even help me?
Or will she ...
...
SHIVER
!
SHF
JUMP
I'd better get back to my own house!

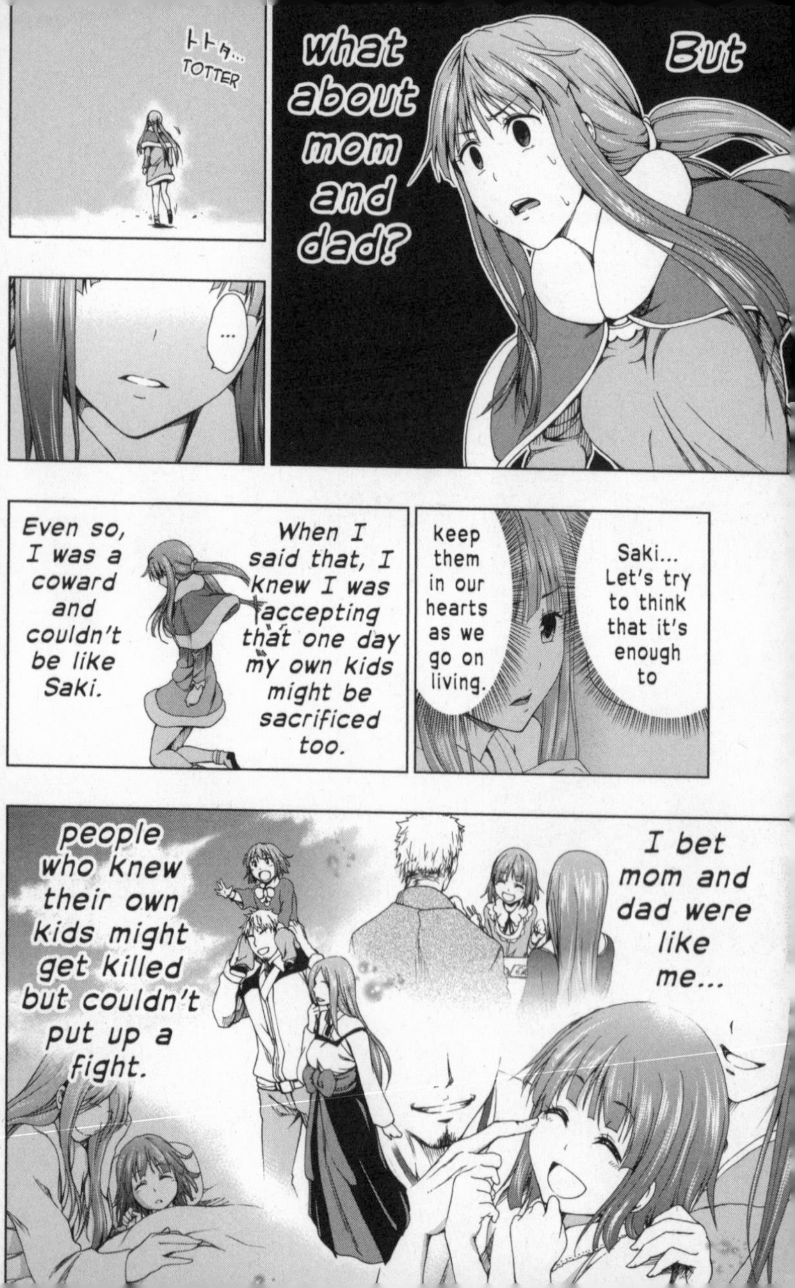
But
what about mom and dad?
トトタ...
TOTTER
...
Saki... Let's try to think that it's enough to
keep them in our hearts as we go on living.
When I said that, I knew I was accepting that one day my own kids might be sacrificed too.
Even so, I was a coward and couldn't be like Saki.
I bet mom and dad were like me...
people who knew their own kids might get killed but couldn't put up a fight.

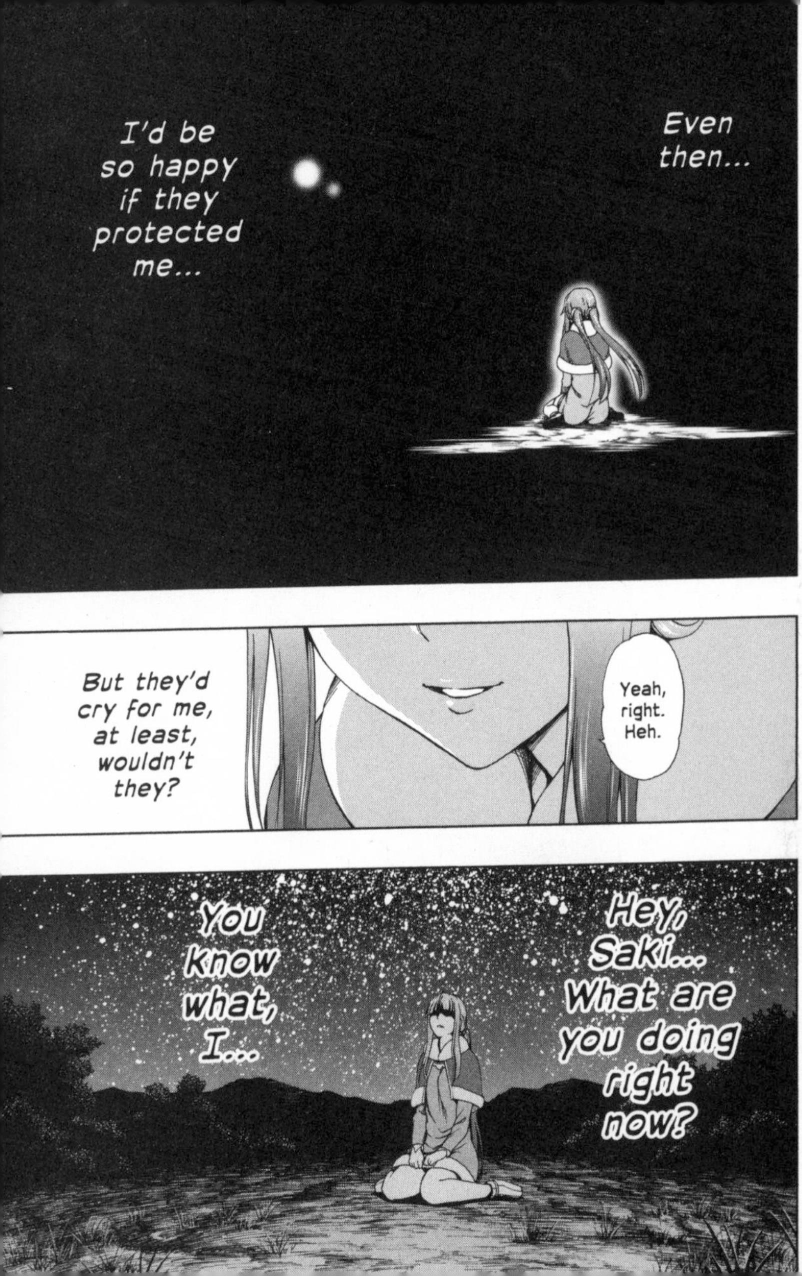
Even then...
I'd be so happy if they protected me...
Yeah, right. Heh.
But they'd cry for me, at least, wouldn't they?
Hey, Saki... What are you doing right now?
You know what, I...

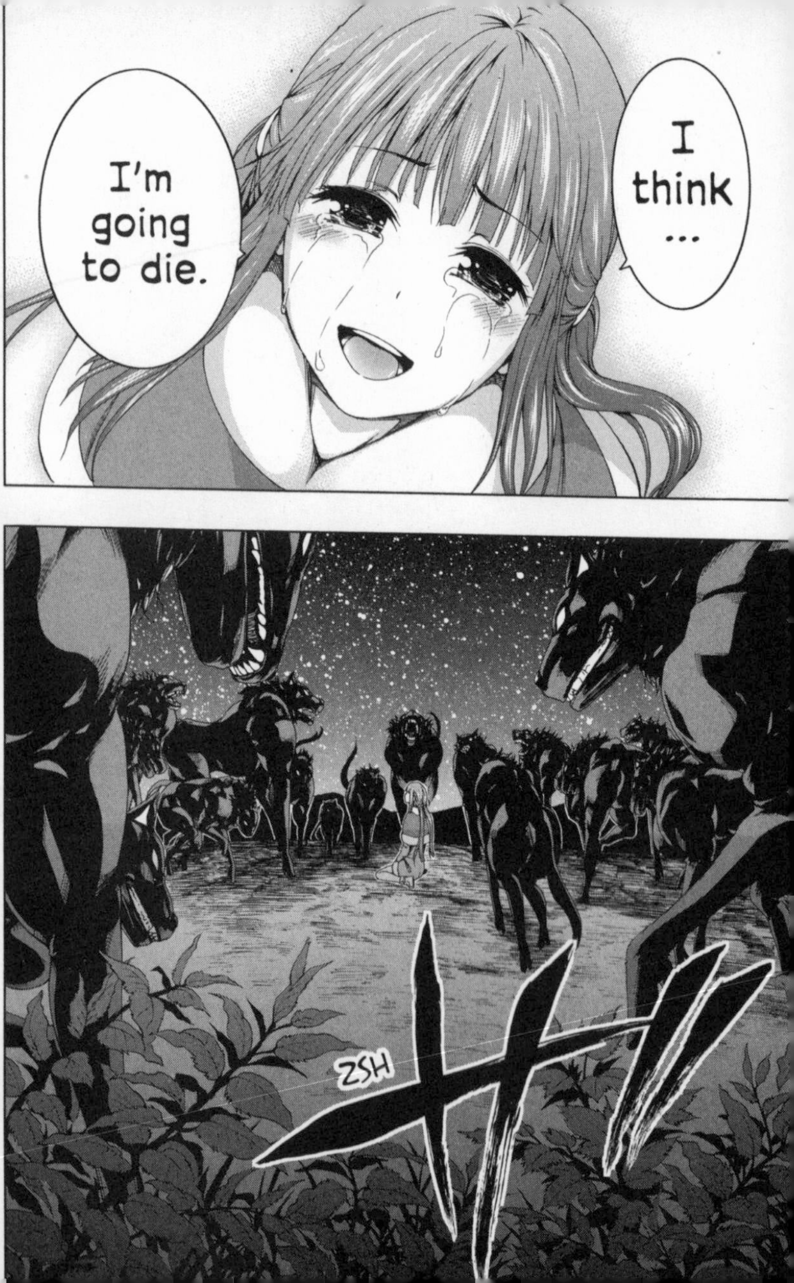
I think ...
I'm going to die.
ZSH

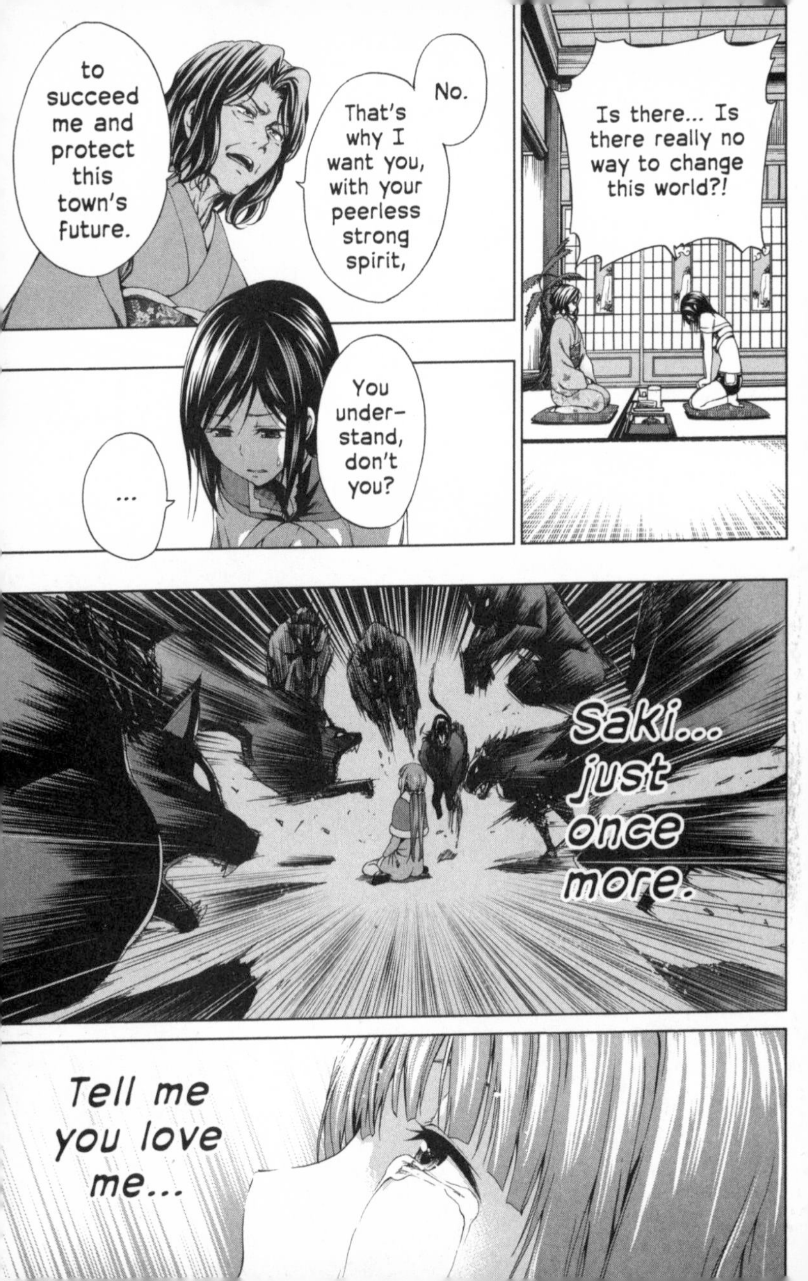
Is there... Is there really no way to change this world?!
No.
That's why I want you, with your peerless strong spirit,
to succeed me and protect this town's future.
You under-stand, don't you?
...
Saki... just once more.
Tell me you love me...

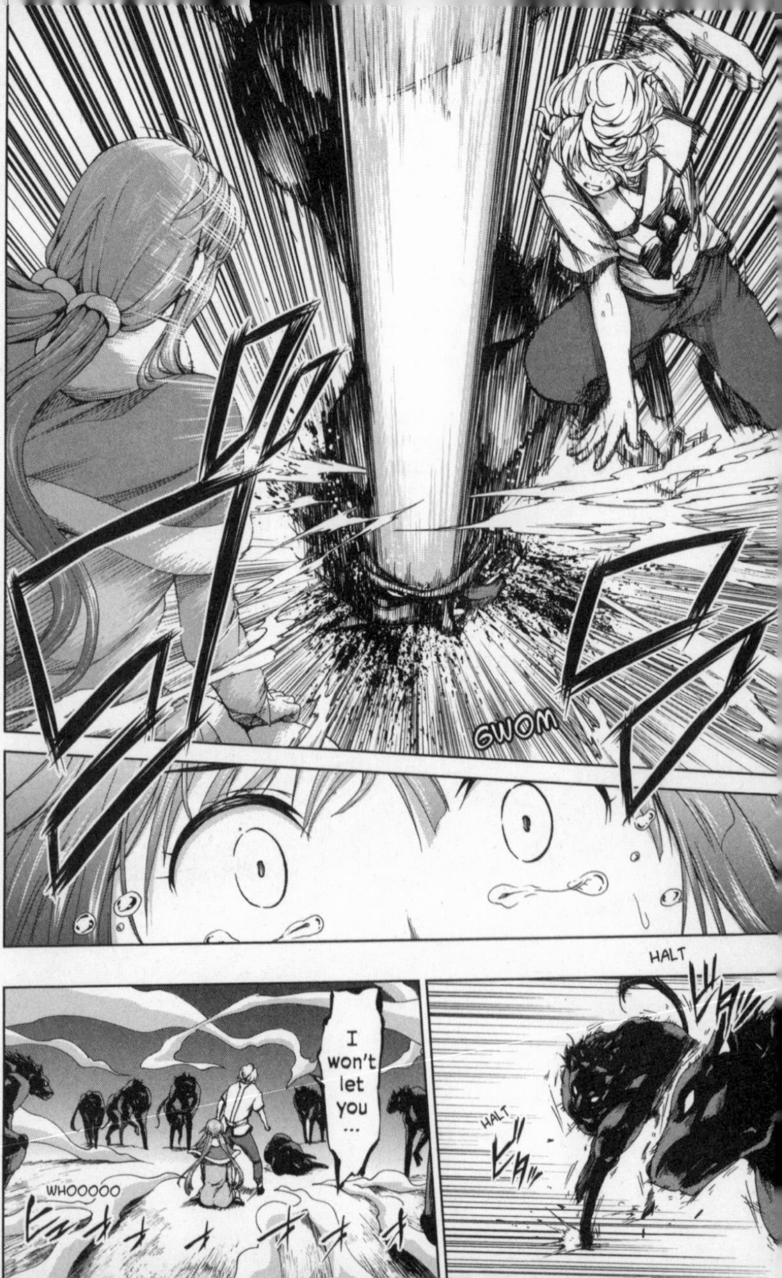
GWOM
HALT
HALT
I won't let you ...
WHOOOOO

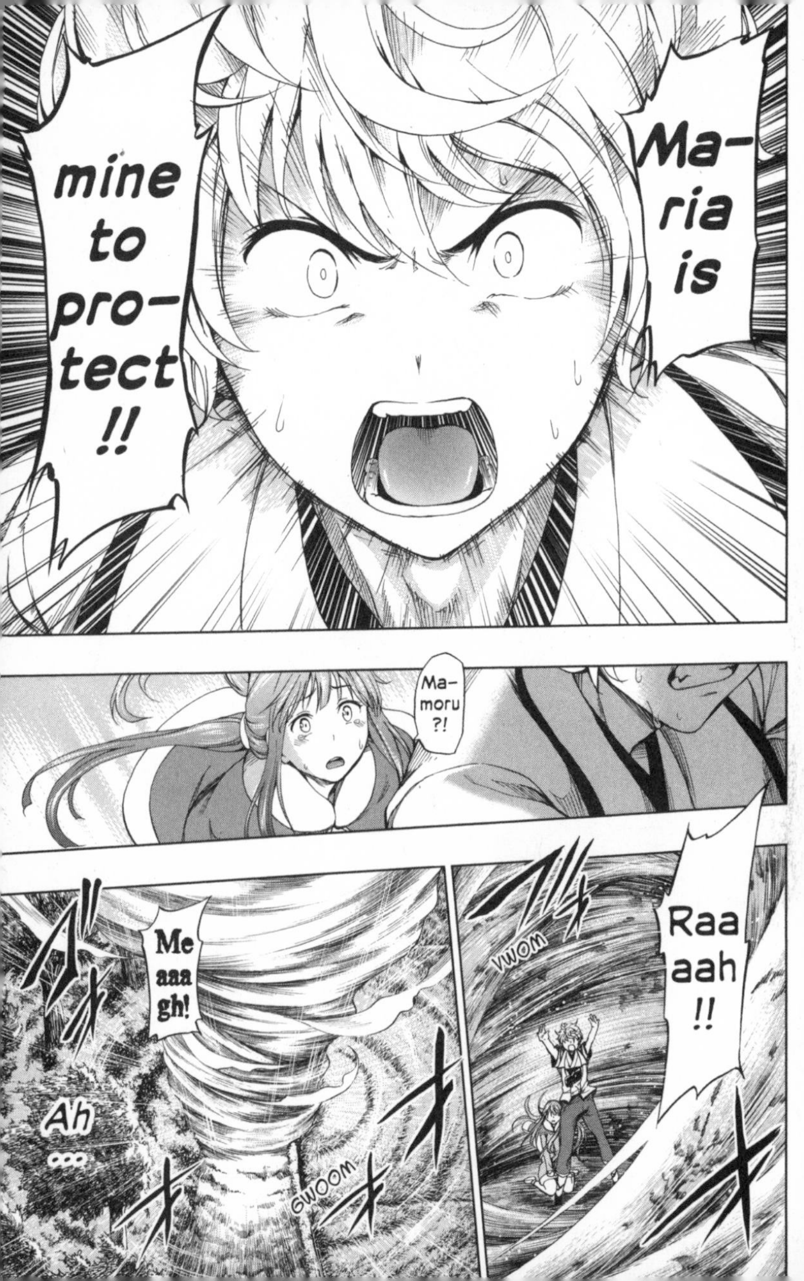
Ma-ria is
mine to pro-tect!!
Ma-moru?!
Raa aah!!
VWOM
Me aaa gh!
Ah...
GWOOM

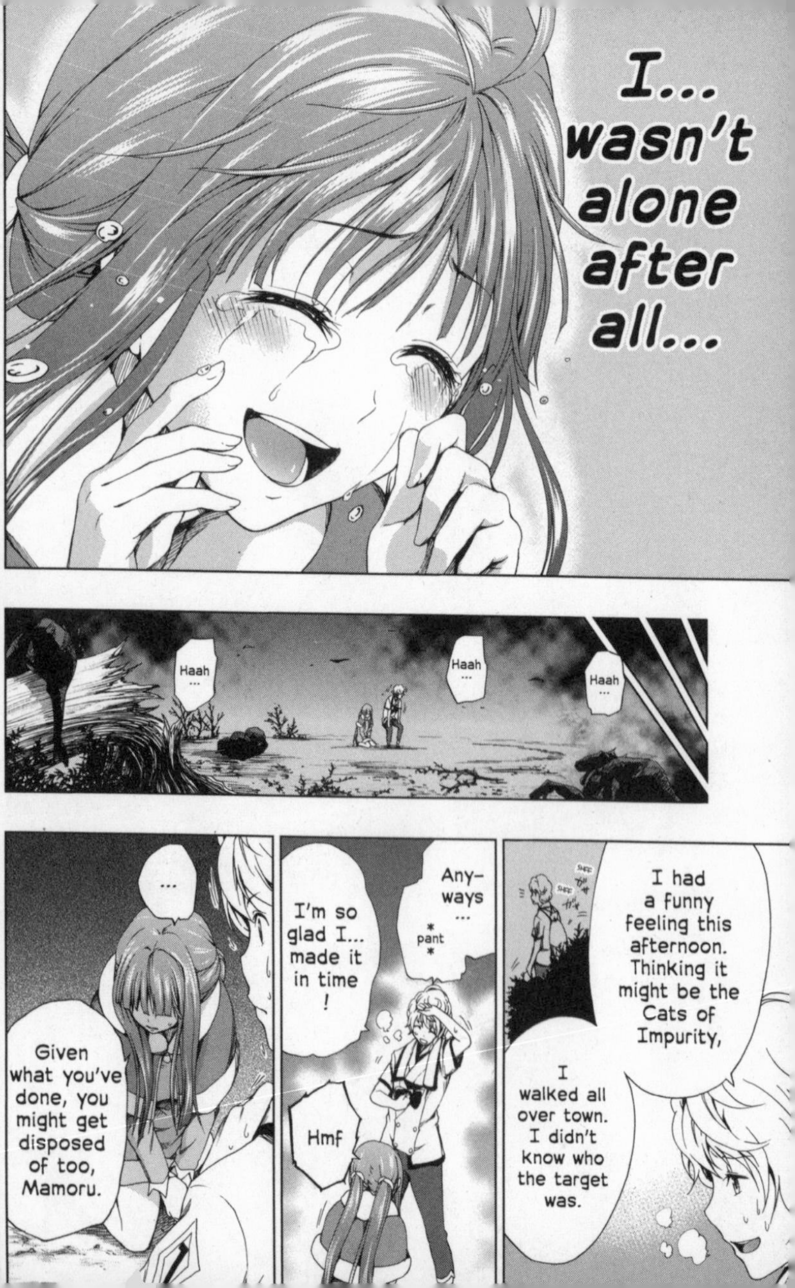
I... wasn't alone after all...
Haah...
Haah...
Haah...
I had a funny feeling this afternoon. Thinking it might be the Cats of Impurity,
I walked all over town. I didn't know who the target was.
Any-ways...
pant
I'm so glad I... made it in time!
Hmf
...
Given what you've done, you might get disposed of too, Mamoru.

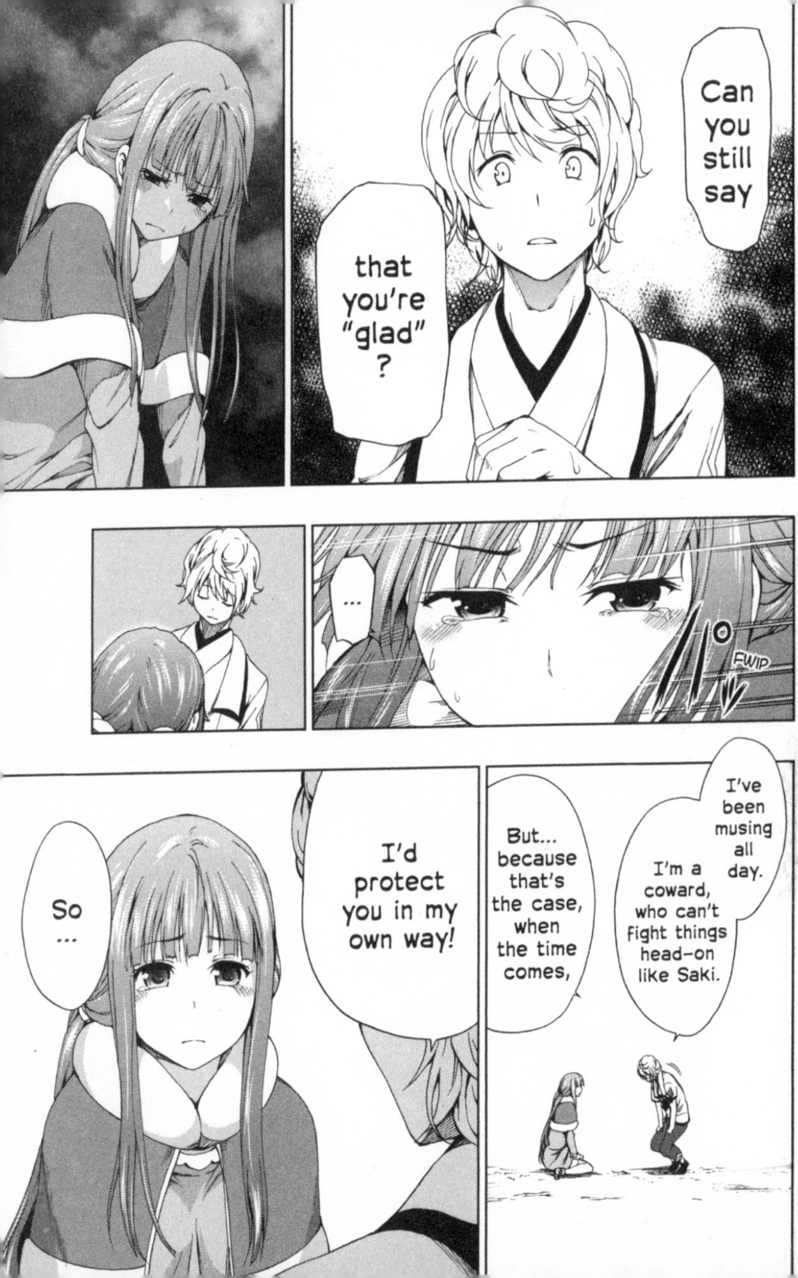
Can you still say
that you're "glad" ?
...
FWIP
I've been musing all day.
I'm a coward, who can't fight things head-on like Saki.
But... because that's the case, when the time comes,
I'd protect you in my own way!
So ...

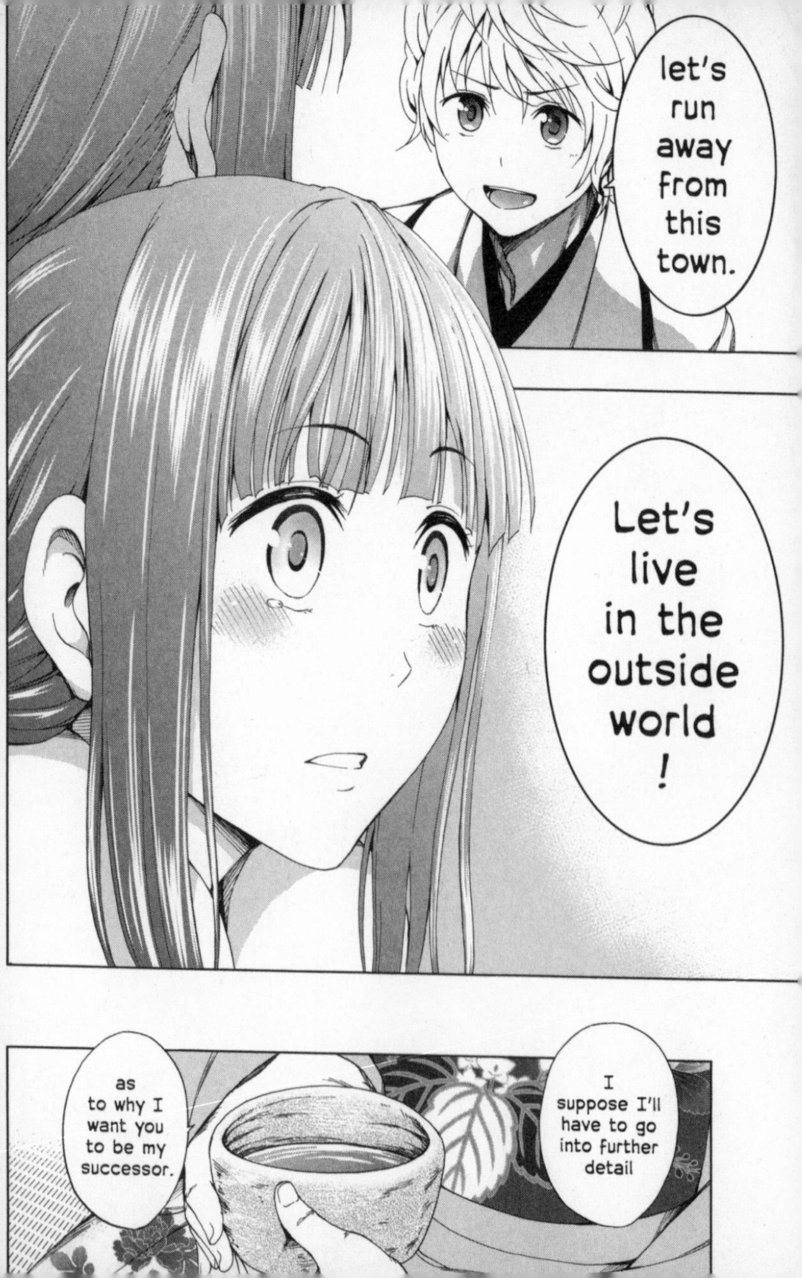
let's run away from this town.
Let's live in the outside world!
I suppose I'll have to go into further detail
as to why I want you to be my successor.

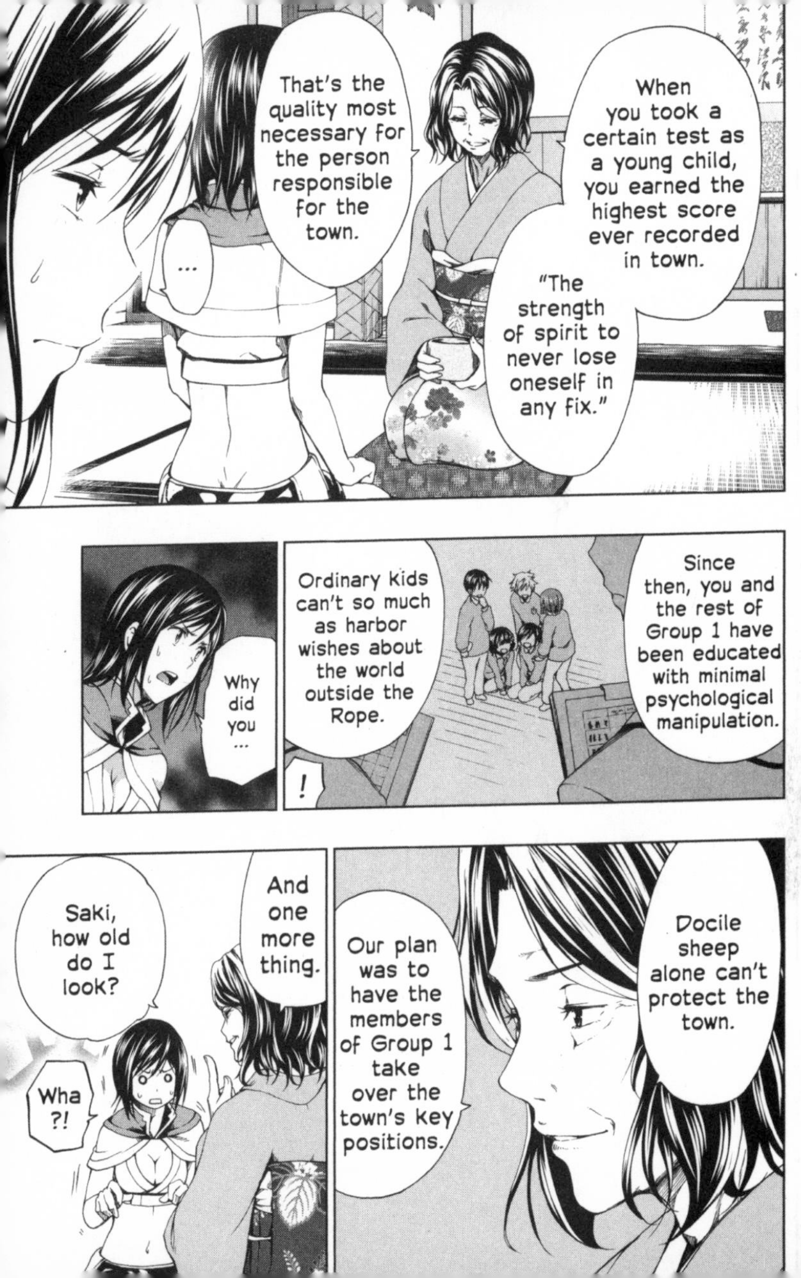

When you took a certain test as a young child, you earned the highest score ever recorded in town.
"The strength of spirit to never lose oneself in any fix."
That's the quality most necessary for the person responsible for the town.
...
Since then, you and the rest of Group 1 have been educated with minimal psychological manipulation.
Ordinary kids can't so much as harbor wishes about the world outside the Rope.
!
Why did you ...
Docile sheep alone can't protect the town.
Our plan was to have the members of Group 1 take over the town's key positions.
And one more thing.
Saki, how old do I look?
Wha?!

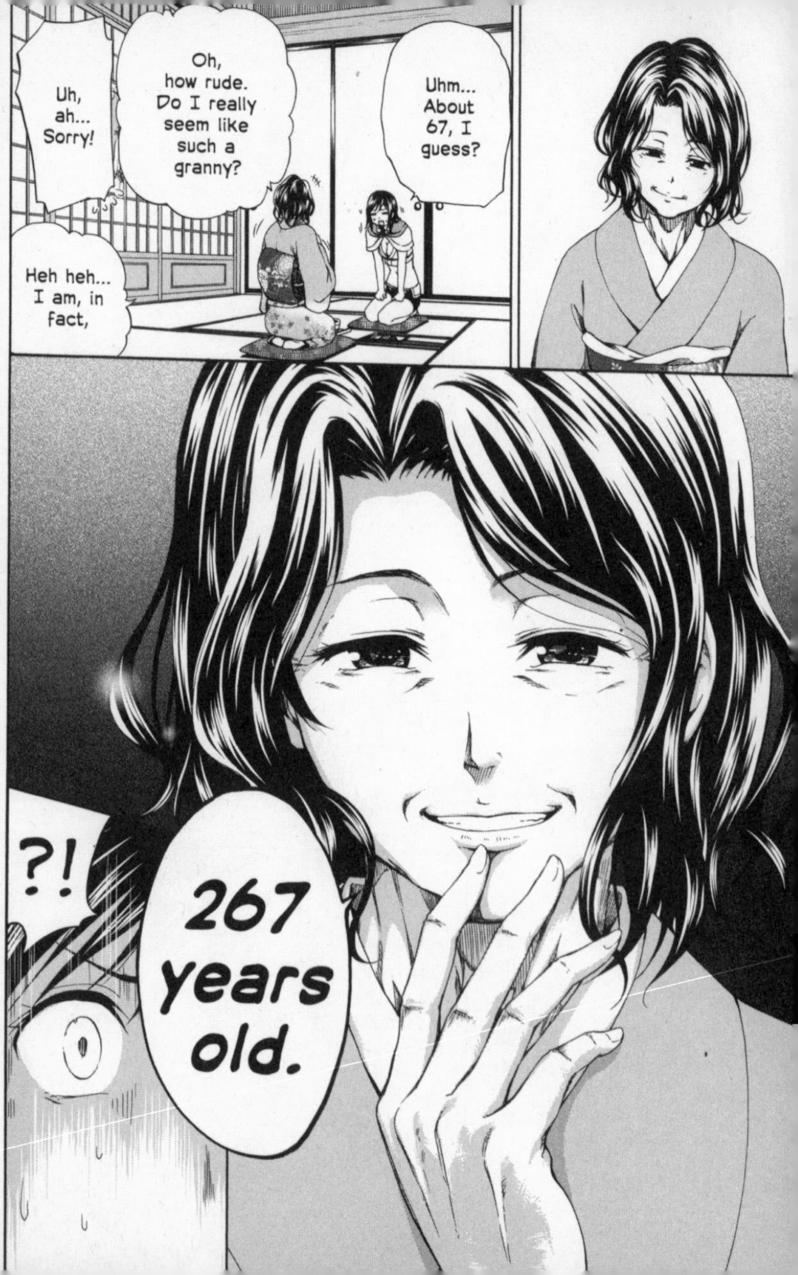
Uhm... About 67, I guess?
Oh, how rude. Do I really seem like such a granny?
Uh, ah... Sorry!
Heh heh... I am, in fact,
267 years old.
?!

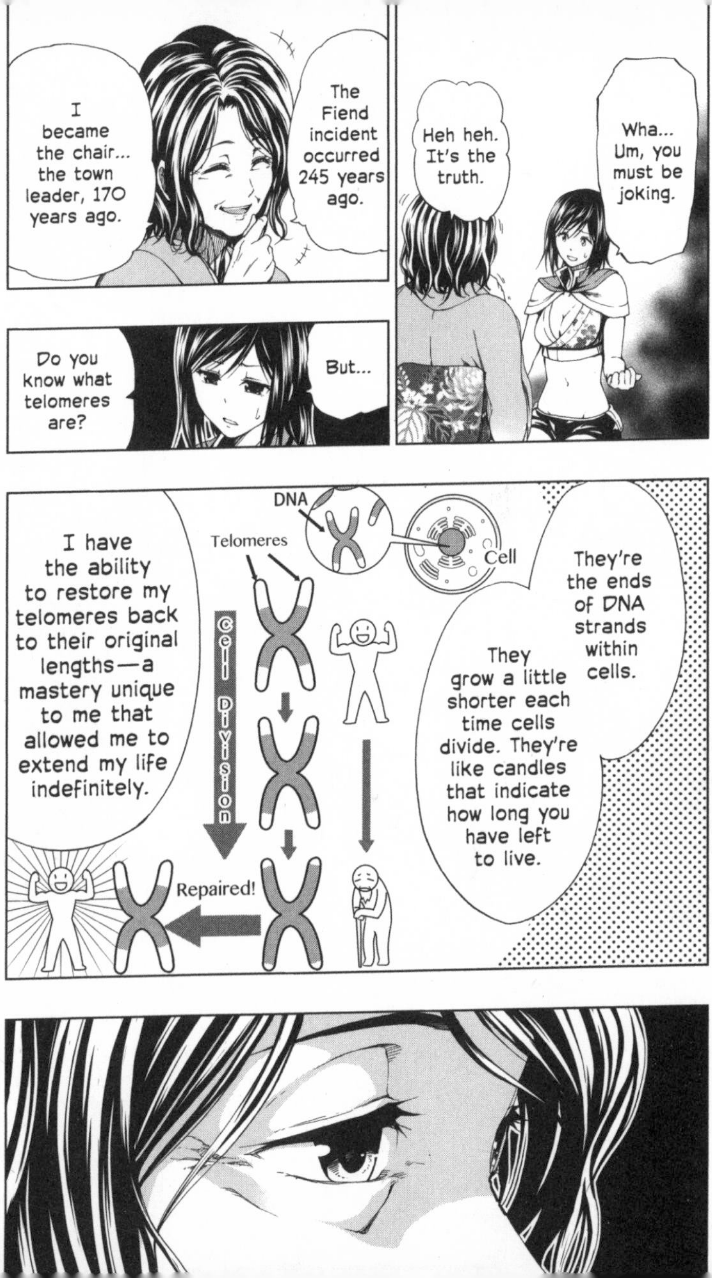
Wha... Um, you must be joking.
Heh heh. It's the truth.
The Fiend incident occurred 245 years ago.
I became the chair... the town leader, 170 years ago.
But...
Do you know what telomeres are?
They're the ends of DNA strands within cells.
They grow a little shorter each time cells divide. They're like candles that indicate how long you have left to live.
Cell
DNA
Telomeres
Cell Division
Repaired!
I have the ability to restore my telomeres back to their original lengths—a mastery unique to me that allowed me to extend my life indefinitely.

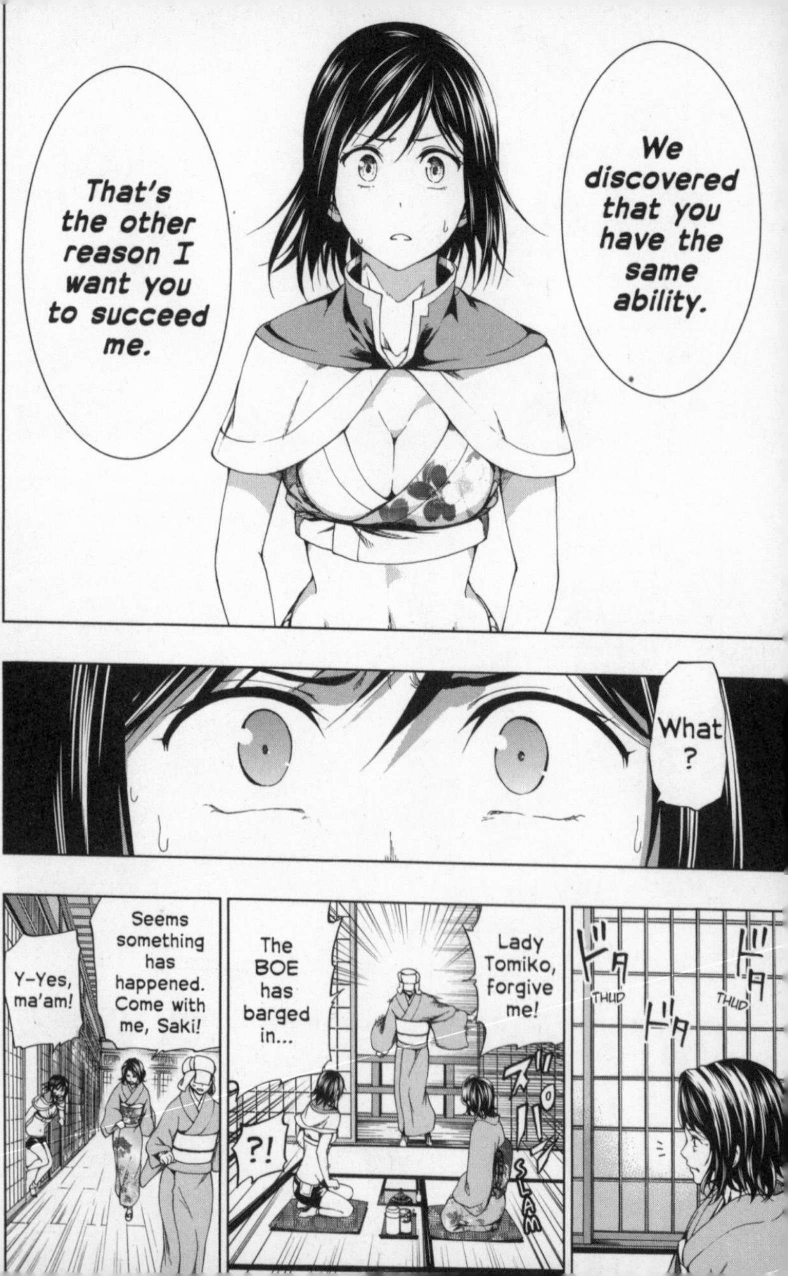
We discovered that you have the same ability.
That's the other reason I want you to succeed me.
What?
THUD
THUD
Lady Tomiko, forgive me!
SLAM
The BOE has barged in...
?!
Seems something has happened. Come with me, Saki!
Y-Yes, ma'am!

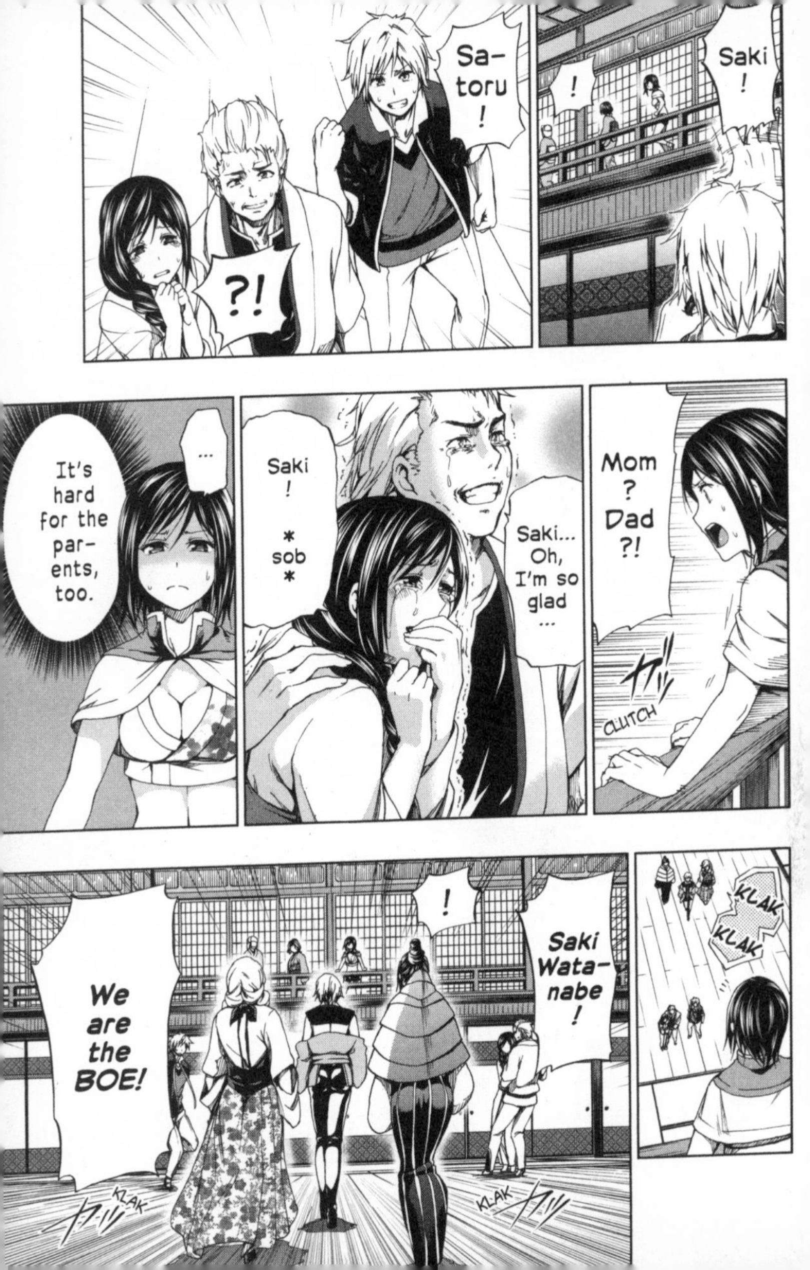
Saki !
!
Sa-toru !
?!
Mom ? Dad ?!
CLUTCH
Saki... Oh, I'm so glad ...
Saki ! * sob *
...
It's hard for the par-ents, too.
KLAK
KLAK
!
Saki Wata-nabe !
We are the BOE!
KLAK
KLAK

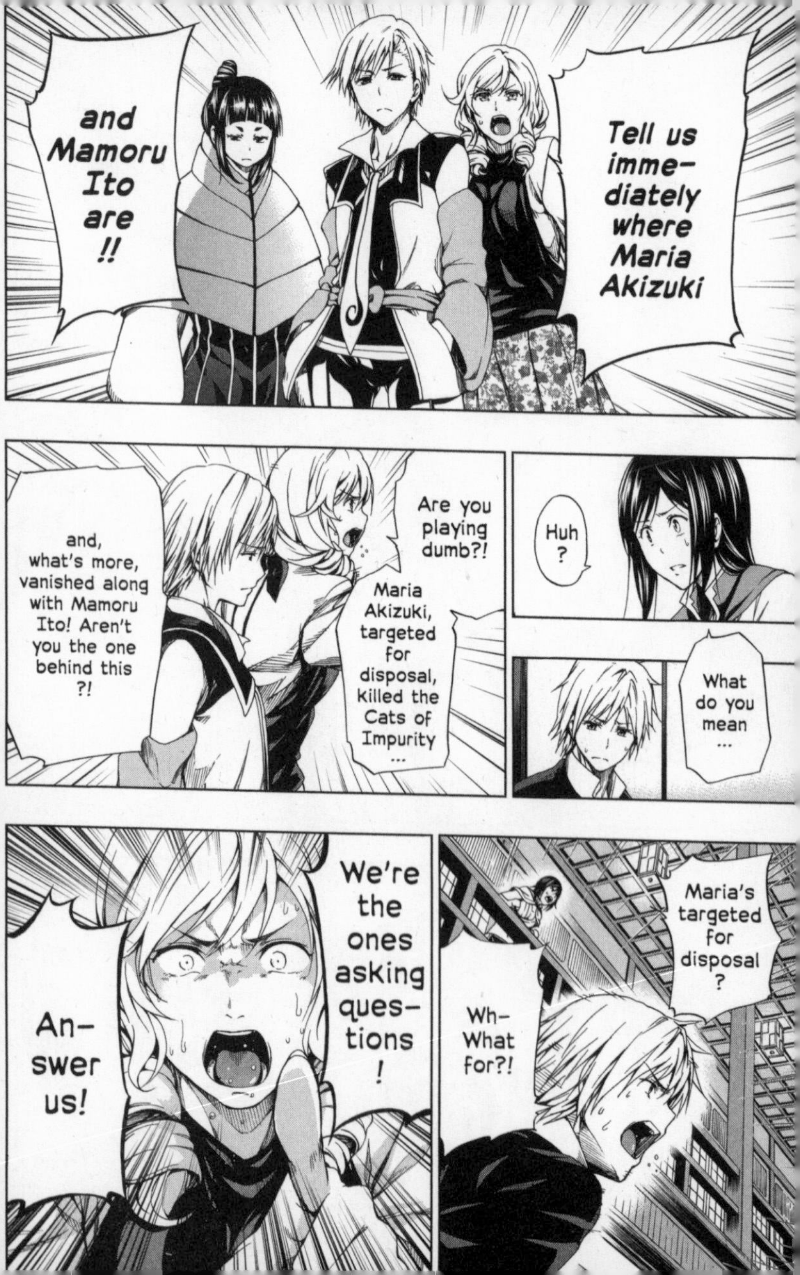
Tell us immediately where Maria Akizuki
and Mamoru Ito are!!
Huh?
What do you mean...
Are you playing dumb?!
Maria Akizuki, targeted for disposal, killed the Cats of Impurity...
and, what's more, vanished along with Mamoru Ito! Aren't you the one behind this?!
Maria's targeted for disposal?
Wh-What for?!
We're the ones asking questions!
Answer us!

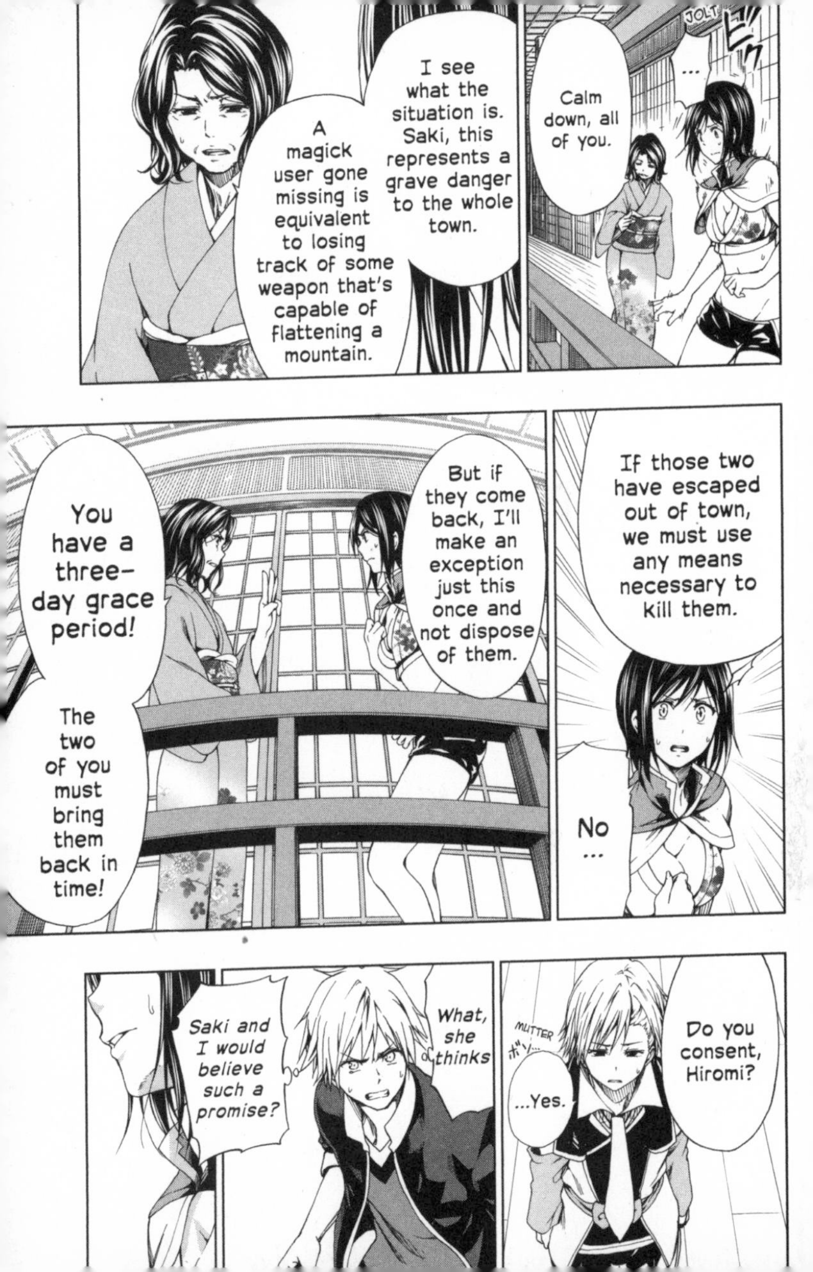
JOLT
...
Calm down, all of you.
I see what the situation is. Saki, this represents a grave danger to the whole town.
A magick user gone missing is equivalent to losing track of some weapon that's capable of flattening a mountain.
If those two have escaped out of town, we must use any means necessary to kill them.
No ...
But if they come back, I'll make an exception just this once and not dispose of them.
You have a three-day grace period!
The two of you must bring them back in time!
Do you consent, Hiromi?
MUTTER
...Yes.
What, she thinks Saki and I would believe such a promise?

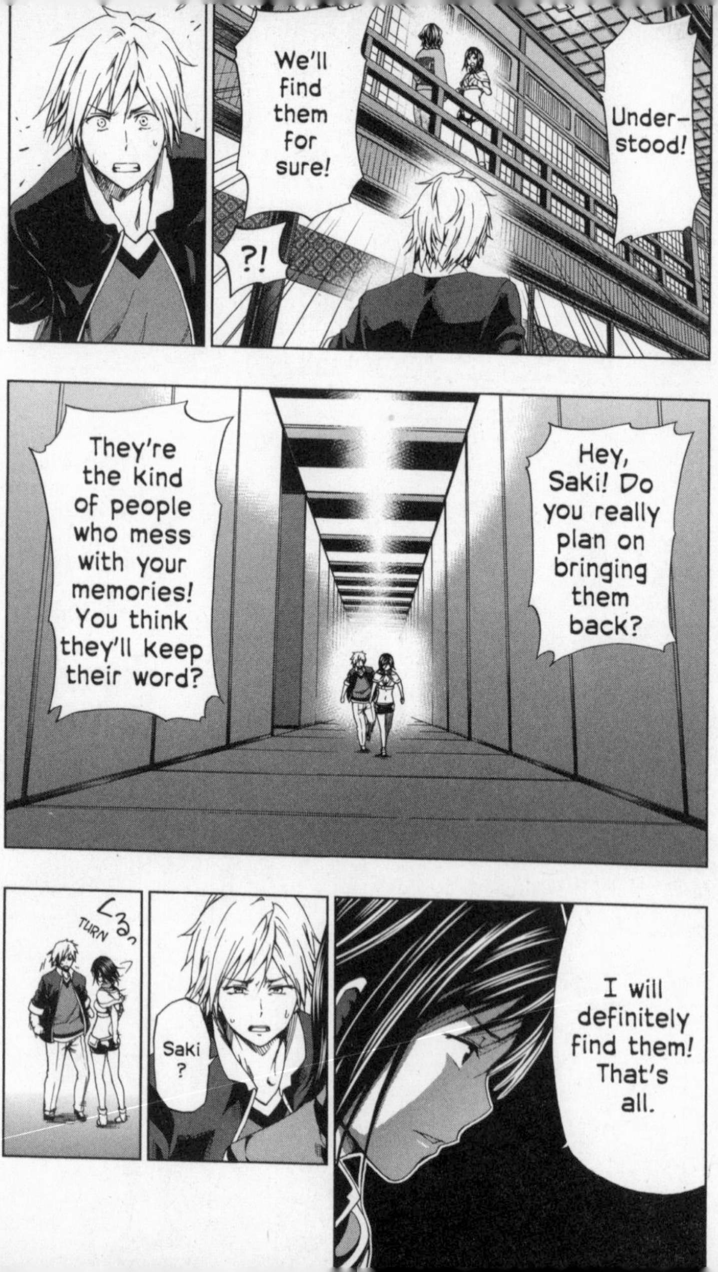
Under-stood!
We'll find them for sure!
?!
Hey, Saki! Do you really plan on bringing them back?
They're the kind of people who mess with your memories! You think they'll keep their word?
I will definitely find them! That's all.
Saki?
TURN

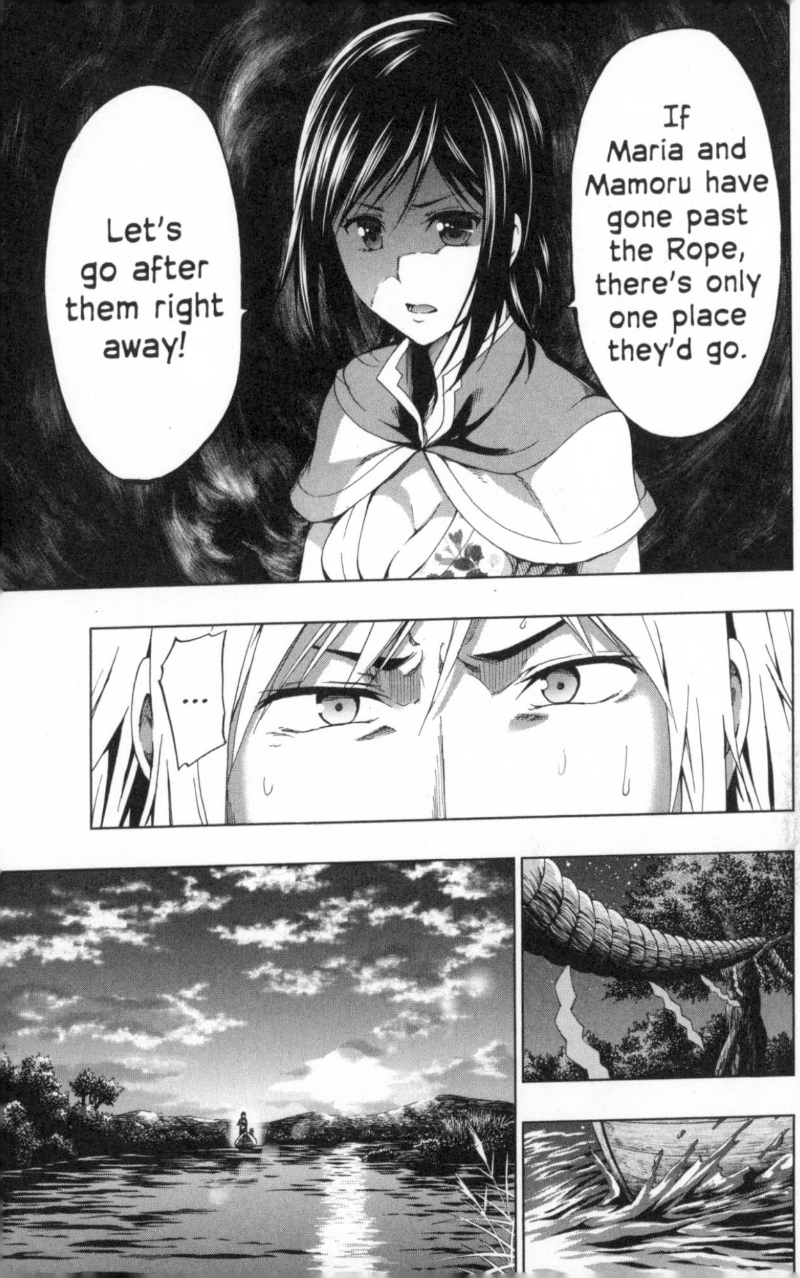
If Maria and Mamoru have gone past the Rope, there's only one place they'd go.
Let's go after them right away!
...

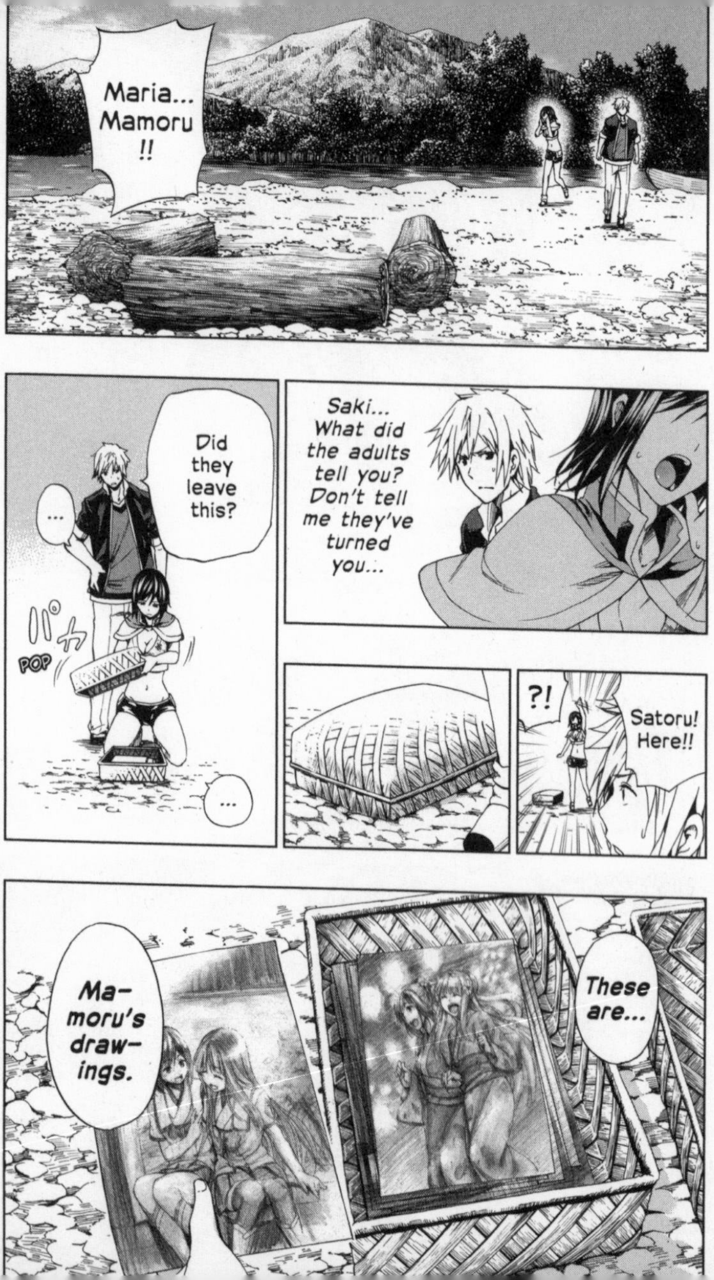
Maria... Mamoru !!
Saki... What did the adults tell you? Don't tell me they've turned you...
?!
Satoru! Here!!
Did they leave this?
...
パカ
POP
...
These are...
Ma-moru's draw-ings.

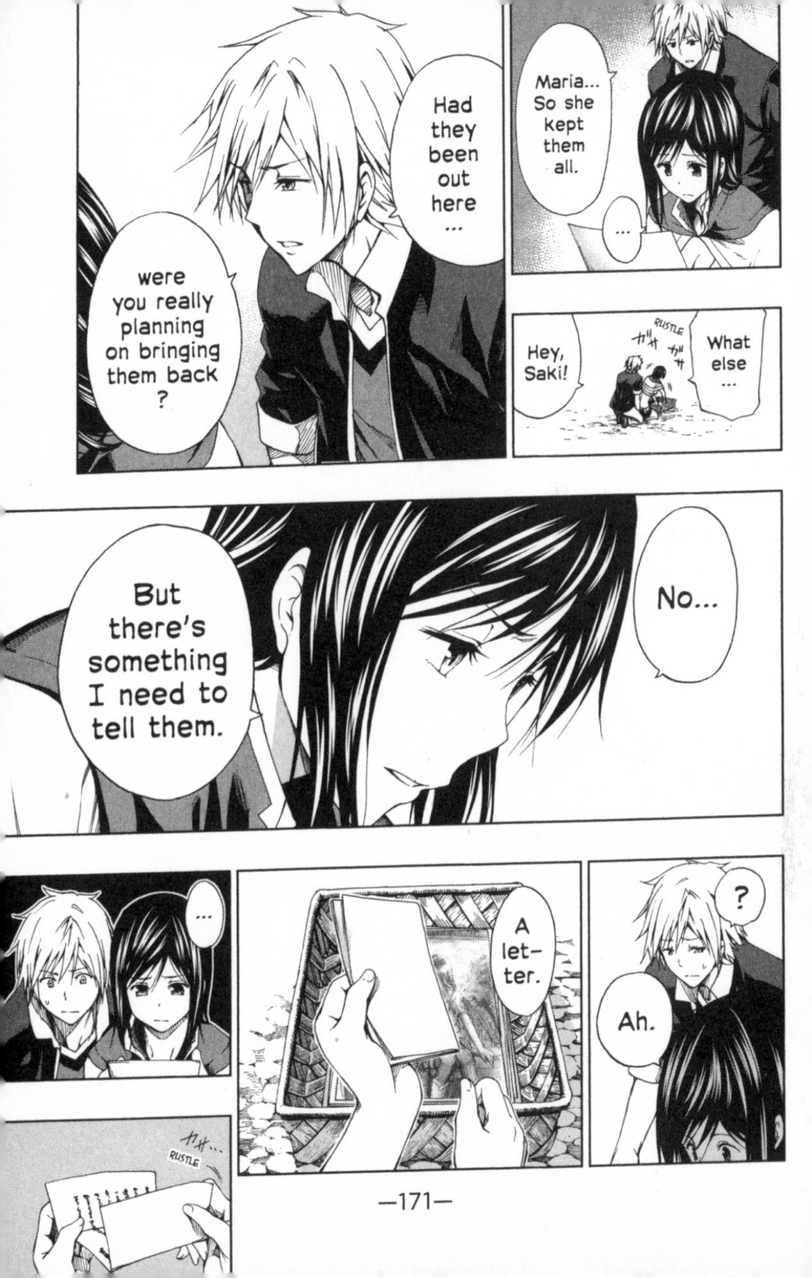
Maria... So she kept them all.
...
What else ...
RUSTLE
Hey, Saki!
Had they been out here ...
were you really planning on bringing them back ?
No...
But there's something I need to tell them.
?
Ah.
A let-ter.
...
RUSTLE

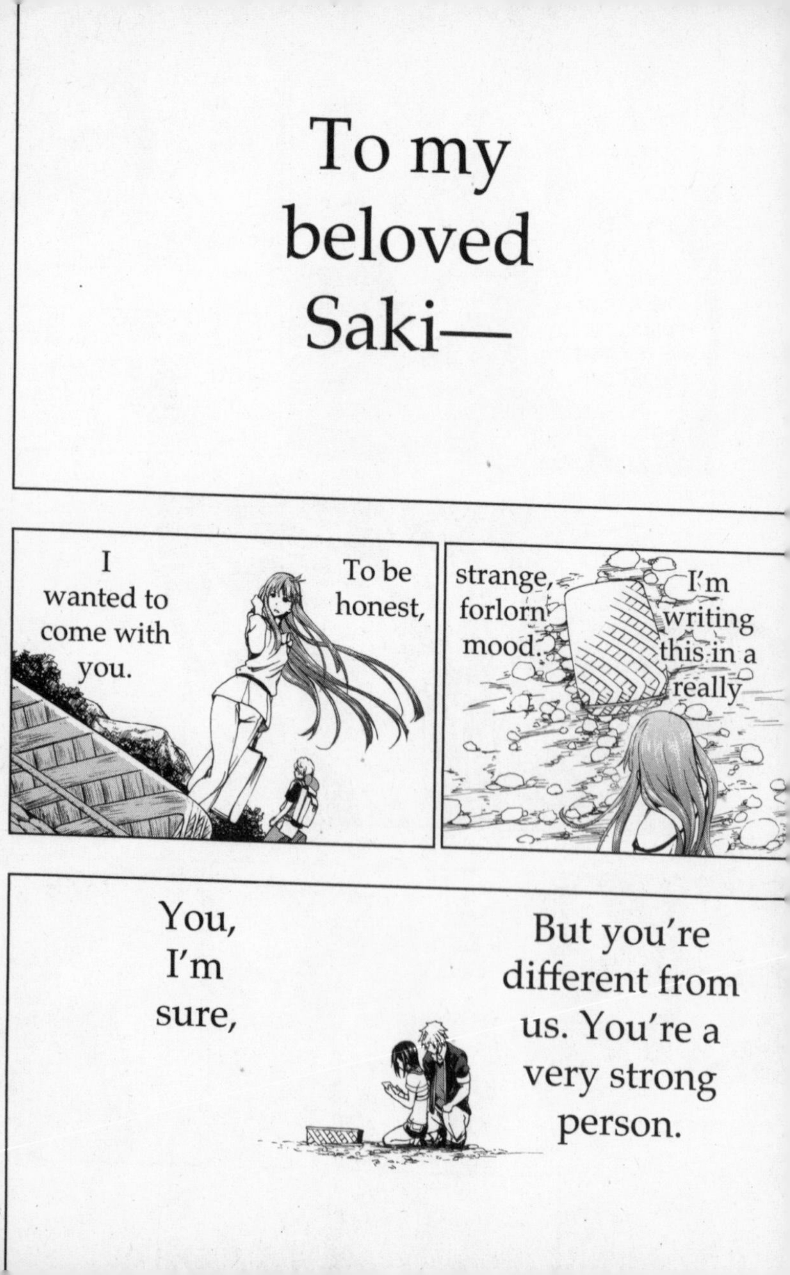
To my beloved Saki—
I'm writing this in a really
strange, forlorn mood.
To be honest,
I wanted to come with you.
But you're different from us. You're a very strong person.
You, I'm sure,

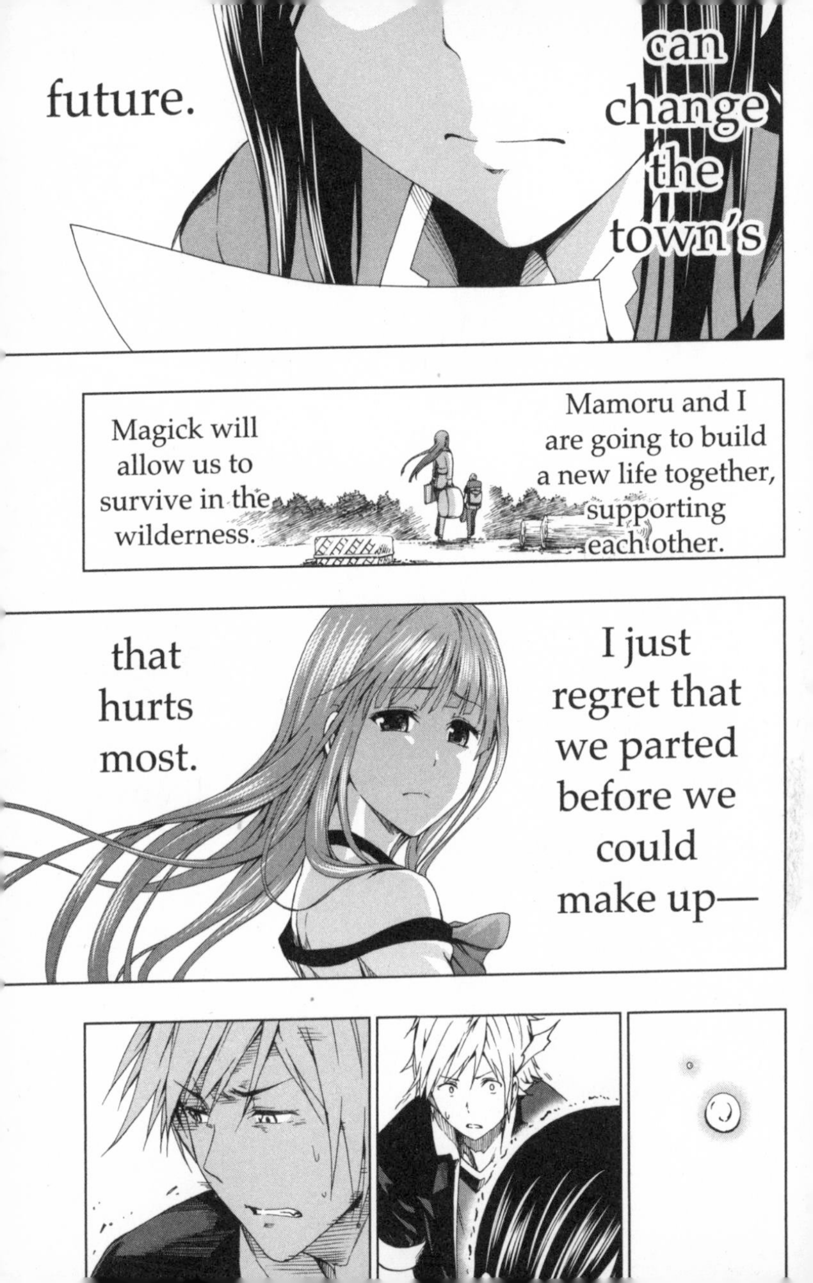
can change the town's
future.
Mamoru and I are going to build a new life together, supporting each other.
Magick will allow us to survive in the wilderness.
I just regret that we parted before we could make up—
that hurts most.

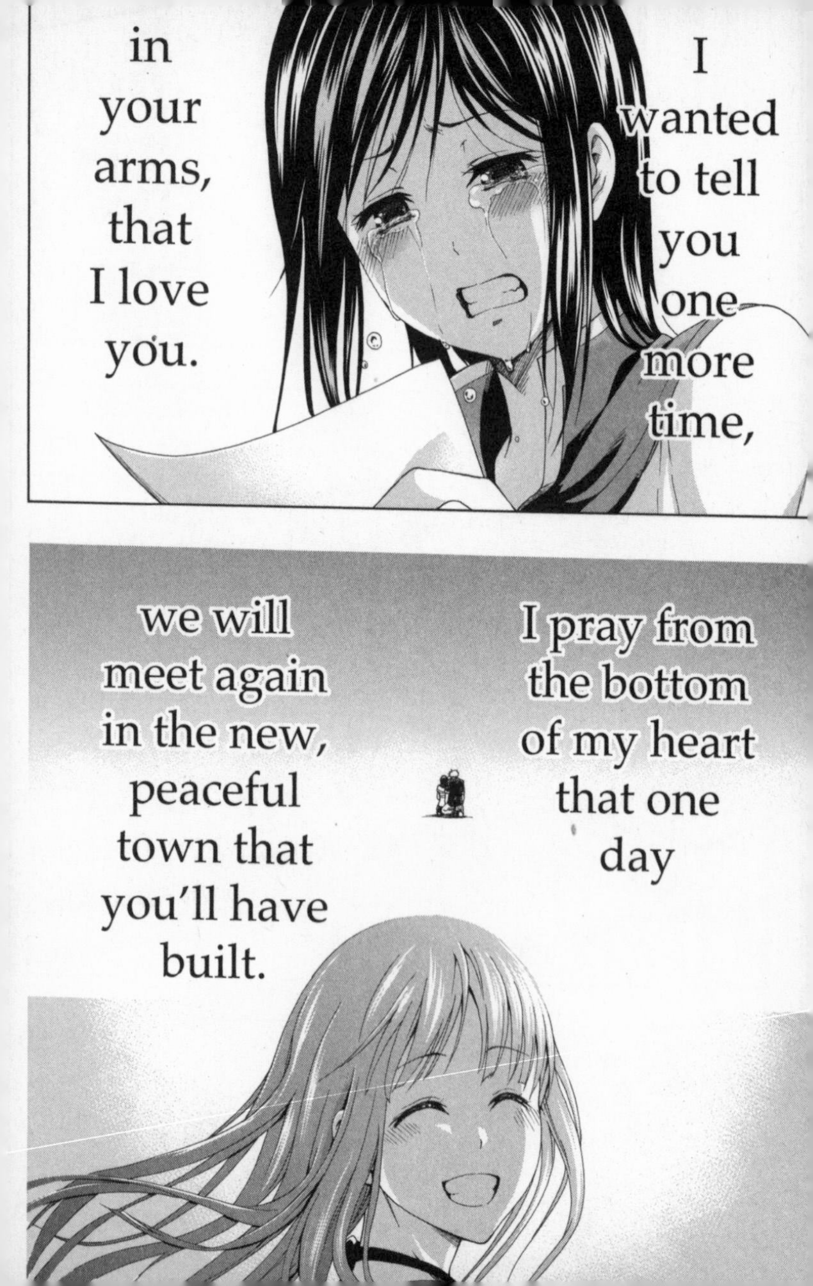
I wanted to tell you one more time,
in your arms, that I love you.
I pray from the bottom of my heart that one day
we will meet again in the new, peaceful town that you'll have built.

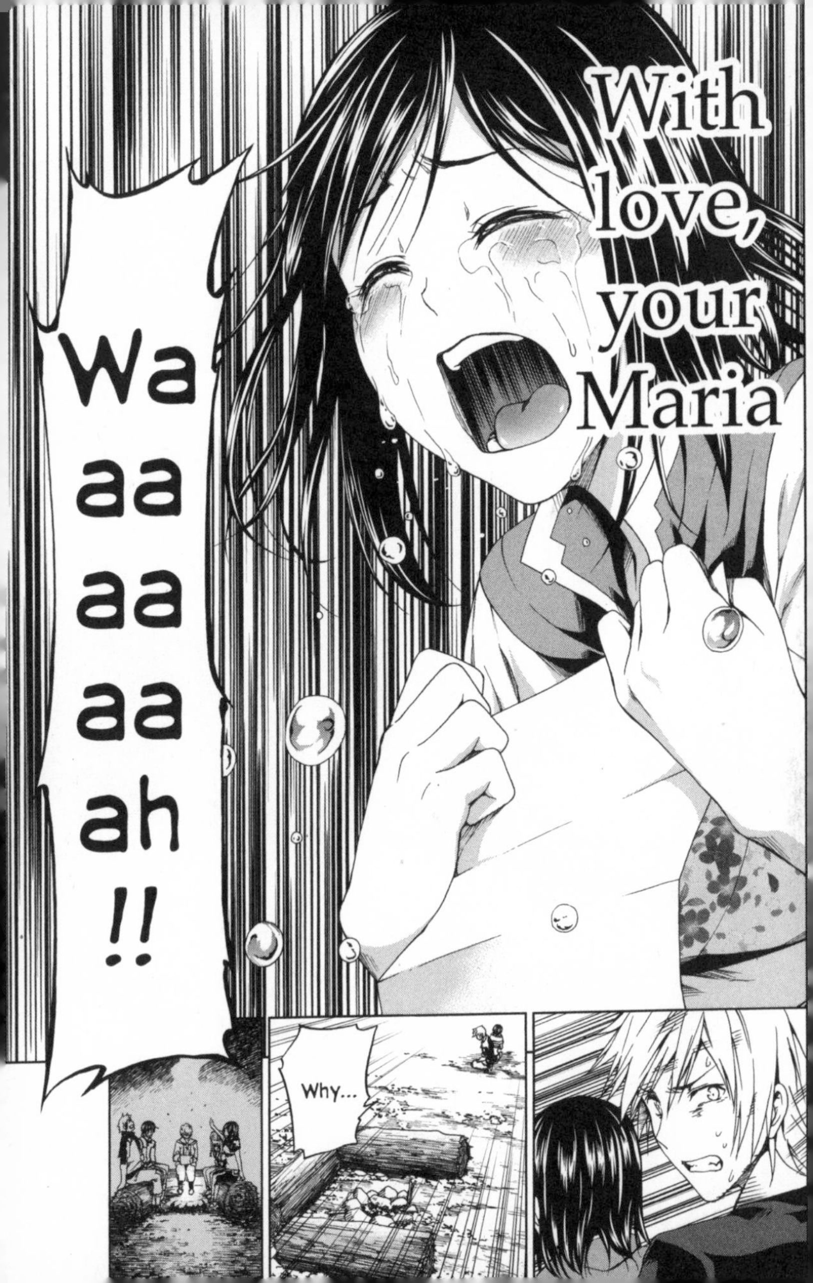
With love, your Maria
Waaaaaaaaah!!
Why...

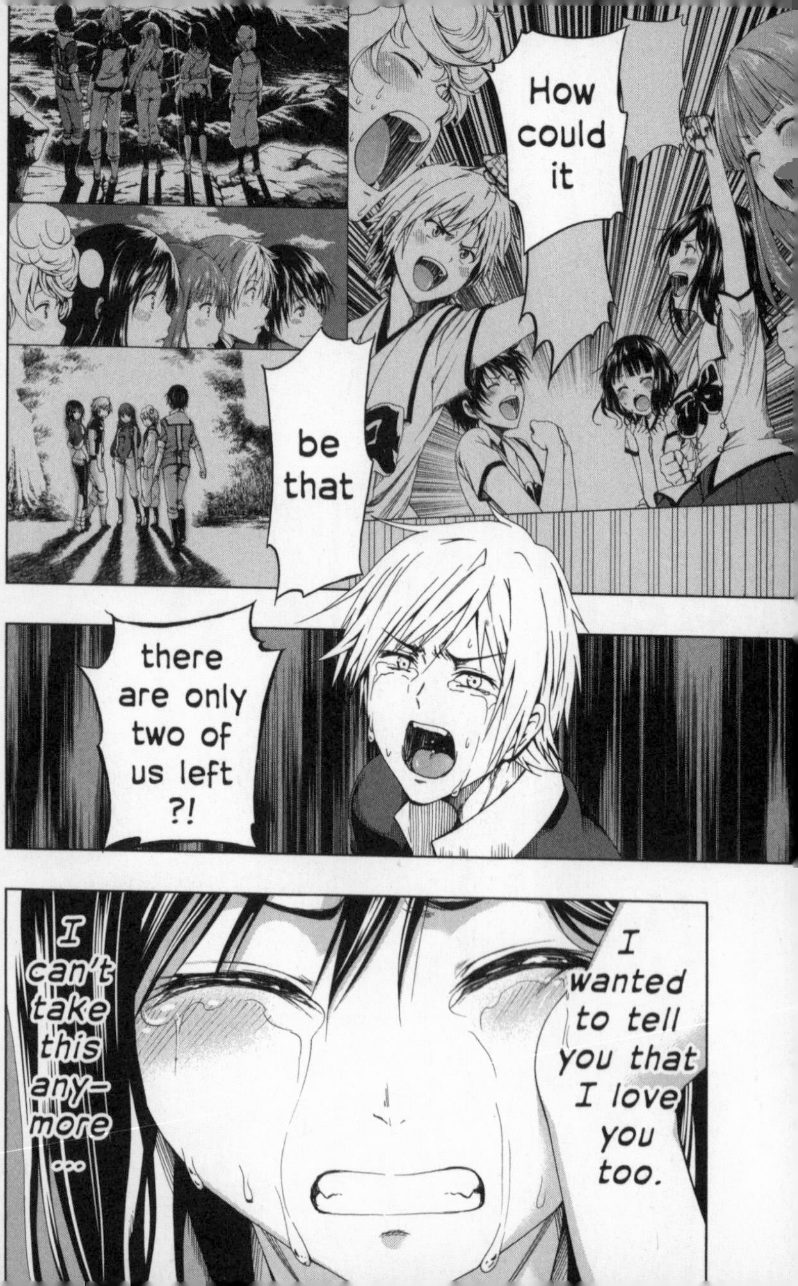
How could it
be that
there are only two of us left ?!
I wanted to tell you that I love you too.
I can't take this any-more ...

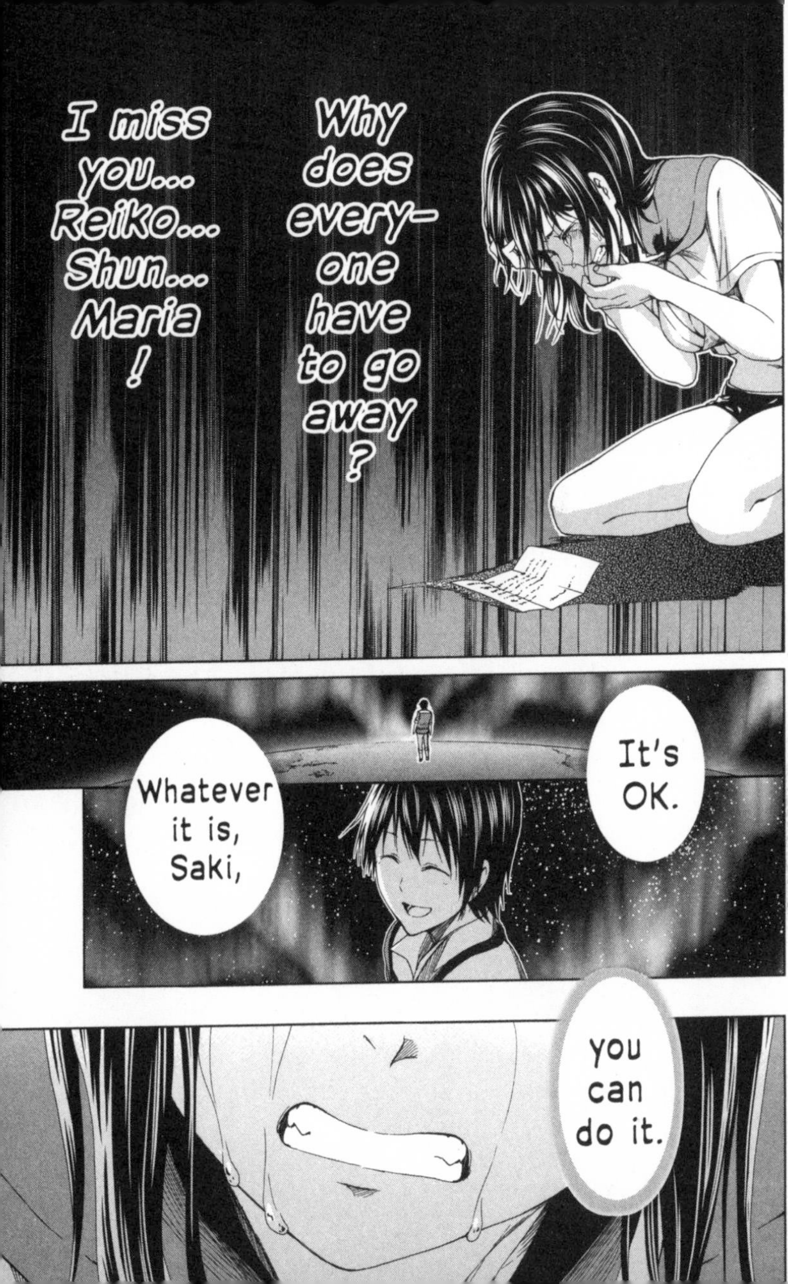
Why does every-one have to go away?
I miss you... Reiko... Shun... Maria!
It's OK.
Whatever it is, Saki,
you can do it.

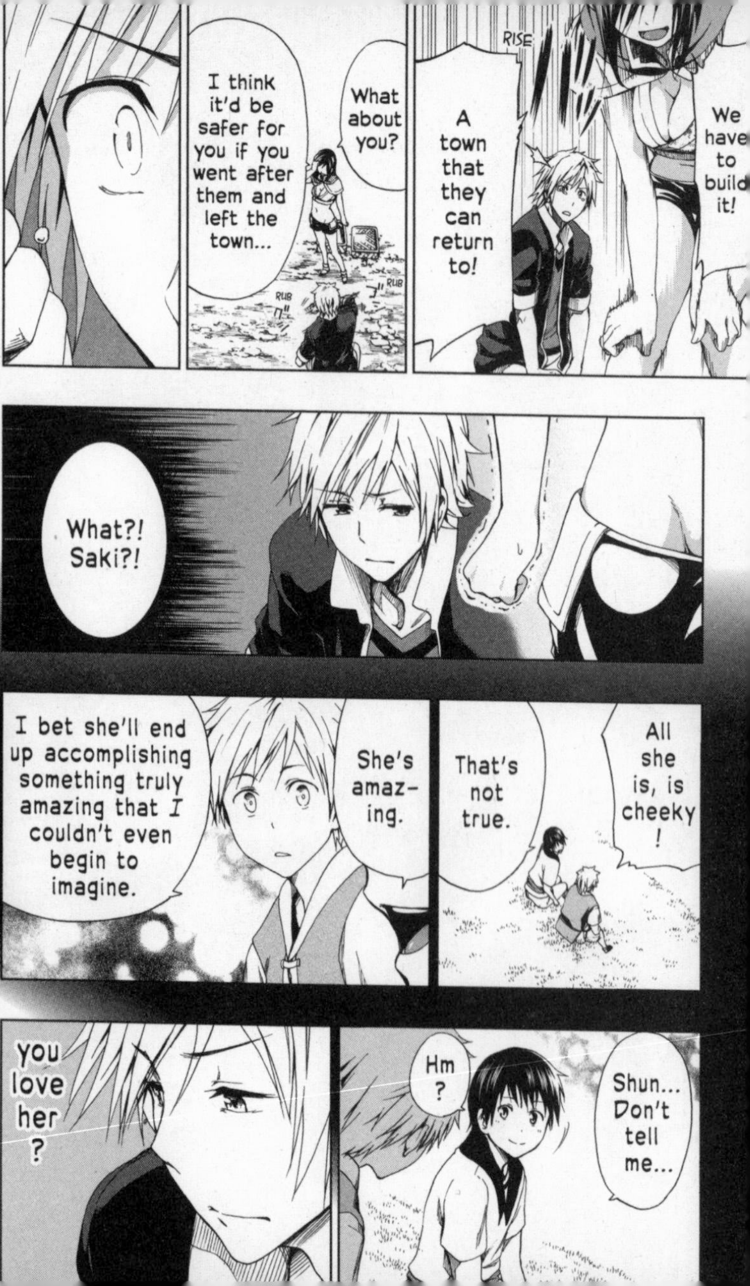
RISE
We have to build it!
A town that they can return to!
What about you?
I think it'd be safer for you if you went after them and left the town...
RUB
RUB
What?! Saki?!
All she is, is cheeky!
That's not true.
She's amaz-ing.
I bet she'll end up accomplishing something truly amazing that I couldn't even begin to imagine.
Shun... Don't tell me...
Hm?
you love her?

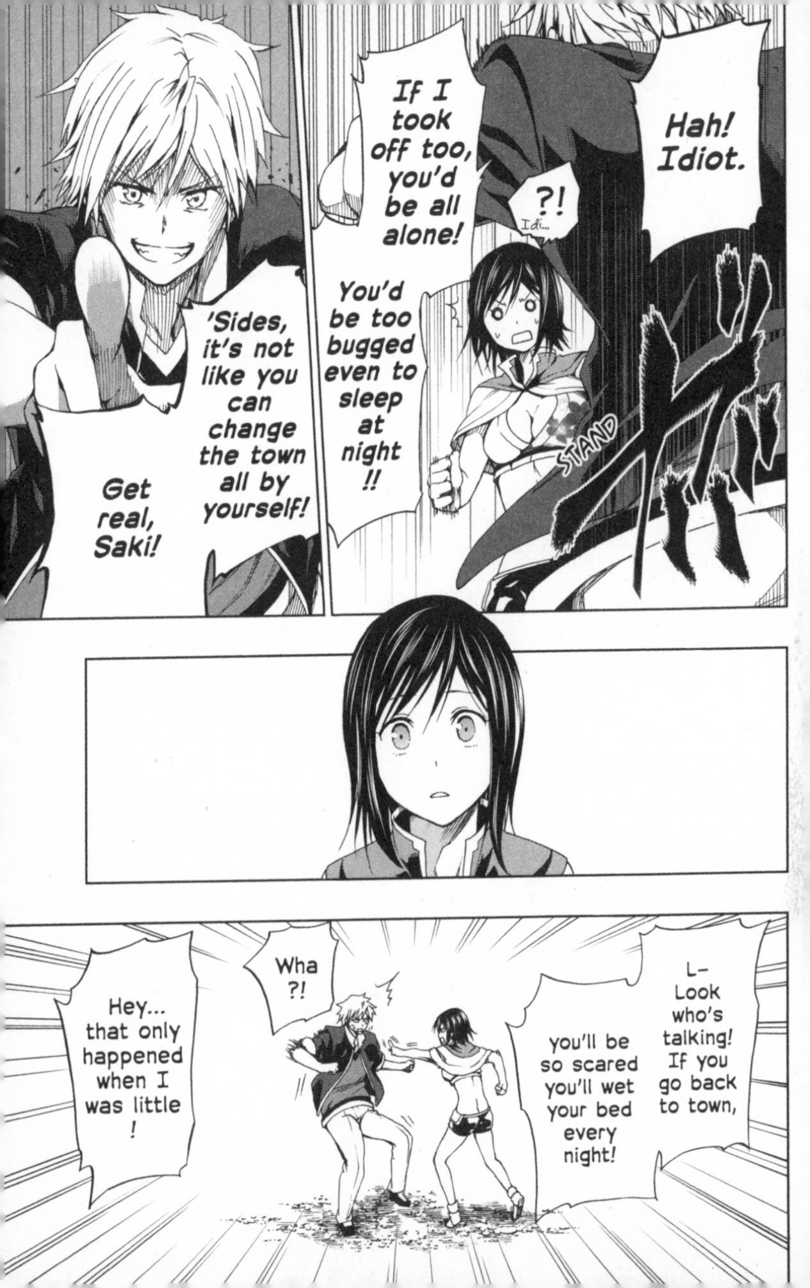
Hah! Idiot.
?!
Idi...
If I took off too, you'd be all alone!
You'd be too bugged even to sleep at night!!
STAND
'Sides, it's not like you can change the town all by yourself!
Get real, Saki!
L- Look who's talking! If you go back to town,
you'll be so scared you'll wet your bed every night!
Wha ?!
Hey... that only happened when I was little!

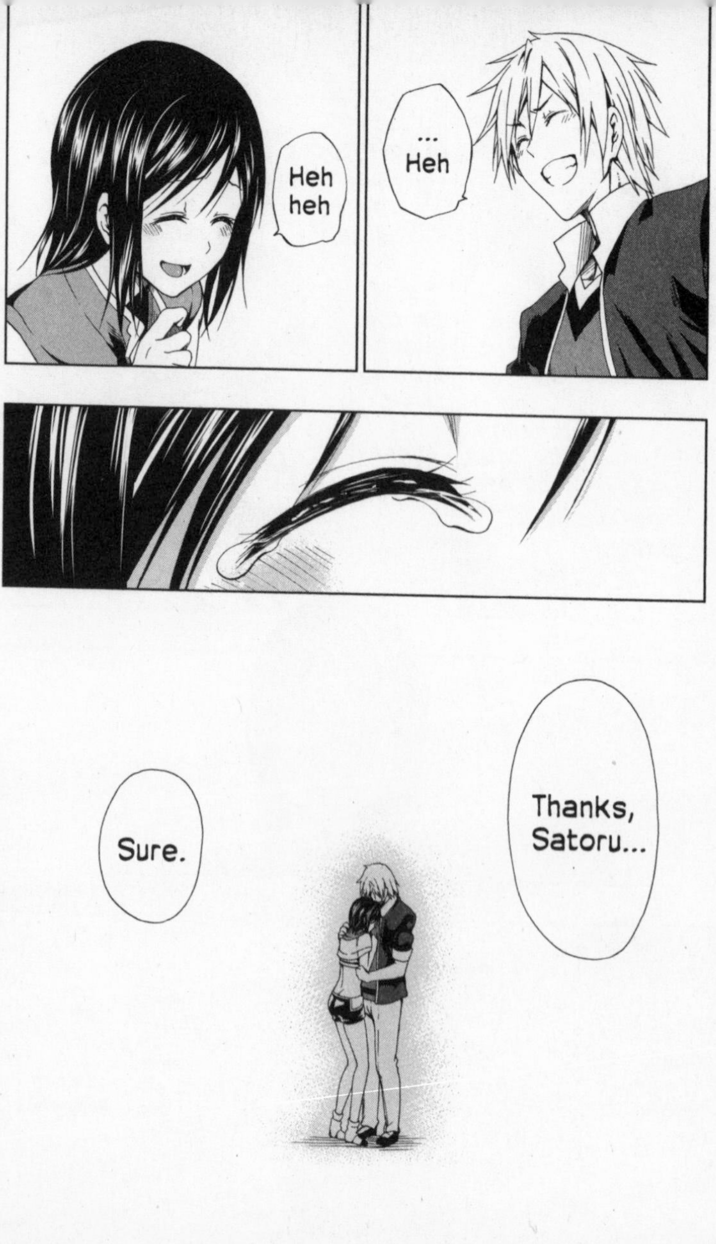
... Heh
Heh heh
Thanks, Satoru...
Sure.

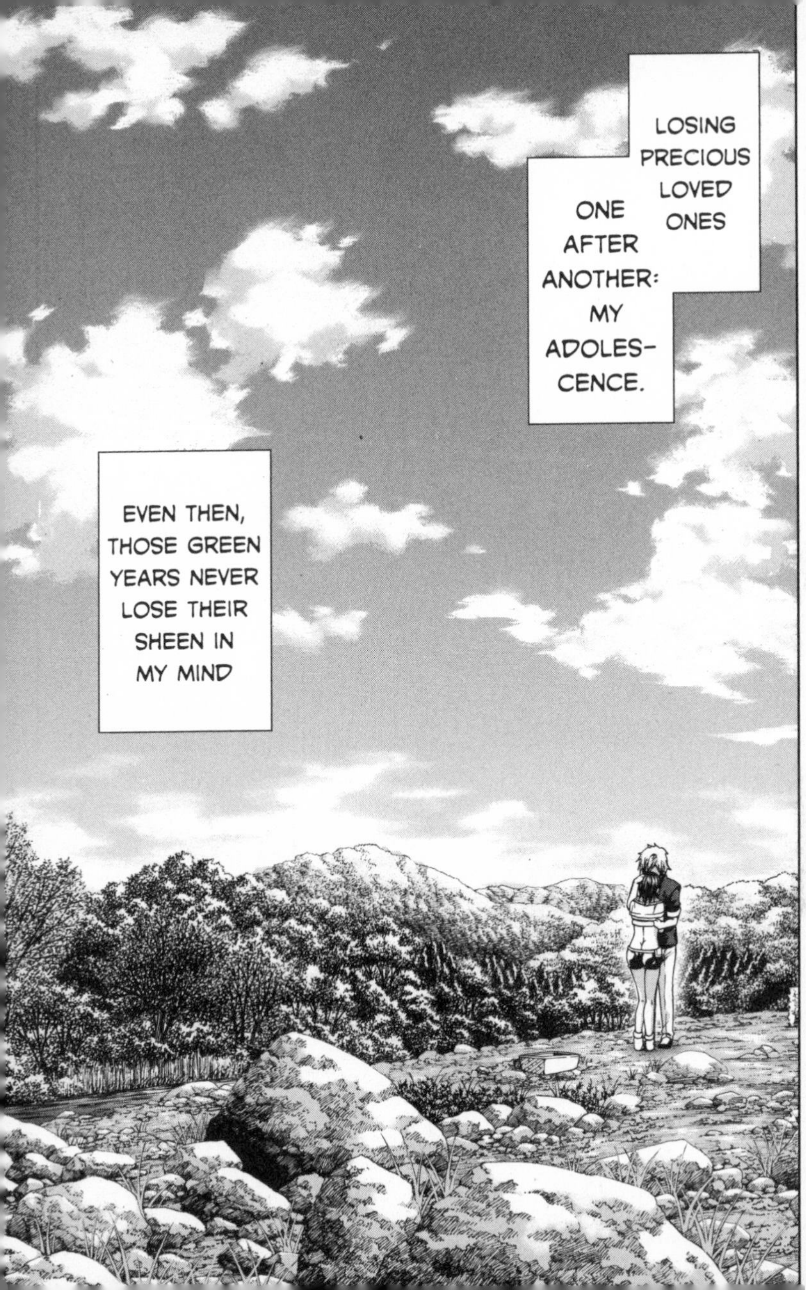
LOSING PRECIOUS LOVED ONES
ONE AFTER ANOTHER: MY ADOLES-CENCE.
EVEN THEN, THOSE GREEN YEARS NEVER LOSE THEIR SHEEN IN MY MIND

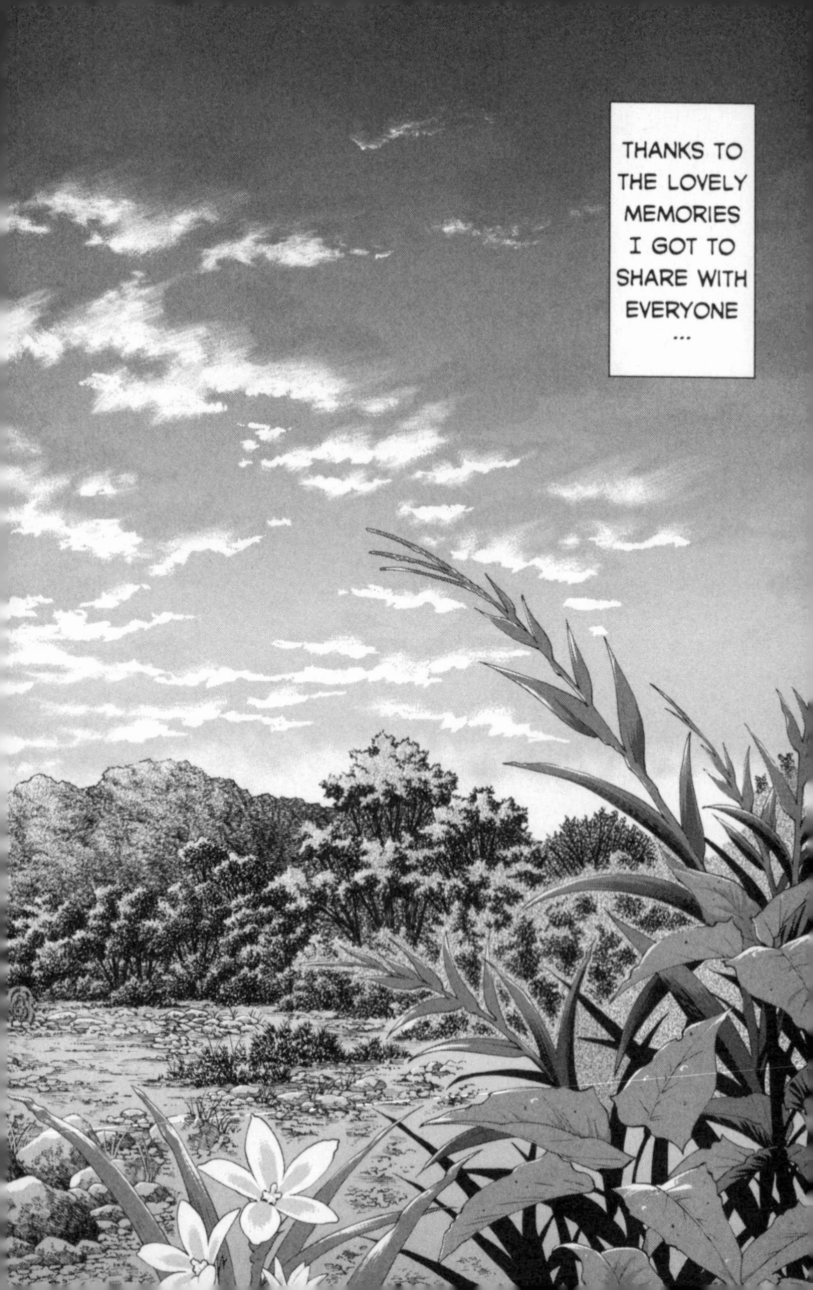
THANKS TO THE LOVELY MEMORIES I GOT TO SHARE WITH EVERYONE ...

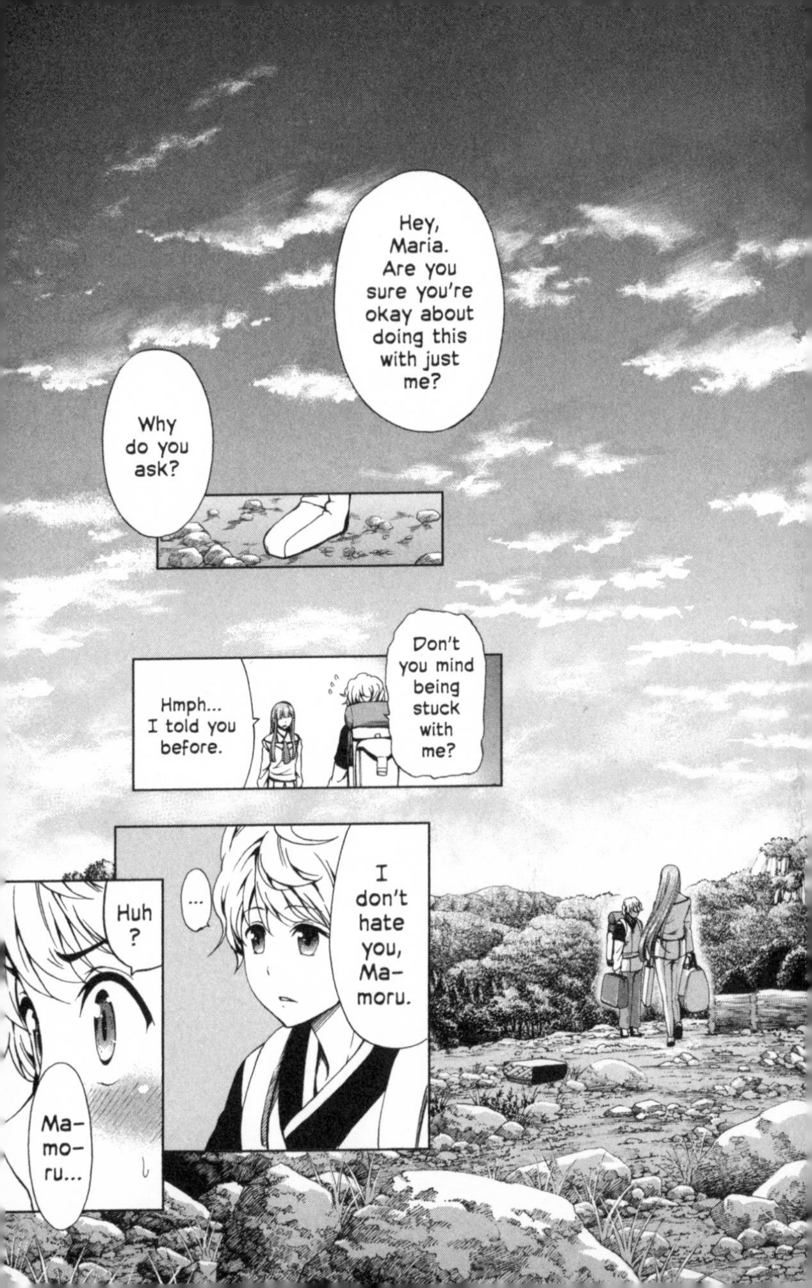
Hey, Maria. Are you sure you're okay about doing this with just me?
Why do you ask?
Don't you mind being stuck with me?
Hmph... I told you before.
I don't hate you, Ma-moru.
...
Huh?
Ma-mo-ru...

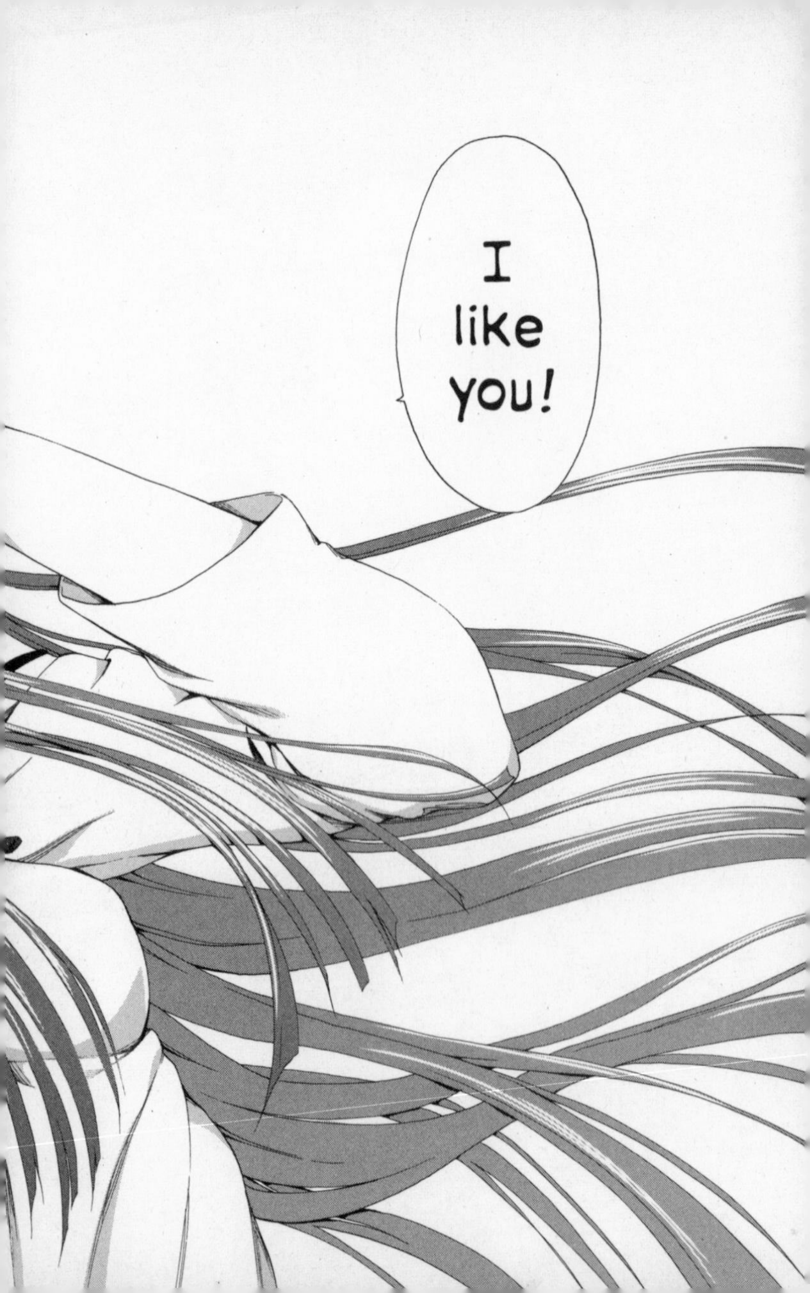
I like you!

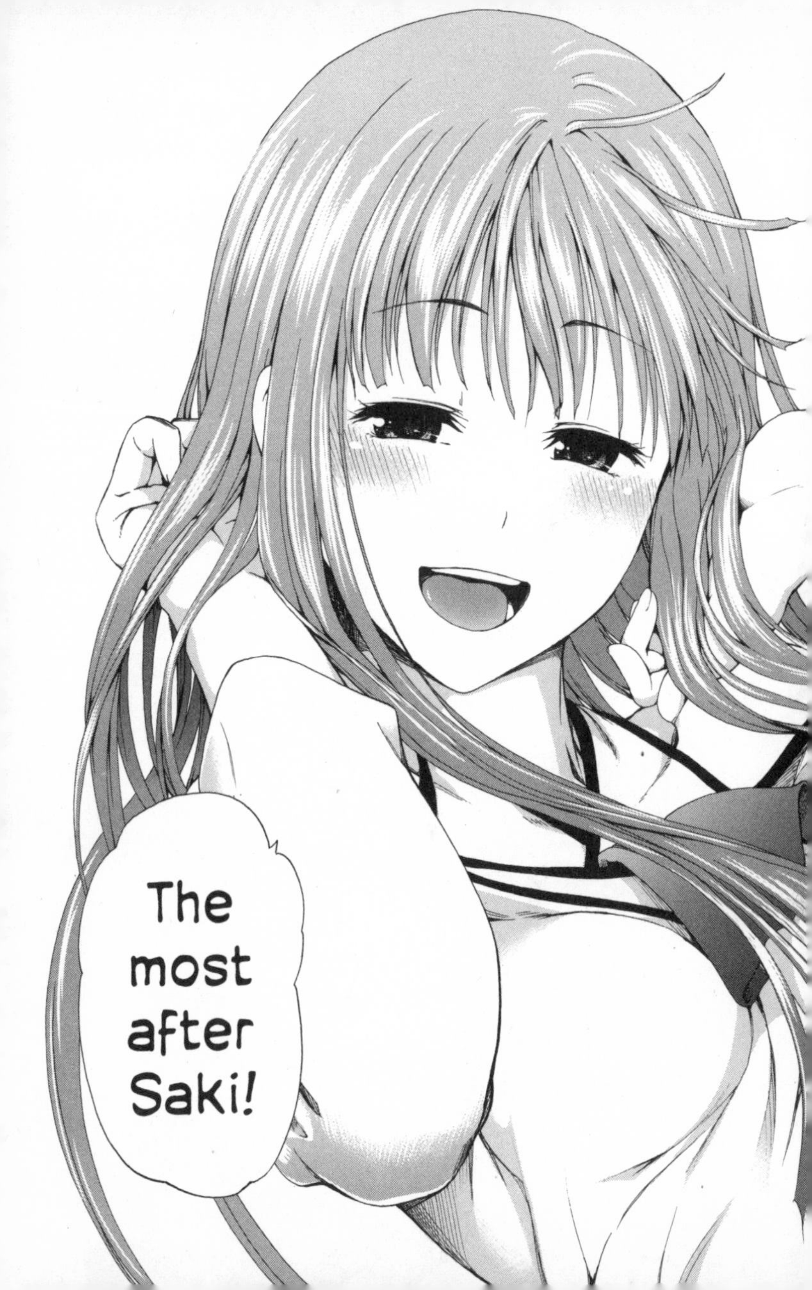
The most after Saki!

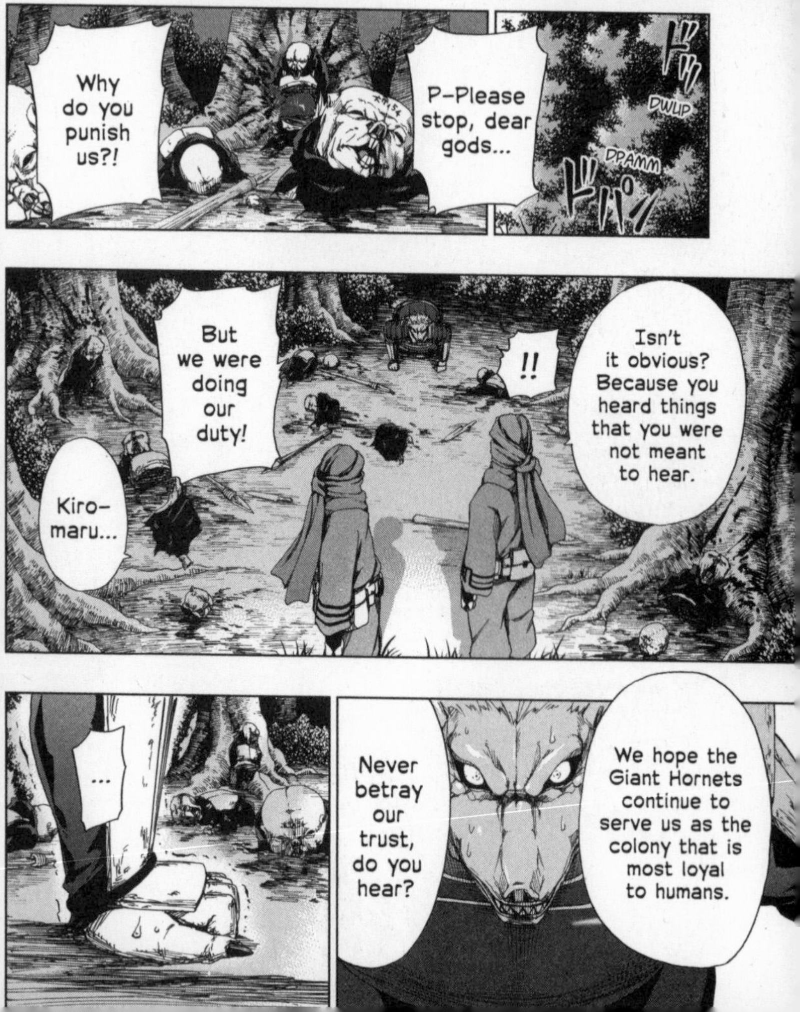
DWLIP
DPAMM
P-Please stop, dear gods...
Why do you punish us?!
Isn't it obvious? Because you heard things that you were not meant to hear.
!!
But we were doing our duty!
Kiro-maru...
We hope the Giant Hornets continue to serve us as the colony that is most loyal to humans.
Never betray our trust, do you hear?
...

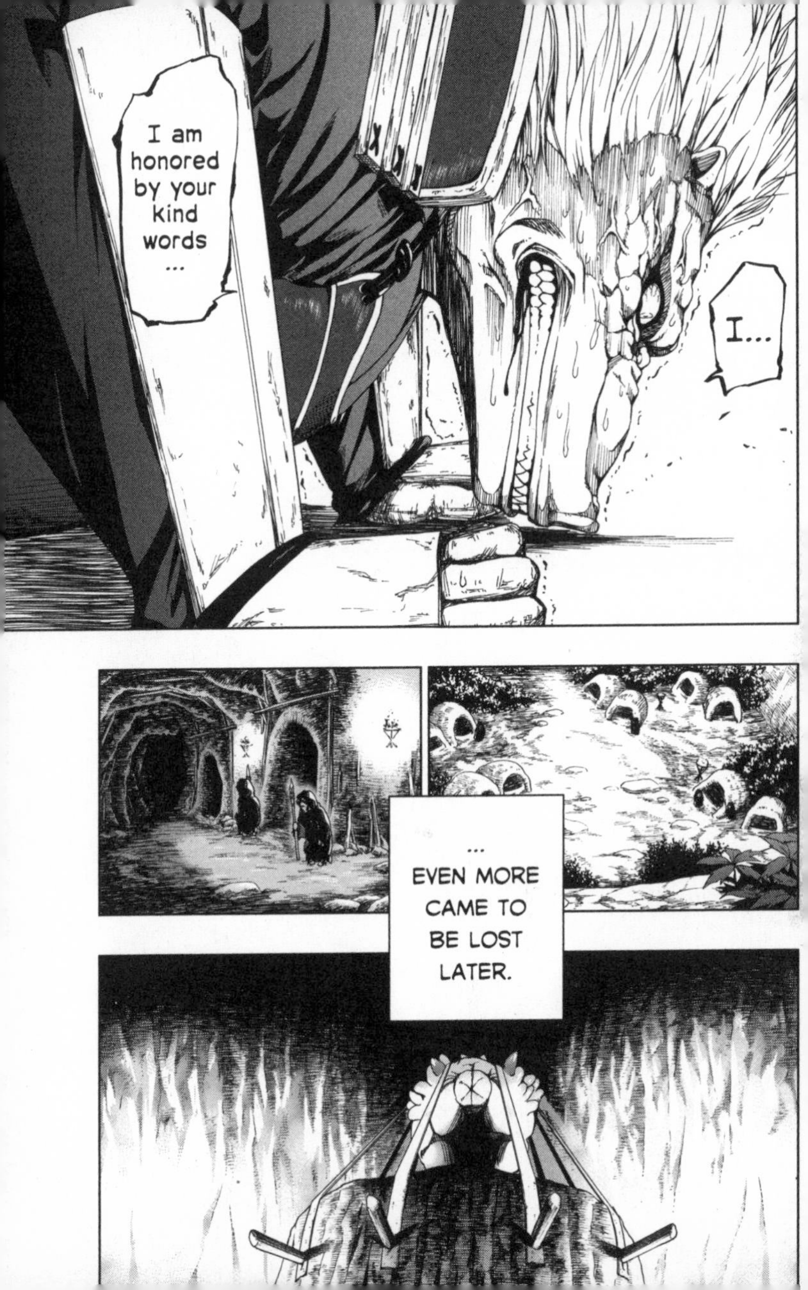
I...
I am honored by your kind words ...
... EVEN MORE CAME TO BE LOST LATER.

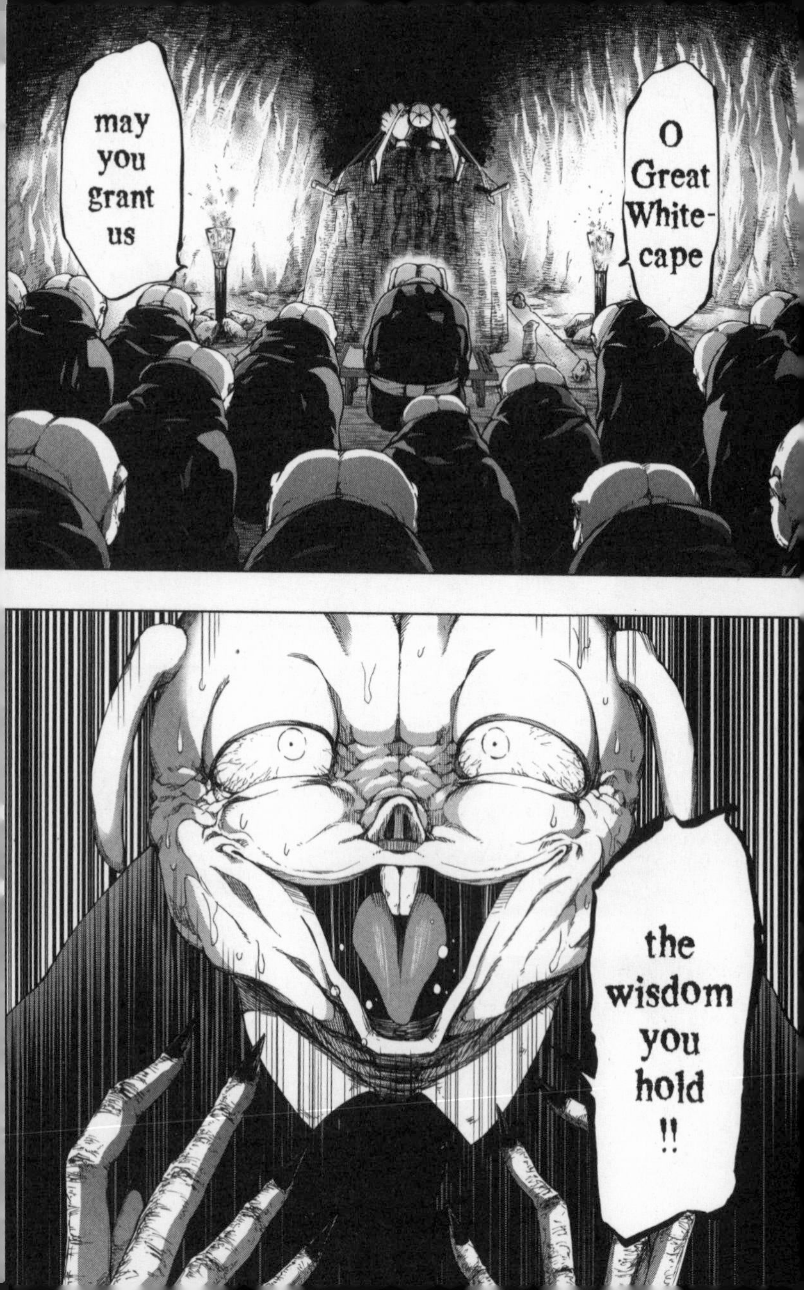
O Great White-cape
may you grant us
the wisdom you hold !!

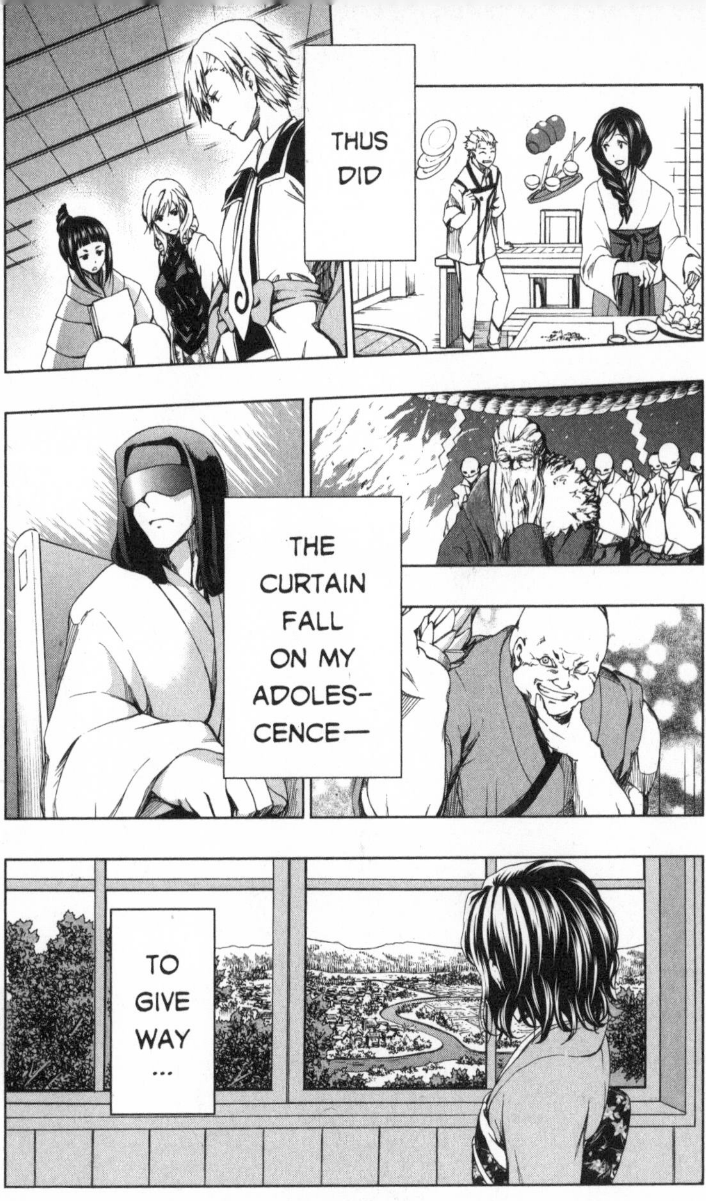
THUS DID
THE CURTAIN FALL ON MY ADOLES- CENCE—
TO GIVE WAY ...

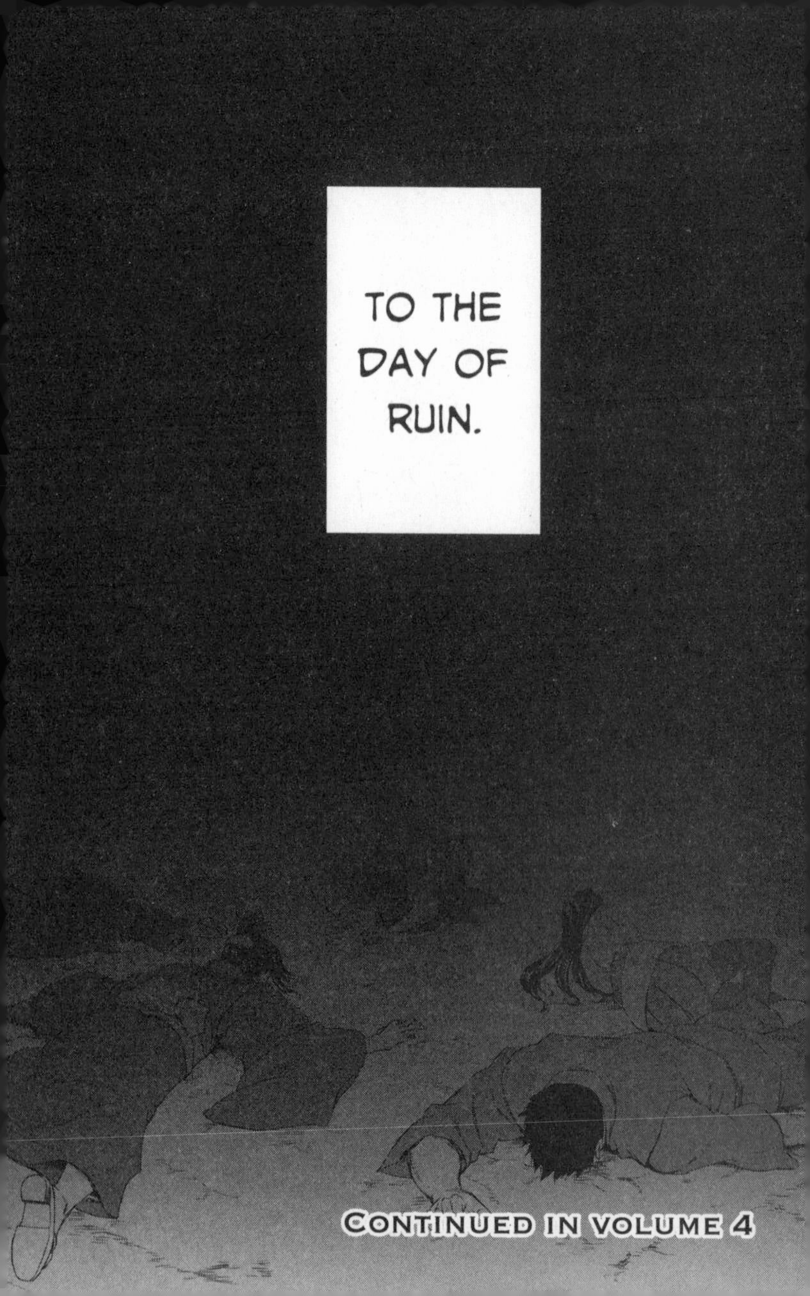
TO THE DAY OF RUIN.
CONTINUED IN VOLUME 4

MORE THAN A DECADE
AFTER "THAT SUMMER"...

WITH ONLY THE TWO OF
THEM LEFT, SAKI AND
SATORU HOLD FAST TO
WHAT THEY PROMISED
THEIR FRIENDS AND
CONTINUE TO RESIST
DESTINY—UNAWARE
OF THE FOOTFALLS OF
PERDITION THAT CREEP
INSIDIOUSLY CLOSER.

THE WORLD CONTAINS
YET MORE *LIES*.
DIVE INTO A SHOCKING
NEW CHAPTER.

FROM THE NEW WORLD

4

VOLUME 4 ON SALE MAY 2014

From the New World
Volume 3

Production: Grace Lu
Anthony Quintessenza

First published in Japan in 2013 by Kodansha, Ltd., Tokyo
Publication rights for this English edition arranged through Kodansha, Ltd., Tokyo
English language version produced by Vertical, Inc.

Translation provided by Vertical, Inc., 2014
Published by Vertical, Inc., New York

Originally published in Japanese as *Shin Sekai Yori 3* by Kodansha, Ltd.
Shin Sekai Yori first serialized in *Bessatsu Shonen Magazine*, Kodansha, Ltd., 2012-

This is a work of fiction.

ISBN: 978-1-939130-29-7

Manufactured in Canada

First Edition

Vertical, Inc.
451 Park Avenue South
7th Floor
New York, NY 10016
www.vertical-inc.com